W9-DGM-772

Tobias George Smollett

Updated Edition

Twayne's English Authors Series

Bertram H. Davis, Editor

Florida State University

TEAS 75

Tobias George Smollett (1721–71). Artist unknown.
Courtesy of the National Portrait Gallery, London.

Tobias George Smollett

Updated Edition

By Robert Donald Spector

Long Island University

Twayne Publishers
A Division of G. K. Hall & Co. • *Boston*

Tobias George Smollett, Updated Edition
Robert Donald Spector

Copyright 1989 by G. K. Hall & Co.
All rights reserved.
Published by Twayne Publishers
A Division of G. K. Hall & Co.
70 Lincoln Street
Boston, Massachusetts 02111

Copyediting supervised by Barbara Sutton.
Book production by Gabrielle B. McDonald.
Book design by Barbara Anderson.

Typeset in 11 pt. Garamond
by Compositors Typesetters, Cedar Rapids, Iowa.

Printed on permanent/durable acid-free paper
and bound in the United States of America.

Library of Congress Cataloging-in-Publication Data

Spector, Robert Donald.
    Tobias George Smollett / by Robert Donald Spector. — Updated ed.
      p.   cm. — (Twayne's English authors series; TEAS 75)
    Bibliography: p.
    Includes index.
    ISBN 0-8057-6971-4
    1. Smollett, Tobias George, 1721-1771—Criticism and
  interpretation.   I. Title.   II. Series.
PR3697.S6 1989
823'.6—dc19
                                      88-21512
                                        CIP

For Stephen Brett, Eric Charles,
and their Grandparents

Contents

About the Author
Preface
Chronology

Chapter One
From Grub Street to Parnassus   1

Chapter Two
Roderick Random: The Rogue Sets Forth   24

Chapter Three
Peregrine Pickle: The Rogue in High Society   44

Chapter Four
Ferdinand Count Fathom: Smollett's Iago   67

Chapter Five
Launcelot Greaves: Quixotic Picaresque   85

Chapter Six
Humphry Clinker: The Picaresque Ménage   104

Afterword   121
Notes and References   125
Selected Bibliography   140
Index   152

About the Author

Professor of English and director of the Division of Humanities at Long Island University, Robert Donald Spector is the author of six books and editor of ten others. He has published more than four hundred articles and reviews in scholarly and commercial journals and collections. Recipient of fellowships from the Huntington, Folger, and Newberry libraries and of a travel grant from the Swedish government, he was named as a 1978 winner of the first annual Long Island University Board of Trustees' Award for Scholarly Achievement. In addition to the original edition of *Tobias George Smollett,* he is also the author of *Arthur Murphy* in Twayne's English Authors Series and *Pär Lagerkvist* in Twayne's World Authors Series. His other works include *English Literary Periodicals, Tobias Smollett: A Reference Guide,* and *The English Gothic.*

Preface

Together with Henry Fielding, Samuel Richardson, and Laurence Sterne, Tobias Smollett raised the novel to literary respectability in eighteenth-century England. His reputation, sufficiently high in his own lifetime, reached its peak early in the next century, only to suffer a sharp decline through Victorian attacks on his candid, sometimes brutal and coarse, portrayal of existence. However, with renewed scholarly interest in the picaresque form, a growing concern for eighteenth-century literature generally and the novel in particular, and a radically altered critical attitude toward literary realism, twentieth-century critics have been reevaluating Smollett's writing.

When I wrote the preface to the first edition of this study in 1968, a genuine revival of interest in Smollett had already begun to manifest itself. Shortly before publication of my book, works about Smollett by Donald Bruce and Robert Giddings had appeared. All three were followed by an important festschrift to Lewis Knapp, the preeminent twentieth-century Smollettian. At almost the same time, Paul-Gabriel Boucé produced his monumental study of Smollett's novels—first in French and then in a helpful, although abridged, translation. Subsequently, Damian Grant offered an excellent appraisal of Smollett's style; Alan Bold edited a collection of essays on *Smollett: Author of the First Distinction;* and George S. Rousseau presented his *Tobias Smollett: Essays of Two Decades.* Annual bibliographies of eighteenth-century literature suggest a sustained interest in Smollett's work—serious and substantial, although not equal to that in his major contemporaries.

For all that, Smollett remains the major eighteenth-century novelist least accessible to the modern reader. Unlike Fielding, he does not temper his harsh realism with strains of optimism. He does not appeal to current concerns for feminism that have aroused attention to the work of Richardson. His humor fails to capture the whimsical and fanciful tone that marks Sterne's idiosyncratic treatment of a tragic view of life that twentieth-century readers find compatible with their own angst when confronted by the overwhelming anxieties about existence. Not surprisingly, then, many general readers may turn away from a novelist unrelenting in his realistic depictions of experience and find him cruel, depraved, and indecent. Even a "distinguished eighteenth-century scholar," cited by Rousseau, can find no reason for offering a new edition of a writer whose mind is depraved and rotted and whose novels present "just random and perverse human indecency."[1]

Such judgments are themselves perverse. Smollett is a novelist of the first rank. His work is as lively, interesting, and readable as that of any of his contemporaries. He creates his own fictional world with an intensity that has a Dickensian appeal. In major and minor novels his gallery of characters has a vitality that Dickens himself admired. As a storyteller Smollett stands alongside the best in the English language. From novel to novel he displays his virtuosity in fictional experimentation. Given the chance to experience his work, unencumbered by prejudicial Victorian critics and those who echo them, alert to the values that characterize his novels and the passion that informs their attack on injustice and arbitrary power, the average twentieth-century reader will find much to admire in Smollett's novels. It is for such a reader that I have written this study. Like his friend the artist William Hogarth, Smollett may be an acquired taste, but it is one well worth acquiring.

To that end I offer a full-scale analysis of Smollett's literary achievement with this book. In a preliminary survey of his career, I have sought to present the fundamental values and techniques in his minor writing—his poetry, plays, histories, journalism, *Travels,* and *Adventures of an Atom*—that also characterize his novels. Subsequent chapters deal in depth with each novel, showing its place in the canon, measuring its successes and failures, and analyzing its structure, themes, and fictional devices. In this updated edition I present additional discussion of much of Smollett's minor work, particularly his histories, the *Atom,* and the *Travels,* and I have taken account of subsequent criticism of the novels. I deal with questions raised about the extent of Smollett's modification of the picaresque in the Afterword. To permit the reader to benefit from the increased scholarly interest in Smollett's work, I have considerably expanded the annotated bibliography.

Contrary to most critical opinion, I argue that Smollett maintained the picaresque form throughout his five novels, that *Humphry Clinker,* no less than *Roderick Random,* belongs to that genre. To be sure, no great novelist— and Smollett was that—could be content with merely repeating his technique from one work to the next, let alone in five successive novels. Smollett did not. In *Roderick Random* he came as near as any English writer to the traditional picaresque. *Peregrine Pickle* altered the form by adding a more specific moral significance, a change that influenced the development of the picaresque in the great English novels of the nineteenth century. With *Ferdinand Count Fathom* Smollett took another turn and set his rogue hero (or antihero) against the background of a kind of fairy tale, giving the work the qualities of a moral fable. Moreover, he effectively applied to the novel devices drawn from the drama of his own and Shakespeare's times. *Sir Launcelot Greaves,* combining an imitation of *Don Quixote* with contemporary satire, added another dimension to the picaresque. Even *Humphry Clinker,* so often described as a complete change in Smollett's technique, as a world apart from his first two novels, continues his experimentation. The epistolary devices and the dual picaros in his final novel demonstrated once more the multiple possibilities in adapting the traditional form for use in the writer's own age.

About Smollett's importance as a novelist there can be no disagreement. And yet another aim of this study is to show that his talents were not limited to *Roderick Random* and *Humphry Clinker,* which have received the bulk of twentieth-century critical attention. *Peregrine Pickle,* upon examination, proves to be a work just below the very top rank in the fiction of its time. Even *Ferdinand Count Fathom* and *Sir Launcelot Greaves* have been too readily dismissed. To be sure, they are not altogether first-rate novels, but they give evidence of Smollett's remarkable narrative ability, and in some of their scenes show his writing at its very best.

In order to make my arguments clear and emphatic, I have repeatedly repudiated previous critical appraisals. As a result, my own work sometimes suggests less indebtedness than actually exists. But there should be no doubt of my obligations to the scholarship recorded in my bibliography. To the late Lewis Knapp my gratitude is both personal and scholarly. I am equally indebted to the kindness and scholarship of Paul-Gabriel Boucé and George S. Rousseau, from both of whom I have learned much over the years. To Long Island University I owe thanks for the invaluable gifts of pleasant working conditions and accommodations of time. The late James R. Foster introduced me to Smollett and the eighteenth century, and I am grateful.

Robert Donald Spector

Long Island University

Chronology

1721   Tobias George Smollett baptized 19 March in parish church of Cardross, Dumbartonshire, Scotland. Third child of Archibald Smollett and Barbara Cunningham Smollett, whose marriage without parental consent had angered Sir James Smollett, the novelist's grandfather and head of a family of Whigs and Presbyterians. Death of Archibald Smollett, shortly after Tobias's birth, leaves family without income and probably dependent upon James Smollett of Bonhill, a cousin.

1727   Enters Dumbarton grammar school. Its Headmaster, or 1728   John Love (1695–1750), an outstanding teacher, later and erroneously described as model for schoolmaster in *Roderick Random*.

1731   Death of grandfather, Sir James Smollett, probably the original for the village tyrant in *Roderick Random*.

1735   Begins work in Glasgow dispensary. Perhaps enrolled at Glasgow University. No record of matriculation or graduation, but matriculation not compulsory for other than "gown" students in Art planning for degree and students voting in Rectoral elections; but even this requirement not strictly enforced. Writes satires during this time.

1736   Apprenticed to William Stirling and John Gordon, Glasgow surgeons. Recorded on 30 May; begins in April five-year term to run until April 1741. Gordon perhaps the original for satirical portrait of Potion in *Roderick Random*.

1739   Arrives in London after June, after release from apprenticeship upon developing cough in 1738. Financial difficulties at home. Brings with him to London completed manuscript of *The Regicide,* a tragedy, which he tries unsuccessfully for eight years to have produced.

1740   Passes examination for naval service. On 10 March obtains warrant from the Navy Board. Qualified for "second mate of a third rate," equivalent to surgeon's second mate.

1740–1741   Serves on the *Chichester,* beginning 3 April 1740. May have been on the tragic expedition to Cartagena in 1741.

1741–1744   Biographical data lacking (21 September 1741–May 1744). Naval service possible; residence in Jamaica certain. Probably in England in 1742 and then in Jamaica 1742–44. Marries (1743?) Anne Lassells, heiress of a Jamaican plantation owner.

1744–1745   Sets up as surgeon, May (?) 1744, in Downing Street, London, until following March.

1744   First publication, *A New Song,* issued with music by James or 1745   Oswald; printed in revised form in *Roderick Random.*

1746   Moves to Chapel Street, Mayfair; remains there until 1748. Writes *The Tears of Scotland*—poem on atrocities of Duke of Cumberland's troops at Culloden during Jacobite Rebellion; put to music by James Oswald. In September *Advice,* verse satire and first example of his satirical writing, appears.

1747   *Reproof,* sequel to *Advice.*

1747   Only child, Elizabeth, born (before April 1748). or 1748

1748   January, *The Adventures of Roderick Random,* written in 1747. Moves to more spacious quarters in Beaufort Street, St. Clement Danes, Savoy Ward; remains until 1750. Visits Oxford, Blenheim, and Stowe in June. Translation of Le Sage's *Gil Blas.*

1749   *The Regicide* published on Royal Paper in May; for public, in June. In summer, visits France, Flanders, Holland.

1749–1750   Plans to have Rich produce his *Alceste*—an opera, tragedy, and masque—fail to materialize. Manuscript subsequently lost, but a lyric from the work survives (*Modern Language Notes,* February 1948). Unsuccessful attempts to produce the comedy *The Absent Man* (manuscript now lost).

1750   Receives medical degree from Marischal College, Aberdeen and moves to Old Chelsea in June; remains until 1763. Probably visits Paris in summer. Le Sage's *The Devil upon Crutches,* translation almost certainly Smollett's.

1751   *The Adventures of Peregrine Pickle,* 25 February. Parts of the novel apparently written before his trip to Paris in 1750.

1751–1752   Publishes three book reviews in Griffiths' *Monthly Review:* John Cleland's *Memoirs of a Coxcomb;* Dr. William Smellie's *Treatise on the Theory and Practice of Midwifery;* Dr. John Pringle's *Observations on the Diseases of the Army.*

1752   *Essay on the External Use of Water* (March) exposes unhygienic conditions at Bath and defends Archibald Cleland, a surgeon under attack for taking a similar stand. *A Faithful Narrative . . . of Habbakkuk Hilding,* an attack on Fielding attributed to Smollett, also appears.

1753   *Adventures of Ferdinand Count Fathom,* apparently written in 1752. Tried in the King's Bench for assault on Peter Gordon, who had refused to repay loan, and Edward Groom, Gordon's landlord; forced to pay damages and costs. Trial before 23 February, after 23 January. June, visits Scotland for about five months. Increased signs of an asthmatic condition.

1754   Publishes his edition of Alexander Drummond's travel book, *Travels through Different Cities of Germany, Italy, Greece and Several Parts of Asia.* Translation from French of *Select Essays on Commerce.* Edits second volume of Dr. Smellie's *Cases in Midwifery.* 16 March makes proposals in *Public Advertiser* for translation of *Don Quixote.*

1755   25 February translation of *Don Quixote,* begun as early as 1748.

1756   Commences publication of the *Critical Review* 1 March; editor until 1763. General editor of *A Compendium of Authentic and Entertaining Voyages,* a seven-volume anthology, published in April

1757   April, first three volumes of his *Complete History of England. The Reprisal; or the Tars of Old England,* a farce, produced at Theatre Royal, Drury Lane, 22 January; published 1 February.

1758   Revised edition of *Peregrine Pickle*; omits earlier attacks on
         Garrick and others. Fourth volume and complete revision of
         Complete History. May, review of Admiral Charles Knowles's
         defense of his conduct at Rochefort. Sued for libel. To save
         Archibald Hamilton, publisher, from prosecution, acknowl-
         edges authorship on June 2. Between June and October, trip
         to Continent for health.

1759   Publication begun of *The Modern Part of the Universal
         History;* continued until 1765, with Smollett as one of
         the editors.

1760   January, begins publication, with Oliver Goldsmith, of *Brit-
         ish Magazine, or Monthly Repository*. Remains as co-editor
         until 1763. Weekly publication in parts of *Continuation of
         the Complete History of England* begins May. Throughout the
         year and until December 1761, *The Adventures of Sir
         Launcelot Greaves* serialized in *British Magazine;* first seriali-
         zation by important novelist. Visit to Scotland likely. Impris-
         oned in King's Bench, November, for Knowles's libel.

1761   Released from prison, probably before completion of
         three-month sentence. First volume of translation of *The
         Works of . . . Voltaire,* done with Thomas Francklin and
         concluded in 1769.

1762   March, *Sir Launcelot Greaves*. Publishes the *Briton* from 29
         May until 12 February 1763. Defends Lord Bute's ministry
         against attacks of John Wilkes and Charles Churchill in the
         North Briton. Death of mother-in-law, Mrs. Leaver, in De-
         cember, leaving inheritance to Smollett's wife.

1763   Daughter Elizabeth dies 3 April. Journeys to France and Italy
         in June; spends most time in Nice; remains away from En-
         gland until July 1765.

1765   Returns to London, July. Travels for health to Bath and Hot
         Wells (Bristol). October, fifth and final volume of *Continua-
         tion of the Complete History of England* published.

1766   Visits Scotland in spring. Very ill. At Bath until at least May
         1768. *Travels through France and Italy.*

1767   Rejected for consulship for third time (first in Pitt's adminis-
         tration in 1756–58; second in Bute's, 1762). Possible publi-

cation of second edition of *An Essay on the External Use of Water.*

1768   First weekly number of the *Present State of All Nations* 25 June; completed in 1769. Leaves England for Pisa, Italy, in fall.

1769   *The History and Adventures of an Atom,* about 1 April. By October settled at Leghorn, Italy.

1770   Death of mother, in Scotland.

1771   *The Expedition of Humphry Clinker,* about 15 June. First two volumes and portion of third probably composed from 1765 to 1768; concluded in 1770. Dies on 17 September from acute intestinal infection. Buried on 19 September in English cemetery at Leghorn.

1773   *Ode to Independence.* Monument erected in Leghorn cemetery.

1776   Translation of Fénelon's *Adventures of Telemachus.*

1791   Death of Anne Smollett, his wife.

Chapter One
From Grub Street to Parnassus

To the imaginative young men arriving from the British provinces or from the hinterlands of Ireland and Scotland, eighteenth-century London must have seemed an attractive mistress. Whatever her moral failings, however soiled her physical charms, she promised recent arrivals an excitement and adventure not to be found in the generally quiet, superficial purity of their former domesticity. A Jonathan Swift, having engaged in the capital's nasty political intrigues, from which he might well have been expected to desire escape, regarded instead his appointment as Dean of St. Patrick's in Dublin as a kind of exile. London was a place where an Irishman like Oliver Goldsmith, quartered through compelling financial circumstances among the booksellers of Grub Street, could come intellectually alive in the society of Samuel Johnson from Lichfield, or where David Garrick, Johnson's former student, could cast off his provinciality on the stage of the Drury Lane and step forth into the world of English aristocracy. Even a Scotsman like James Boswell, familiar with the not unattractive intellectual atmosphere of Edinburgh, grew bored and restless outside London's social and literary activity.

For a writer, especially, London must have held an inescapable fascination. In St. Paul's Churchyard, Little Britain, and Paternoster Row; on Fleet Street, St. James's, and in the Strand—booksellers and publishers abounded. Journalists, playwrights, poets, essayists, and novelists congregated in the numerous coffeehouses. Drury Lane, Covent Garden, and smaller unlicensed theaters offered dramatists display cases for their talents. If a young writer wanted to succeed in the English world of letters, London surely beckoned irresistibly.

The Outsider

It was natural, then, for Tobias Smollett, in ill health and desperate financial need, a completed tragedy in his pocket, to come from Glasgow to try his luck in the London theater in 1739. But like so many others who courted her favor, he discovered that London was a hard mistress, slow and unwilling to yield to his demands, never easily acquiescent. For someone of his temperament, for someone in his situation, whatever her initial attractiveness, London could not long retain her charm. And it was only after eight long years—years of disappointment with theater managers, of naval service aboard one of His Majesty's men-of-war, of unsuccessful medical practice—only after some little recognition through two verse satires and the greater acclaim of a successful novel, that he was able to have his play published, and that without the work's creating much stir.

Moreover, Smollett, like Goldsmith and Boswell, learned that in the England dominated by John Bull's insular nationalism, British subjects from Ireland and Scotland were almost unalterably outsiders. Smollett quickly recognized the distance that separated him from the mainstream of London life; and, throughout his years of fervid activity there, he remained ever conscious "of his alien Scottish origins."[1] For him England was a "land of indifference and phlegm where the finer sensations of the soul are not felt, and felicity is held to consist in stupifying Port and overgrown buttocks of Beef."[2] Writing to his friend Alexander Carlyle, even after the success of *Roderick Random,* Smollett bemoaned this country "where genius is lost and taste extinguished" and expressed an obvious nostalgia for Scotland. Smollett was an outsider. Unlike the majority of eighteenth-century writers, he belonged to no literary societies, no clubs. He was, in fact, a member of no social organizations except a small group of Scottish physicians.[3]

Despite the contention of Lewis Knapp, his chief biographer, that evidence for Smollett's isolation from English life should not be overemphasized, Knapp himself acknowledges that it "may mean that Smollett felt exiled from English personalities of similar interests and achievements" and that he "probably moved chiefly in Caledonian circles."[4] The fact that Smollett was "socially gifted" and generous in his dealings with even unappreciative Scottish expatriates, who then disappointed him, would have served only to intensify his feelings as an outsider in London.

Both this position as outsider and the normal difficulty of achieving literary success in the great city naturally affected Smollett's development as a writer. His situation accorded naturally with his conservative temperament, his desire for a well-ordered society, and his concern about corrupt standards and distorted values that posed obstacles to his own development.[5] For Smollett the novelist, spiritually and socially apart from the community in which he lived, the satirist's perspective was most accommodating; and the picaresque technique was most appropriate. Satire became not only the dominant tone but the very theme of his novels; the picaresque tradition, in varying degrees and in diverse ways, formed the very foundation of his fiction. As George Kahrl has suggested,[6] Smollett, owing no allegiance to English culture, could concern himself in a peculiar way with its public life: its law courts, resorts, inns, and prisons. In dealing with English characters Smollett emphasizes their foibles; in his treatment of English squires, the symbol of a hierarchy, he is invariably satirical. Even his method of describing these figures from the outside seems attributable, at least in part, to his special position in their society.

The Writer

Smollett, who had started by writing plays and whose reputation rests on his achievements as a novelist, wrote in almost every conceivable genre, but that fact had little to do with his condition as outsider. Varied literary activity characterized the eighteenth-century man of letters who depended on his craft for a livelihood—as well the "true-born Englishman" Henry Fielding, or the grand master of the Establishment, Samuel Johnson, as Scotland's Tobias Smollett or Ireland's Oliver Goldsmith.

From 1739 until his death in 1771 Smollett published an amount of material that in quantity, at least, could hardly have been exceeded by the output of his most industrious contemporaries. Only the blind political prejudice of Horace Walpole could have permitted him to speak of "indolent Smollett."[7] For along with his dramas there was a body of poetry. He translated, as well, the works of Le Sage, Cervantes, and Voltaire; edited a major journal of criticism and a popular magazine; compiled travel books and encyclopedic volumes of history. During the final days of the Seven Years' War he engaged in political controversy in opposition to John Wilkes and the *North Briton*. As a doctor of medicine, he wrote essays on the subject and lent aid to friends whose work required his editorial talents or his journalistic defense. He became a historian who, in popularity, rivaled the enormously successful David Hume. He brought forth his own contentious and controversial book of travels near the end of a life that had been devoted mainly to literature in one form or other.

To be sure, only Smollett the novelist seems important today; and only two of his novels—*Roderick Random* and *Humphry Clinker*—give him any genuine claim to literary eminence. Yet, to ignore the rest of his work not only distorts his image as a writer, it denies any complete understanding of his masterpieces, obscures any true comprehension of what it meant to be a man of letters in eighteenth-century England, and falsely suggests that there is nothing else worthy of study in this massive production.

The Plays

What seem among the least worthwhile in Smollett's canon are, ironically, his plays, particularly *The Regicide,* the heroic drama that first brought him to London. It has every fault of that genre without a single redeeming feature. Its treatment of Stuart's attempt to usurp the throne of James I of Scotland reduces the classical rules of unity to absurdity. At best such heroic tragedy, with its action jammed into twenty-four hours, places enormous demands on the reader's credulity, taxes his power of sympathy in the presence of carnage that piles death upon death with such rapidity that it gives him no time for an expression of sorrow.

Requiring a majestic power of language, a nobility of sentiment, Smollett's play has neither. Its diction is artificial; its characterization, ludicrous. Listening to Eleonora, torn between her love for Stuart, her loyalty to her father, who is James's devoted supporter, and her admiration for the faithful and heroic Dunbar, the reader remains unmoved. Stock characterizations of the villainous Athol and Grime—using Stuart's pretensions to further their own designs—are as unconvincing as the attenuated deathbed orations of Eleonora and Dunbar. Punctuated with "ohs," "alases," and exclamation points, their final speeches border on the comic:

> *Eleon*. That thus our hope,
> Which blossom'd num'rous as the flow'ry spring
> Are nipp'd untimely, ere the sun of joy
> Matur'd them into fruit, repine not, youth—
> Life hath its various seasons, as the year;
> And after clust'ring autumn—but I faint—
> Support me nearer—in rich harvest's rear
> Bleak winter must have lagg'd.—Oh! now I feel
> The leaden hand of death lie heavy on me.—
> Thine image swims before my straining eye—
> And now it disappears.—Speak—bid adieu
> To the lost Eleonora.—Not a word!—
> Not one farewell!—Alas! that dismal groan
> Is eloquent distress!—Celestial pow'rs!
> Protect my father, show'r upon his—Oh! [dies]
> *Dun*. There fled the purest soul that ever dwelt
> In mortal clay!—I come, my love! I come—
> Where now the rosy tincture of these lips!
> The smile that grace ineffable diffus'd!
> The glance that smote the soul with silent wonder!

The voice that sooth'd the anguish of disease,
And held attention captive!—Let me kiss
This pale deserted temple of my joy!
This, chastity, this, thy unspotted shade
Will not refuse.—I feel the grisly king—
Through all my veins he shivers like the north—
O Eleonora! as my flowing blood
Is mix'd with thine—So may our mingling souls
To bliss supernal wing our happy—Oh! [dies]
                                        (5.8)[8]

Everywhere there are borrowings from Shakespeare: the device from *Othello* of using the envious and dissatisfied officer to precipitate the monarch's fall; the material from *Julius Caesar* in which the queen unsuccessfully attempts to thwart the disaster with unheeded admonitions. But nowhere is there Shakespeare's—or even a much less talented dramatist's—ability to delineate character or create a proper respect for the tragedy.

It is impossible to fault the general criticism of the play, to disagree with Knapp, who calls it the "dullest thing Smollett ever wrote,"[9] or David Hannay, who terms it a "crude and boyish production."[10] Only the contemporary *Monthly Review* had kind words for it; and John Cleland, the reviewer, seems to have had some personal grievance with the theater managers who had rejected the play.[11] For clearly, as Arnold Whitridge has noted, its "dialogue is always stilted, usually to the pitch of absurdity";[12] and it has, in Howard Buck's terms, "no intrinsic value, nor does it contain the seed of later achievement."[13] It was, to be sure, a work by a young man; yet Smollett not only continued to have faith in it after its first rejection by the theater managers, but actually revised it many times, so that the published version presumably represents improvements and makes the reader wonder how atrocious it previously must have been.

Nevertheless, the play is important for any study of Smollett. Not only does Smollett's personal experience in trying to get it on the London stage provide the material for Melopoyn's adventures in *Roderick Random,* but the episode itself contributes to his enmity with David Garrick and others who figure in his first and second novels—an enmity that he details in the Preface to the published drama. What is more important, *The Regicide,* in its content and publication history, adds to our understanding of Smollett as man and author. In his persistent attempt to have his drama produced, he revealed that stubborn tenacity that enabled him to overcome the physical and financial handicaps that harassed him throughout his career. In the kind of fury that he expressed with those he felt were being unfair, against what he believed to be injustice, he demonstrated the temperament that led him naturally to satire. He knew how to be angry; he was unafraid to assail what he regarded as improper authority, no matter how powerful its forces.

Out of the failure of his tragedy there are lessons to be learned about Smollett's art. His inability to give life and credence to his heroine, Eleonora; his ineffectiveness with labored and ornate diction; and his more natural inclination to caricature—all foreshadow his problems and techniques as a novelist. It is difficult to believe that deep within himself he did not recognize that the heroic manner was unsuited to his talents. To be sure, he attempted unsuccessfully to produce his tragic opera *Alceste* (even the manuscript of which has disappeared) in the same year as *The Regicide*, but he was also at work trying to bring a comedy—*The Absent Man*—to the boards; and, when he finally produced his next and last play, he turned from the tragic genre to his natural comic art.

The Regicide displays as well some general characteristics of Smollett's writing: his practice of imitation, performed poorly here, was nevertheless his customary approach to literature—Shakespeare, Cervantes, Le Sage, and his contemporaries were all more important to him than his own powers of invention. Despite his use of the picaresque and realistic traditions, his learning and his attitudes were classical; and it was most natural for him to incline toward imitation and, in his first literary effort, attempt something in a characteristically classical genre.

Smollett's only other surviving play—the comedy *The Reprisal; or, The Tars of Old England*—has a little more to recommend it than *The Regicide*. It clearly reflects his journalistic methods and displays, unlike his tragedy, his characteristic manner. Written and produced at the beginning of the Seven Years' War, his comedy is a piece of political propaganda, a "broad farce glorifying the British sailor and depicting the [enemy] French as a nation of *petits maîtres*."[14] It has, to be sure, a flimsy plot, describing the capture by a French man-of-war of a British pleasure boat that is captained by a rapacious but inefficient scoundrel who cannot even control the Irish and Scottish officers in his employ. After a comedy of errors, the hero escapes and returns with a British warship to rescue the heroine and to make the Frenchman grovel for mercy.

Smollett was, in journalistic fashion, taking advantage of topical interest. Ridiculing the enemy French with stock characterization, he appeals mainly to the nationalistic interest aroused by the war. Yet the play also reveals his talents as a caricaturist, his fondness for dialect humor, and his easy familiarity with naval life. "Devil burn me!" the Irishman Oclabber exclaims, "but my bowels wept salt water to see her sweet face look so sorrowful!" (act 1, scene 2). And the idiom suggests the speech of Bowling and Trunnion in Smollett's novels. There is also in the play's broadly farcical spirit some of that "colorfully grotesque gallery" of characters and "not a little of that stanchness enjoyed by all Smollett's sea-pieces."[15] Whatever its dramatic limitations, *The Reprisal* anticipates Douglas Jerrold's *Black Eyed Susan* and even Gilbert and Sullivan's *Pinafore;*[16] and, despite rude treatment by contemporary reviewers, it enjoyed some popular success on the stage.[17] And for Smollett there must have been great satisfaction in the fulfillment of the ambition to be a playwright that had brought him to London some eighteen years before.

Yet despite his promise in the epilogue to *The Reprisal,* he never again came before the public as a dramatist. Perhaps he was too busy with his journalistic and editorial ventures. Or perhaps he simply recognized that his talents were not dramatic, for certainly Knapp is right, after all, to say that his plays are "negligible . . . as literature."[18]

The Poetry

Whether his poetic talents—some of which were, in fact, displayed in *The Reprisal*—were greater than the dramatic may be questionable; but the poetry, like the drama, remains important for understanding the man, his work, and particularly his temperament. For whatever judgment may be made of his small body of poetry, as Buck has declared, "without [his poetical temperament], what would [his novels] be? In his prose fiction . . . —his only surely immortal work—it was the poet that was in him that is the leaven of the lump."[19]

Judged solely as poetry, at least four of Smollett's works command attention; and each has significance in revealing traits of his personality or illuminating points in his biography or success in his novels. The first of these poems—*The Tears of Scotland*—was also likely his initial means of catching the public's eye. An ode responding to the reported atrocities of the Duke of Cumberland's army at Culloden after the victory over the Jacobite forces, the poem had the advantage, at least for Scots, of appealing to aroused sympathies and to a sense of outrage. With what passion could those exiles from North of the Tweed respond to the lamentation in Smollett's opening stanza:

> Mourn, hapless Caledonia, mourn
> Thy banish'd peace, thy laurels torn!
> Thy sons, for valour long renown'd,

> Lie slaughter'd on their native ground;
> Thy hospitable roofs no more
> Invite the stranger to the door;
> In smoky ruins sunk they die,
> The monuments of cruelty.

In itself, Smollett's verse may suffer, as Goldsmith noted, from an imperfection in its "numbers and language,"[20] a serious defect in a short work. Yet it conveys his youthful idealism and ardor; and, in his willingness to bring it before an English public, it suggests his characteristically independent spirit and "the scorn of consequence . . . which was the ruling passion of Smollett's life."[21] Moreover, it gives further evidence of his feeling as an outsider in his London surroundings; for, if the poem does not surely indicate, as his enemies insinuated, that he was a Jacobite sympathizer, it nevertheless asserts the depths of his Scottish patriotism.

In similar ways, Smollett's verse satires—*Advice* and *Reproof*—now seem more important for an understanding of the novelist than for any intrinsic literary qualities that they may possess, although they are at least as respectable as the many imitations of Alexander Pope written at the time.[22] *Advice* is a dialogue—imitative of Pope's form in the Horatian satires but written in the vigorous bludgeoning spirit of Juvenal—[23] between the poet and a friend. Listening to the friend's cynical counsel on how to succeed in the literary world, the poet stubbornly responds, "Two things I dread, my conscience, and the law"; to which the friend replies, "Too coy to flatter, and too proud to serve / Thine be the joyless dignity to starve" (lines 220, 236–37). What better summary of Smollett's character and his relation to society! Whether his insistence that he satirizes vice out of a sense of obligation rather than from misanthropy is more than the conventional apologetics of the satirist seems ultimately less consequential than this dedication to independence, this determination to strike down what he believes to be wrong, without personal fear, without regard for the strength of his opposition.

In its first edition *Advice* includes as its most sustained attack a passage devoted to sexual perversion. The character of Sir John Cope, the main target for Smollett's satire in *Reproof*, bears the brunt of the assault. By now, of course, it is impossible and relatively unimportant to determine the justification for Smollett's charges, although he was not reluctant to repeat them in print.[24] What mainly concerns the critic, however, is the writer's preoccupation with the subject. Smollett, like Fielding, is a strongly masculine novelist; and sexual deviance arouses his wrath. His poetry strikes out upon the subject with all the vigor of Pope's satire, and *Advice* recalls Smollett's portrait of

Captain Whiffle in *Roderick Random* and the many passages on sexual aberrations and suggestions of transvestism in *Peregrine Pickle*.

But *Advice* is not limited to this subject. It very nearly catalogues Smollett's characteristic attitudes, his manner, and his likes and dislikes. He clearly thought of himself as an Augustan satirist in the tradition of Pope and Swift; and, in fact, he was their spiritual heir. His commonsense approach led him to a derision of the dunces of Grub Street, to a mockery of the impracticalities and absurdities often recorded in the transactions of the Royal Society, and to a general denunciation of the entrenched Whig oligarchy. His particular affinity is to Swift, not only in the antipapist commentary and the assault on the falsities of literary patronage, but also in the rough, physical, and frequently vulgar humor that for both men perhaps made prose the most logical vehicle for their satire.

Not much distinguishes the second verse satire from *Advice,* to which it is linked by the opening lines in which the friend chides the poet for having published his private counsel and the poet replies by arguing the necessity for honesty. Despite Buck's claim that *Reproof* is better general satire,[25] both poems suffer from personal allusions interesting to contemporaries but now requiring annotation. Here again Smollett insists that not rancor but flourishing vices and corruption evoke his wrath. What distinguishes the two poems, however, is Smollett's greater concentration in *Reproof* on a particular topic: his renewed attack on Sir John Cope, whose unheroic military conduct against the Highlanders had made him the subject of national ridicule and had also led to his trial. Using animal allegory, in which Cope is depicted as Sir Ape, Smollett parodies the events; asking for help from their monarch, the beasts get what they request:

> Their pray'r was heard, and by consent of all,
> A courtier ape appointed general.—
> He went, he led, arrang'd the battle stood,
> The savage foe came pouring like a flood,
> Then pug aghast, fled swifter than the wind,
> Nor deign'd in threescore miles to look behind;
> While ev'ry band for orders bleat in vain,
> And fall in slaughter'd heaps upon the plain:
> The scar'd baboon (to cut the matter short)
> With all his speed could not outrun report;
> And, to appease the clamours of the nation,
> 'Twas fit his case should stand examination.
>
> (lines 57–68)

This kind of attack "utilized the weapon of satire, which, in turn, involved libel, even personal libel."[26] And just such an attack was to lead the novelist, as editor of the *Critical Review,* into those difficulties with Admiral Knowles that culminated in his imprisonment.

Smollett's fourth noteworthy poem—the posthumously published *Ode to Independence*—also remains more important today for what it tells about the man than for its deft use of the Pindaric ode, a form which has no great appeal to a modern audience.[27] Fortunately, there is no doubt about the authenticity of Smollett's authorship and, consequently, the poem stands as a tribute to the determination that was his spirit. By 1765, the probable date of its composition, Smollett was a man broken in health, defeated in political enterprise, and saddened by the death of his only child. The vigor of the poem arouses admiration for his tenacity, the courage of his spirit. From the "moving power" of its opening lines, the "strength of [his] soul" that runs throughout the poem can be felt:

> Thy spirit, Independence, let me share,
>   Lord of the lion-heart and eagle-eye;
> Thy steps I follow with my bosom bare,
>   Nor heed the storm that howls along the sky.

And, in the fine lines that close the third strophe, there is a summary of Smollett's own resolute determination to stand by his ideals, for which he paid so dearly in the course of his life:

> He, guardian genius, taught my youth
> Pomp's tinsel livery to despise:
>   My lips by him chastis'd to truth
> Ne'er paid that homage which my heart decries.[28]

As anyone familiar with Smollett's novels knows, these are not his only poems. In his fiction he scatters examples of serious lyrics, parody, satire, and burlesque. Some of these had a popularity of their own, appearing, along with other original verse, in contemporary magazines and drawing praise in his own day and for some years to come.[29] And yet the greatest value of his poetry rests, as has been noted, in what it reveals about the man and his temperament and in the way that it affected his novels, giving shape to scenes and providing the tone for his satire.[30]

Journalist, Historian

To an even greater degree than his poetry and drama, Smollett's enormous editorial and journalistic labor finds its main interest today as evidence of what appealed to an eighteenth-century audience, as testimony to his amazing industry, and as an influence upon his style. On the last point, especially, George Kahrl and Louis Martz have been insistent, arguing reasonably that Smollett's editorial and related labors gave a precision and refinement to his writing in his final novels.[31]

Compendiums of travel and history—appealing to the dominant taste of the times—engaged Smollett's attention and efforts to an extent remarkable even for an eighteenth-century man of letters. Whatever his satirical remarks about the labors of Grub Street drudges, he himself toiled in similar manner to meet the same financial needs. But it is again characteristic of his fundamental honesty that his ventures were more than merely the customary pilfering from other sources. If he sometimes "lacked candor in his use of sources" for such a work as the *Compendium of Voyages,* as Martz has pointed out, "[he] strove honestly to compile his collection from the best sources available . . . , and . . . did not follow the ordinary practice of stealing ready-made abstracts from other compilations." Martz has described the "integrity of [Smollett's] editorial standards" as he "filled out . . . original accounts with additional details from a variety of other books."[32] Although Smollett had the aid of a team of assistants for the mechanical processes of compilation, his own supervision was at all times "rigorous"; the selection of material and the revision were his; and much of the work is characterized by his unmistakable style.[33]

For his two popular and massive encyclopedias of modern history, his labor was not less; writing, compiling, and closely supervising the printing of the works, he was at the same time busy giving advice to the publisher and trying to increase sales by reviewing his own work in his own literary review. Again, as in his travel books, there are obvious relations to his novels: the encyclopedias contain material important for a study of *Humphry Clinker* and *The History and Adventures of an Atom,* as well as characteristic expressions of social, religious, and political attitudes.[34]

In this respect, Smollett's *History of England,* with its *Continuation,* is even more significant. The work has a strong Tory bias, and Smollett realized in advance that his history would draw the Whigs' wrath.[35] He claimed, however, that he had begun objectively—even with "a warm side to those [Whig] principles in which I was educated"—but that facts were, after all, facts; and these had convinced him of the scurrility of the Whig ministers.

No doubt he honestly believed in the truth of this statement, but facts are

indeed facts; and it seems apparent that, whatever his earlier political training, Smollett was naturally inclined to the Tory conservative stance of the
mid-eighteenth century. Like the earlier Tory satirists, Swift and Pope,
Smollett distrusted change, feared the aroused passions of the public, and
sought stability for the state; he did not identify such views with the new mer-
cantile interests that were coming to dominate the Whig party. Moreover, as
David Hannay, his nineteenth-century biographer, remarks, when Smollett
met the exiled Scottish Jacobites on his visit to France in 1750 (seven years
before the publication of his history), "he felt and wrote as he had done four
years before [in *The Tears of Scotland*], . . . as a man who was not a Jacobite,
but who was Tory enough and Scotchman enough to feel for his unfortunate
countrymen."[36]

In a spirited essay that seeks to defend Smollett's *History* from charges of
"poverty of style, intellectual shallowness, and gross partisanship,"[37] Donald
Greene's major concern is to challenge the view that the work expresses
Smollett's Tory sentiments. He briefly demonstrates the superiority of
Smollett's style to that of David Hume's history and, less convincingly, argues that Smollett's "businesslike but attention-holding prose" is more satisfactory than Macaulay's "brilliant stylistic pyrotechnics," which is over-
dramatized and "becomes tiresome and even ludicrous."[38] On the matter of
Smollett's politics in the *History*, Greene's argument relies on selective quotation, ignores the consensus of contemporary opinion, and neglects
Smollett's own comment on the effect his work would have on the "West
country whigs of Scotland."[39]

In a brief note to Smollett's letter regarding the reception of his *History*,
Edward Noyes long ago neatly summarized the process whereby Smollett
changed his principles from those of his Whig grandfather and stressed not
only the writer's reaction to the Whig repression of the rebellion of 1745, but
the fact that, like his Tory friends Home and Hume, he was "essentially aristocratic, and hated the mob, and the London mob was at this time largely
Whig in sympathy."[40] Those like Donald Greene and Robin Fabel,[41] who in-
sist that Smollett's political responses in his *History* and admittedly polemical works were based on interest in issues rather than parties, fail to note that
issues ultimately determine parties and that it was Lord Bute, a Tory, who selected Smollett as his chief spokesman in the partisan literary struggle at the
end of the Seven Years' War. Any further question of Smollett's Tory sentiments should be silenced by John Sekora's extensive discussion of the *History*, which details the manner in which he used the work to trace "the
continuity of present and past, discovering the source of contemporary ills in
the parliamentary victory he disdained to call glorious."[42]

Whatever its politics, Smollett's history was certainly a vehicle for express-ing his personal prejudices. He uses it to alter his earlier historical judgment of events, and he finds its pages convenient for making amends to former en-emies and rivals.[43] Garrick, Fielding, Lord George Lyttelton, Mark Akenside, and James Quin are praised where earlier they had been targets of attack; and even his detested political opponent, John Shebbeare, now (in 1761–62) an ally in defense of Lord Bute's administration, receives kind words from Smollett.

As for the literary merits of the history, which at the time hurt the sale of David Hume's already popular volumes,[44] they appear—contrary to Greene's judgment—not considerable, but sufficient. Smollett's work re-sembles H. G. Wells's kind of historical treatment, and at no time was it con-sidered a significant or serious contribution to historical knowledge. Yet David Hannay's judgment, which does not belittle Smollett's labor, is worth-while to recall because it still seems a justifiable conclusion:

Whoever will turn to his history without expecting more than he ought to expect, will find a well-written narrative, belonging, for the most part, to the same order of work as the summaries of the year printed by some newspapers, only decidedly better done than such things usually are.[45]

Editor, Translator, Publisher

Less need be said for Smollett's work as a translator of *Gil Blas* and *Don Quixote* and of Voltaire, for whose prose he also provided historical and crit-ical notes in the volumes he edited with Thomas Francklin. The transla-tions were journeyman's work; and, as he commented on *Gil Blas,* "it was a Book-seller's job, done in a hurry [and] I did not chuse to put my name to it."[46] Yet the picaresque, which he was familiar with long before he trans-lated it, was a primary influence on his own novels. The rendering of Voltaire subsequently proved serviceable in his composition of *The History and Adventures of an Atom.* As for the work on Cervantes's masterpiece, which has been characterized as consisting "principally of plagiarizing, par-aphrasing, rewriting, and inverting [Charles] Jarvis' translation,"[47] it, too, had a continuing effect on Smollett's fiction, particularly in its later use as a model for *Sir Launcelot Greaves.*

Of all Smollett's Grub Street productions, however, two—the *Critical Re-view* and the *Briton*—have particular significance for an understanding of his vitality, personality, and attitudes. The *Critical* was one of the two major re-views of the eighteenth century. When Smollett, as part of his plan for an academy of belles lettres,[48] with the publisher Archibald Hamilton and a "Society of Gentlemen" struck out on a venture that was to keep him engaged in journalistic controversy for more than seven years,[49] he had first to challenge the position of Ralph Griffiths's *Monthly Review,* which had stood alone in the field for almost a decade. That Smollett was successful is apparent not only in the fact that the *Critical Review,* with which he gained an immediate identification, was so well founded that it continued long after his connection with it had ended, but also in the measures that Griffiths was forced to take, almost at once, to meet the competition.[50]

Hurt by the impact of the new review, Griffiths required financial assistance and attempted circulation drives to counter the challenge. He increased the size of his periodical and borrowed features from his rival. In keeping with his projected plan for an academy of belles lettres, Smollett had introduced accounts of foreign publications; proudly proclaimed communication points in Paris, Rome, Lucca, Florence, Berlin, and The Hague; and later extended his list by eight cities. The *Monthly* responded with a foreign articles section of its own. To inform the *Critical* with a genuine air of intellectual interest, Smollett introduced a section on painting and engraving, subjects almost altogether neglected by the journalistic practices of the time. Griffiths's *Monthly,* with less success, followed suit. Within half a year of its first number, Smollett's review had gained a respectability and status equal to that of the *Monthly.* In his first periodicals venture Smollett had displayed the intelligence and industry that characterized his creative energy.

Since articles in the *Critical* were unsigned, the extent of Smollett's involvement as a writer used to be a matter of conjecture; but Derek Roper's recent discovery of a marked copy of the first volume supports the accuracy of Knapp's guess that such evidence would prove Smollett to be "the leading reviewer in London for the period from 1756 to 1763."[51] There has never been any question that, as editor, he brought the fullness of his personality, taste, and interests to the pages of the *Critical.* The review, in its record of controversies with Griffiths, John Shebbeare, John Hill, and Smollett's many other foes, was an intellectual, incisive, caustic, vitriolic, and spirited periodical that could have been only his.

Smollett took seriously his projected plan for an academy, and the *Critical* provided a basis for striking out at the literary dunces, medical quacks, and political and religious charlatans. Setting himself and his review up as an authority to pass judgment on the vast body of literary, political, scientific, and religious comment that passed before them, he took on the responsibility of a public defender at enormous cost to his health, reputation, and security. He became the target for venomous attacks that matched his own furious comment but irked his extremely sensitive temperament. Yet he never feared such angry combats as those he had with the sharp-witted poet Charles Churchill, the devious religious opportunist Archibald Bower, or the unscrupulous political hack writer John Shebbeare; and he never hesitated to come to the aid of friends like Dr. William Hunter, engaged in a medical controversy, or Lord Bute, involved in making the peace that ended the Seven Years' War.

To indicate the tone and spirit of the *Critical,* reflecting Smollett's own personality, nothing serves better than the review's pronunciamento to its readers, explaining its purpose and defying its opponents:

The task of professed critics, who undertake to reform the taste of mankind, is like that of cleansing the Auguean [*sic*] stable; they must not only wade through dung-hills of dullness, but also be exposed to the stench and stings of all the vermin hatched amidst such heaps of noisome pollution. . . .

The *Critical* reviewers, secure from personal abuse, will persevere in the execution of their plan, without paying the least regard to the undistinguishing clamour and impotent threats of bad writers, or their employers. . . . Every author who writes without talents is a grievance, if not an imposter, who defrauds the public . . . . (Vol. 1 [April 1756], 288)

Such a challenging stance could only contribute to direct confrontations with abused writers, and it kept Smollett embroiled in controversy. From the very outset he was publicly assumed responsible for what the review printed; and, when one of its articles assailed Admiral Charles Knowles for his conduct at the battle of Rochefort in 1757, Smollett, to protect his printer, acknowledged authorship in the belief that Knowles would seek a gentleman's satisfaction. The admiral, however, went to court; and Smollett was eventually sent to prison for a libel that had as its defense only the then-unacceptable argument of truth.[52]

The Knowles case is merely one example of Smollett's involvement in the *Critical,* an enterprise that greatly consumed the energies and talents of the novelist. Its pages reveal the personality of the satirist and record the characteristic attitudes and values of his fiction. The political, scientific, social, and literary opinions parallel those that govern his novels. During the period when Smollett was editor, the Seven Years' War was being fought; and the judgments, evaluations, and criticisms of men and events in the review are reflected in his fiction. Here are to be found his antagonism toward the Duke of Newcastle and the old Whig oligarchy, support of William Pitt for quelling the dangerous voices of faction, opposition to the alliance with and subsidy of Frederick of Prussia, vituperative treatment of the French, dissatisfaction

with appeasement of the new commercial interests, and arguments defending the peace negotiations of Lord Bute, King George III's Scottish prime
minister.

These attitudes are all consistent with Smollett's conservative view of government, his fear of radical change, and his trepidation at arousing the popular voice in politics. In the *Critical*'s pronouncements on the importance of
stability in church and state, Smollett's voice is clear. In the reviewers'
commonsense approach to religion and science Smollett's position, like
Swift's before, is evident. The conservative literary values of the *Critical* are
Smollett's own: the insistence upon the neoclassical dictum of *dulce et utile,*
admiration for classical antiquity, a reasonable dependence on the rules, arguments for imitation, and adherence to the theory of genres, disapproval of
chinoiserie and the Gothic, rejection of romantic and Rousseauistic primi-
tivism, and denunciation of radical innovation, as much in art, literature, and
language as in religion and politics.

Smollett's work for the *Critical* probably suggested him to Bute as the
man to write a political paper—the *Briton*—that would make publicly pal-
atable the minister's terms for concluding the Seven Years' War. Smollett's
service to the Tory minister required little sacrifice of principle. To be sure, it
brought him into conflict with his erstwhile friend John Wilkes, who was,
with Charles Churchill, editor of the *North Briton,* the foremost opposition
paper; but Smollett truly disdained the appeal to public emotion that was
Wilkes's primary instrument for argument. If loyalty to Bute necessitated
Smollett's rejection of his formerly favorable opinion of Pitt, the new attitude
was at least consistent with his view that the retired war minister was now
working to stir up the "dangerous" voices of faction that he had earlier silenced. Only a more charitable attitude toward the French that the peace negotiations required must have disturbed Smollett's conscience, for his
anti-French sentiment, as his novels disclose, was not superficial. However,
believing that the continuation of the war threatened political and economic
stability, Smollett could suppress his Gallic antipathies.[33]

And yet, with the sincerity of his purpose and all his experience in controversy, Smollett failed entirely with the *Briton.* Not only did he lose his battle
to make the peace terms and Bute himself attractive to the public; he actually
increased the paper warfare against his cause and became a conspicuous and
rather defenseless target for the opposition. The reasons for his defeat had little to do, however, with his journalistic ability. To an England aroused by military success, anything but the utter capitulation of the enemy was likely to be
unattractive. For Smollett to convince the public that Bute's peace terms
were fair and appropriate, he had to persuade his readers that they were either

greedy themselves or dupes of those whose avarice insisted upon making unnatural demands. He had to defend the Bute ministry at a time when it was
both waging war and negotiating and when each victory increased the public
expectation of reward and each defeat challenged the competency of the ministers. While Wilkes and Churchill had all the advantages of opposition, allowing them to choose the grounds of debate and giving them the initiative in
argument, Smollett could only parry in defense, waiting for the next assault.
Bute was no help, often informing the writer only after having taken action.
Moreover, as a Scot, the minister was an easy object of ridicule, hardly to be
defended by a Scottish author, who could be labeled a foreign mercenary, a
ministerial hireling, and, worst of all, a Tory Jacobite.

As polemical literature, the *Briton,* while not in the ranks of Swift's *Examiner,* seems no worse than the generality of such topical writing. Its devices are
those customary in eighteenth-century political journalism; and, if its use of
historical allegory, heavy irony, and name calling now seems tedious, it provided what the age demanded. For the modern reader interested in Smollett,
the *Briton* offers additional evidence of his conservative temperament. As
Byron Gassman has argued, by 1758, with *The Complete History of England,*
Smollett had rejected his early Whig principles and found himself in accord
with Tory attitudes.[54] Like the earlier Tory satirists, he expresses in the *Briton*
fear of the Whigs' inclination toward innovation and lack of respect for tradition. He opposes the principles of the Glorious Revolution that had de-
throned the majestic symbolism of monarchy. He argues for the king's
prerogative as a right that parliament was trying to usurp. Most important of
all, he is critical of what he regards as the luxury and decadence of the age and
attributes the general moral decline to the corruption of Whig governments.
In his attack upon what he regards as abuses of the language by his journalistic opponents, he appears to be defending one more part of the establishment
against what he believes to be Gothic or barbaric threats to the social and political stability of the state.

Of course, these arguments run counter to the political development of the
times; and Smollett, with the forces of history against him, stood no chance
of winning with the *Briton.* Moreover, like most political writers whose services are no longer needed, he was treated without regard by the king and his
minister. The experience with the *Briton,* together with the difficult and ago-
nizing labors for the *Critical,* left Smollett with a general bitterness and a
specific disgust for politics and politicians. Weary and sick, depressed by the
loss of his only child, he refused to be defeated. He turned to travel, and in
the sad days of his physical decline brought forth two prose works—excellent
in their kind—that reflect his mood and that belie the view that *Humphry*

Clinker is the result of a mellowed spirit. Indeed, as Gassman notes, the political views Smollett expresses in the *Briton* "are given imaginative expression through the observations, comments, and experiences of Matthew Bramble and his fellow travelers."[55]

Travel Writer

To point out the biographical significance of Smollett's *Travels through France and Italy* is not to return to the earlier mistaken view that the book is a fragment of autobiography. Older critics did believe that the travel book presents no more than the gathering of letters that Smollett had written during the journey he had taken with his wife, their servant, and two young ladies in 1763–65.[56] To some extent, Smollett's comments to correspondents might have seemed to justify such conclusions;[57] but, even where actual letters are used in the *Travels,* they are clearly "rearranged and replaced for publication."[58] Despite Laurence Sterne's simple identification of "Smelfungus" Smollett—irritable and irascible—with the traveler, it seems abundantly clear that Smollett's book is a fictionalized account, with a persona that bears a relationship to him personally similar to that of Matt Bramble in *Humphry Clinker* to the novelist who created him.[59]

Smollett carefully develops that persona to express the artistic intention of his collection of letters. Recent critics "who have learned to balance the autobiographical detail and Smollett's craftsmanship" have focused upon the characteristics of the persona and the manner in which they enable Smollett to turn his *Travels* into something more than the guidebooks that constituted a kind of genre of Grand Tour literature.[60] In an essay identifying the persona with contemporary literary and medical ideas of the melancholic man, John F. Sena pointed the way to a better understanding of the purpose of the *Travels,* relating the work, with its persona's quest for health, to Matt Bramble's similar journey in *Humphry Clinker.* Sena details the traveler's preoccupation with matters of diet, exercise, and climate and relates it to an aesthetic purpose, suggesting a didactic intention that achieves unity in a seemingly loosely assembled series of letters.[61] Scott Rice, expanding on a suggestion first advanced in Ronald Paulson's study of Smollett's satire, goes further than Sena in exploring Smollett's artistry. For Scott Rice the persona is drawn from a Juvenalian model of the public defender and is spurred on in his purpose by "righteous indignation." Smollett's pose allows him to reconcile "the nationalistic demands of the tour book and the condemnatory demands of satire by assailing . . . domestic vices in a foreign setting."[62] Rice regards him as a satiric spokesman fused with "Smollett's literal identity as an M.D. and a convalescent," bringing together "autobiographical, travel, and satiric materials into a single design."[63]

Although Rice and Sena offer significant insights into Smollett's methods and provide ample evidence of the artistic design of the *Travels,* neither perceives the essential change in the persona, who leaves England in an act of self-imposed exile as an expression of disgust for his native land, and concludes his journey as a celebratory spokesman for his country's virtues. The *Travels* is ultimately an exercise in *dulce et utile.* Smollett's spokesman serves his countrymen with a plethora of costs, prices, routes, and conveniences designed to protect them from the various villains and extorters they are likely to encounter on the Continent. He warns English travelers against foreign deception and affectation. For Englishmen likely to be intimidated by French arrogance, the persona insists on the superiority of the British character. For those too easily impressed by French products, institutions, and manners, he argues their inferiority to what is to be found at home. English small beer is preferable to French wine; English bridges are better constructed than French; roads at home are more convenient; French conditions are less sanitary, and French manners are pompous and dishonest.

With Italy Smollett's persona is unsparing. Its bridges cannot compete with Westminster or the one being prepared at Black-Friars. Italian gardens are nothing when set against Stowe, Kensington, and Richmond. Italian public houses offer lodgings comparable to those in British prisons. For both France and Italy the domination of Roman Catholicism undermines every aspect of the lives of their citizens; it vitiates the very taste and art of nations and under the oppressiveness of their religion "no country was ever known to prosper."[64] Strongly opinionated, as the subsequent French diatribes against him attest to, but determined to present himself as a meticulous, reliable, and concerned observer, Smollett's persona presents his letters in a design intended to serve a didactic purpose. His overall structure seeks to convince his reader that England, whatever its faults, presents the best prospect for happiness on earth.

But it is not the persona alone that gives Smollett's work an aesthetic value to go along with its biographical interest. Both Martz and Kahrl have demonstrated to what extent the letters in the *Travels* represent a literary device and how distinct his account is from the actual journey he had taken.[65] They have provided some of his sources and disclosed his methods; moreover, they have accurately commented upon the development of his style, the polish and precision of his diction, and the appeal to contemporary interest in his compilations of historical facts.[66] The result is a work artfully using the epistolary and travel forms to convey impressions and opinions that Smollett sincerely believes in and that are given a special sharpness by his acerbic mood.

Despite the newly expressed interest in the *Travels* as a work of literature, its conformance to genre expectations and its biographical value cannot be ignored. Smollett's nationalistic defense of England, while obviously expressing his personal views and written more vigorously and effectively than the majority of such books, fits the pattern of travel literature, a genre whose excessive patriotism Swift had earlier ridiculed. As for Smollett's persona, whatever its artistic functions, it is, after all, an alter ego of the author. The range of interests in the work is characteristically Smollett's and altogether appropriate to the genre of the travel book. His comments deal with classical antiquity, fine arts, religion, national differences, practical science, food, and natural beauty. There are opinions on Salvator Rosa, landscapes, waterfalls, ruins, and agriculture. Without allowing his judgment of the Continent— "its people, history, commerce, art, and culture"—to be influenced by petty considerations, he demanded "honesty, cleanliness, and a modicum of decency" in his travels.[67] On conditions for travelers, as Kahrl notes, "he was expressing with power and finality what all endured and only feebly and inadequately condemned."[68] Even when wrongheaded, his iconoclastic statements on art, which most aroused the criticism of his contemporaries, are an attempt to tear down what he genuinely believes to have been overpraised. Whatever may be said for his judgment and taste,[69] Smollett discloses no awe for accepted opinions. Others might blindly repeat the praise of the "famous Venus Pontia, commonly called *de Medicis*"; Smollett finds "no beauty in the features of Venus" and calls "the attitude . . . aukward and out of character" (236). The Parthenon, for all his "veneration for the antients," he can describe only as "a huge cockpit, open at top" (269).

It matters less whether modern judgment has come to support him on many points[70] than that he wrote with Johnsonian vigor and feeling about what had become the commonplaces of fashionable criticism in the contemporary guidebooks. The fullness of Smollett's power makes his *Travels* stand out today as a literary work, regardless of the accuracy of its aesthetic judgments. How dreary, as Kahrl says, would be "the mass of history, sociology, art criticism, archaeology, and natural history comprising the factual substance of the *Travels* . . . were it not animated by Smollett's own personality."[71] Its interest is biographical, certainly, because it reveals Smollett in a savage mood after the literary and political battles he had fought. But it endures, as well, as a work of literature, as one of the "most consistently praised of Smollett's works" today.[72] Even V. S. Pritchett, who finds little to approve of in Smollett's novels, unhesitatingly recommends his travel book.[73]

Satirist

Until recently few such recommendations were forthcoming for his other prose work of the period—a savage political satire entitled *The History and Adventures of an Atom*—although the work was favorably received by Smollett's contemporaries. Its indecency always has presented a target for attack, but in the eighteenth century there was at least some qualified praise.[74] With the exception of Arnold Whitridge, however, early modern scholars were generally content to discount it as "violent and unpleasant,"[75] "a coarse roman à clef whole only point is political satire."[76] Only Whitridge, in a fairly extensive account of "Smollett the Satirist," makes a staunch defense of the work in which "Smollett went forth to slay the same dragons that excite the indignation of all great satirists. The brutal stupidity of statesmen, the fickleness of the mob, hypocrisy masquerading as patriotism."[77] Whitridge acknowledges the weaknesses of a satire so tied to its time that it requires a key for later generations to understand it. He recognizes its "laborious filth and outlandish nomenclature."[78] Nevertheless, in a study that carefully illuminates its historical setting, Whitridge clearly appreciates the artistic power of the *Atom*.

In the past few years other critics have discovered that, "despite its scurrilous matter . . . and its unsavory techniques [making it] unquestionably the most scatological book-length work in English literature," the *Atom* deserves respect and serious scholarly attention.[79] Relating the satire to contemporary political prints and noting the function of its "thematic cluster of icons," Wayne Douglass has argued that the "directness, crudity, and intemperance of Smollett's satire can no longer be interpreted merely as an attempt to communicate with his readers using terms familiar to them" in the political controversy of the day.[80] Damian Grant's treatment of the *Atom* in his analysis of Smollett's prose style goes farther than any previous criticism in depicting the virtues of Smollett's work, its expression of his brilliance and inventiveness as a form of "comic fantasy."[81] Grant accurately describes the *Atom* as "an intellectual tour of political England during the Seven Years' War," recognizes how its fictional form yields wholly to its political satire, and presents in precise detail its revelation of Smollett's "linguistic sensibility."[82]

However one assesses its merits as literature, the *Atom* remains a work of considerable biographical and literary interest. Fictionalizing the history of Great Britain from 1754 to 1768, particularly the events of the Seven Years' War, Smollett recounts circumstances with which his work as editor of the *Critical* and the *Briton* had made him familiar. The thin mask of analogy—using Japan for England, Scotland, and Ireland; China, for France; Corea, for

Spain, Tartary, for Germany—does not hide his comments on contemporary history. It merely provides security for his expression of contempt for partisan political parties, his disillusionment with Pitt, his disappointment in Bute, and his characteristic distrust of popular government.

Whatever Smollett's earlier praise of Pitt, in the *Atom* Pitt has altogether lost favor with the novelist, who now presents him as a turncoat who has allowed public acclaim to turn him from his proper duties. Despite his former activities on behalf of Bute, Smollett—in the bitterness of his own withdrawal from the political scene and perhaps his sense of betrayal by the manner in which Bute terminated the *Briton*—can now see in that minister the artificialities and the hypocrisies of the politician. To be sure, Smollett is less severe with the Tories than with the despised Whigs, but by this time his political disgust has brought him to view the game of politics and its participants as nasty and mean-spirited, as leading to the natural dissidence of the mob.

Important as a source for revealing Smollett's characteristic attitudes toward political strife and his final assessment of the conduct of the war and the making of the peace, the *Atom* is also a bit of significant evidence for Smollett's general literary manner. His was never a simple inventive genius; he borrowed his materials and, through his powerful style, his own verve, gave them a personality that was his. From the picaresque *Roderick Random* to his last novel, he uses tradition and models to give impetus to his own talents.

The borrowings in the *Atom* are many. His major narrative device—a migratory atom, a transmigratory atom, settles in the mind of Nathaniel Peacock, a Briton; and it gives him a full account of an era in Japanese history that turns out to be parallel with British events of his own period—is attributable to such sources as Charles Johnstone's *Chrysal; or, the Adventures of a Guinea,* an essay in the *Spectator,* another in the *Adventurer,* and Voltaire's *Micromegas.* It also owes something to Swift, Le Sage, Fielding, and Lucian. There is further indebtedness in the *Atom* to Dr. John Shebbeare's *History of the Sumatrans,* Smollett's own history of Japan, the enormous vogue of "Oriental" literature, and the fashion of chinoiserie. And yet, such is Smollett's technique that the result is a work that could only belong to him.

As long ago as 1953, without any genuine external evidence of Smollett's authorship, James R. Foster was able to demonstrate from internal analysis—the power of the slashing style, the dominance of certain interests—that the spirit and the manner make it unquestionably Smollett's work.[83] Scatological detail, devices of syntax, characteristic attitudes—all tend to support Foster's conclusions. And subsequently, not only have Wayne

Douglass and Damian Grant added to Foster's argument for Smollett's authorship of the mysteriously and anonymously published *Atom* by citing parallel passages with his other work and offering detailed examinations of his satiric style, but Robert Day has clinched the attribution with solid external evidence.[84]

It is of some importance to be able to identify the *Atom* as Smollett's. Written at a time when he was supposed to be growing milder and turning completely away from the picaresque tradition, the book retains all of the old vitality and picaresque techniques. From *Roderick Random* to *Humphry Clinker* there is, therefore, a consistency in Smollett's fictional world that has sometimes been obscured by criticism of his final novel; and the *Atom* is a warning to those who choose to see a marked dichotomy in his work.

Chapter Two

Roderick Random: The Rogue Sets Forth

Published in 1748 when it had to vie for its early attention with Richardson's *Clarissa* and with Fielding's *Tom Jones, The Adventures of Roderick Random* successfully met the challenge.[1] Its popularity, as Lewis Knapp has declared, was "immediate, impressive, and prolonged," confirming in Smollett the "self-confidence and pride" that were his lifelong qualities.[2] In this instance he had sufficient reason to be proud; for by November 1749, less than two years after its publication, the novel had been through three editions and sixty-five hundred copies, rivaling the commercial achievement of Fielding's *Joseph Andrews,* a first novel written when its mature author already had acquired some reputation as journalist and playwright.

Part of the contemporary approval of *Roderick Random* may have been attributable to the topical interest of the novel's naval scenes; part to the preparation of an audience through Fielding's first novel and the caricature techniques of William Hogarth's engravings; and part, perhaps, to the public's mistaken notion that *Roderick Random* was the creation of Fielding.[3] Yet the fame of Smollett's first novel ultimately carried well beyond its immediate appeal, finally becoming that "book above all others which has ever since been associated with his name."[4] To do so, it had to offer more than the accidents attendant upon its publication; it had to have some inherent values to enable it to remain even today one of the half dozen highly regarded eighteenth-century novels, worthy of comparison with *Clarissa, Joseph Andrews, Tom Jones,* Sterne's *Tristram Shandy,* and Smollett's own *Humphry Clinker.*

In assessing those values, it is important to begin with the fact that *Roderick Random* was the work of a young novelist and that it has the characteristic vitality of a young man's book. Smollett wrote it in apparent bursts of enthusiasm over an eight-month span, during which there were several pauses of two, three, and even four weeks.[5] In his Scottish scenes, his naval episodes, and his satire on London theatrical groups he was close to the materials of his fiction. His robust picaresque narrative reveals his youthful enthusiasm for the manner of Le Sage, whose *Gil Blas* he was translating. No wonder, then, that there are a freshness and verve in *Roderick Random* that enhance its "vivid narrative style" and an authenticity in its descriptions of sights, sounds, and the very odors of eighteenth-century life that creates a verisimilitude in even the occasional gross exaggerations of its plot.[6]

Biography and literary tradition, although no substitutes for criticism, suggest convenient points of departure for analyzing Smollett's first novel. Both, however, require some general outline of the narrative for the reader to comprehend how Smollett transformed them into the material of art.

The Plot

In an episodic, panoramic style *Roderick Random* sets forth the adventures of a young Scotsman. The "orphaned" Roderick is left to the care of his grandfather, a tyrannical village squire, who has rejected the boy's father because of an "improvident" marriage. Sent to school to be out of his grandfather's way, Roderick displays a brightness and pride that incur the wrath of his schoolmaster. With the appearance and intervention of Lieutenant Tom Bowling, his mother's seafaring brother, Roderick's fortunes appear to improve; but the unforgiving, ungenerous squire dies, leaving the boy penniless. After revenging himself against the schoolmaster, Roderick goes off with Bowling, who provides for his nephew's education before he himself returns to sea. Young Roderick displays his talents for satirical verse, attacking his female cousins who had formerly mistreated him. Bowling's misfortunes, however, leave Roderick to his own devices; and he becomes the apprentice of Launcelot Crab, a scheming, devious apothecary. To cover up his own affair with a young girl, Crab sends the unsuspecting Roderick to London. Accompanied by the loyally devoted Hugh Strap, whom he has known since childhood, Roderick experiences the hazards of highway and roadside life: treacherous robbers, fraudulent traveling companions, deceitful and cheating innkeepers.

London offers no improvement, as the naive country boys are immediately put upon and duped by city confidence men. While Strap resumes his trade as a barber to support the boys, Roderick seeks a berth as a naval surgeon. He encounters all of the bribery and corruption involved in seeking a political appointment. When he finally comes before an examining board for his warrant as a surgeon's mate, the procedure terminates in a farcical battle between the examiners. Even with papers, Roderick discovers he can get no appointment; and instead he goes to work for a French apothecary, Lavement.

He becomes involved in the complicated liaisons of his employer's wife and daughter with their boarder and narrowly escapes being killed. Once again Roderick retaliates for injuries to his pride and then moves on to another apothecary and to additional domestic intrigues. The climax of this series of episodes comes in Roderick's attempt to marry a woman of means who proves instead to be a prostitute. Despite the further decline in his fortunes and the departure of Strap, whom he has neglected, Roderick befriends the young lady, Miss Williams. Her story of her fall from a good family, betrayal by her lover, and descent into the streets provides a long inset in the narrative.

Ironically, Roderick, who has been unsuccessfully attempting to go to sea, is pressed and put aboard a man-of-war, the *Thunder*. Through a series of fortunate circumstances he becomes surgeon's mate to Morgan, a colorful Welshman. But life on board ship is described in all its stinking misery, which is compounded by the tyranny of Captain Oakum and the brutality of Mackshane, an insensitive surgeon. Under their oppression, Roderick is put in irons; and, during a naval battle preceding the disastrous engagement against the French at Cartagena, he lies chained to the deck. After recovering from a severe fever, Roderick finds himself first under the command of Captain Whiffle, a homosexual, and then transferred to the *Lizard,* where his renewed conflict with Crampley, former mate of the *Thunder,* leads to his being beaten and deserted upon shore after a shipwreck.

Under the care of Mrs. Sagely, reputed to be a witch, Roderick is nursed back to health and then enters the service of a "bluestocking," who is engrossed in mathematics and philosophy and long oblivious of all practical matters. Roderick wins the favor of Narcissa, his mistress's niece, by saving her from attempted rape, and also gains the enmity of Sir Timothy, a rival. Seized by smugglers, however, Roderick is taken from her and cast ashore in France. He encounters his uncle, Tom Bowling, whom he helps return to England; but Roderick enters the French army. Duels, battles, and anti-French satire follow, until he meets Strap, now with some means and in the employ of a French master and as generous as ever to Roderick, who has used him badly.

With Strap he returns to London, seeking a wealthy wife to protect and augment their small fortune. After a series of adventures in the company of Dr. Wagtail, Medlar, Bragwell, Chatter, Slyboot, Banter, and Ranter—whose names suggest their characters—Roderick experiences a rise and fall in his fortunes until he goes in desperation to the resort town of Bath to pursue the unattractive but wealthy Miss Snapper. Bath itself now becomes the object of satire; its odors, deceits, and intrigues are the main targets. When Narcissa appears at Bath, Roderick advances his romance, aided by Miss Williams, who is now her maid. However, his luck runs out, and he is imprisoned for debt. At this point, a long inset about a poet, Melopoyn, fictionalizes Smollett's own unfortunate experiences in London theatrical circles.

Roderick, released from prison by Bowling, who has gained command of his own ship, returns to sea. After a successful engagement in which they take a handsome prize, Roderick discovers that his father is alive and an extremely wealthy plantation owner. Roderick, able to marry Narcissa, makes a triumphal return to Scotland, where he now can parade proudly before his cousins, scorn his enemies, and reward his friends.

Autobiographical Material

Despite the length of this summary, it barely suggests the sweep of Smollett's satirical novel. It does provide, however, some basis for a discussion of the autobiographical features of *Roderick Random* and, even more important, of Smollett's use of the picaresque tradition.

There are some obvious points of relationship between the life of the Scottish novelist and his Scottish hero. Smollett's father *had* difficulties with his family because of his marriage. Smollett *did* experience a Scotsman's customary trials in London; he *did* serve as surgeon's mate aboard a man-of-war, the *Chichester,* during the battle of Cartagena; his marriage was to a young lady who *was* something of an heiress. To the account of Melopoyn's experiences with the London stage managers, Smollett brought his own history of his attempt to produce *The Regicide* some years before. And there is more.

From Smollett we learn that Strap could be identified with his "neighbour John Lewis[,] Bookbinder," although the novelist later qualified his flat statement by remarking that Strap was "partly taken from life."[7] Indeed, five possibilities have been suggested as models for the portrait, and similar candidacies have been advanced for Captains Oakum and Whiffle, Squire Gawky, Crab, and the schoolmaster-landlord.[8] Nor does the list end there: whatever Smollett's own denial, he appears to have used John Gordon, a Glasgow surgeon, to create Potion, and his own grandfather to portray the village tyrant.[9] In the famous Melopoyn incident positive identification of living models was as apparent to Smollett's contemporaries as to modern scholars.[10]

The tie between Smollett and Roderick is at least emotional. Knapp has described the novelist's "temperamental weaknesses"—recognized by Smollett himself—as "pride, obstinacy, jealousy, impetuosity in taking offense, [and] lack of emotional control." For Knapp, the "emotional pattern in Smollett's life" is clear: "an irritating obsession of persecution, and the quick, instinctive reaction . . . of revenge, not only threatened but usually executed with the weapons of satire or even with a cudgel."[11] What could be a better general portrait of Roderick? Smollett himself was aware of the similarity, knew that his hero was "already recognized by the public as the image of his own adolescent pride"; and he revised the novel after the first edition to moderate Roderick's poetic abilities, to lessen "the youthfully naive and egotistic portrait" in this respect.[12]

And yet, what, after all, does this use of autobiographical material amount to? Most novelists, especially young ones engaged in satire, draw upon their own experiences and circumstances, model their characters upon types of people they know. Roderick is *not* Smollett, and this first novel is no more trustworthy as autobiography than his last work, *Humphry Clinker.* To be sure, as Kahrl has pointed out, something of Smollett appears in Roderick, just as in Peregrine Pickle and Launcelot Greaves; but it is "wiser to regard the characters, like the incidents, as founded, not upon particular personal experiences, but upon Smollett's wide observations."[13] Or, as Damian Grant has more recently pointed out, the novel's relationship to Smollett's life lies in its general tone, Smollett's sense of "personal grievance" with the world as he found it. *Roderick Random* was the work of a young man angry with the manner in which "a Whig, Hanoverian England . . . had betrayed Scottish interests," with the atrocities against his countrymen following Culloden, with the treatment of his play by theater managers, and with his situation as he attempted "to set up as a surgeon in London."[14]

Although earlier critics tended to overestimate the particular autobiographical significance of *Roderick Random*,[15] there have always been clear warnings against such reading of the novel. Smollett himself gave the first evidence when he insisted, "The low situations in which I have exhibited Roderick, I never experienced in my own Person."[16] For those who nevertheless have insisted upon the autobiographical reliability of the novel, his letters to his cousins at Bonhill, showing a warmth and friendliness in remarkable contrast to the fictional situation in the early pages of the book, should be sufficient rebuttal.[17]

Perhaps the best examples of the relationship between autobiography and fictional art in his novel are to be found in the episode concerning the disastrous battle of Cartagena and in Smollett's portrait of life aboard a British man-of-war. For a detailed, horrifying description of seafaring conditions, Smollett's is unparalleled. With Swiftian ferocity he recounts Roderick's descent into the ship's sick bay:

Here I saw about fifty miserable distempered wretches, suspended in rows, so huddled one upon another, that not more than fourteen inches of space was allotted for each with his bed and bedding; and deprived of the light of the day, as well as of fresh air; breathing nothing but a noisome atmosphere of the morbid steams exhaling from their own excrements and diseased bodies, devoured with vermin hatched in the filth that surrounded them, and destitute of every convenience necessary for people in that helpless condition.[18]

Or, again, he portrays the brutal and callous attitude toward life in the aftermath of battle: "Such was the oeconomy in some ships, that, rather than be at the trouble of interring the dead, their commanders ordered their men to throw their bodies overboard, many without either ballast or winding-sheet; so that numbers of human carcasses floated in the harbour, until they were devoured by sharks and carrion crows; which afforded no agreeable spectacle to those who survived" (189).

The dependability of his general picture, the hideousness of which apparently stirred subsequent reforms,[19] stands undisputed. For this vividness and accuracy, Smollett's personal experiences were undoubtedly partly responsible;[20] nevertheless, the literary antecedents and sources that clearly affected his treatment suggest that many more than his own adventures were involved.[21] "Again and again," as Kahrl has stated, "Smollett selected secondary events, not necessarily autobiographic, and made them the basis for realistic pictures, of daily life aboard a man-of-war."[22] Moreover, the whole suited his artistic purpose, a portrait of the picaresque world that provided the background for his satire on mankind.

As for his narrative of the Cartagena expedition, even the certainty that these episodes came from his own experiences has been questioned by his most reliable biographer.[23] Indeed, examining Smollett's treatment of this naval action in three separate works—*Roderick Random*, "An Account of the Expedition against Carthagena" in *A Compendium of Authentic and Entertaining Voyages,* and the *Complete History of England*—Louis Martz has used his findings to refute the misconceptions that have arisen from Thackeray's unfounded charge that Smollett had *no* inventive sense.[24] To be sure, Smollett characteristically worked from literary sources and personal experience, but ultimately these provided no more than an outline for his fiction.

By comparing Smollett's treatment of the expedition in his novel with his other accounts of the action, Martz ably demonstrates the distance between the two—one characterized by differences in purpose and technique. Elsewhere Smollett concerned himself with the tactical motives of the military engagement, emphasizing especially the logical reasons for its failure. In *Roderick,* however, following the manner of Le Sage and working to a satiric purpose, he did not attempt either "an accurate relation of his own experiences or a 'history' of naval and military operations." Only one-fourth of the pages devoted to the expedition relate directly to it, and they concentrate on the "bitter satire and denunciation" of the "stupid and insolent [military] leadership" that underlie the vivid picture of misery created by blundering. What exists in the novel is an exaggerated portrait of "misery and ineffi- ciency,"[25] consistent with Smollett's satiric aim and not ultimately dependent upon any *specific* personal experience. Surely the multitude of Roderick's ad- ventures lies beyond the scope of any one man's possible activities. Moreover, the kind of effect that the novel has depends on imaginative detail rather than on any autobiographical fact. For example, there is Smollett's description of Roderick's experience as he lies chained to the deck during the naval encoun- ter just prior to the Cartagena expedition:

The reader [Roderick says] may guess how I passed my time, lying in this helpless sit- uation, amidst the terrors of a sea-fight; expecting every moment to be cut asunder, or dashed in pieces by the enemy's shot! I endeavoured to compose myself as much as possible, by reflecting that I was not a whit more exposed than those who were sta- tioned about me; but when I beheld them employed without intermission in annoy- ing the foe, and encouraged by the society and behaviour of one another, I could easily perceive a wide difference between their condition and mine: However, I con- cealed my agitation as well as I could, till the head of the officer of Marines, who stood near me, being shot off, bounced from the deck athwart my face, leaving me well-nigh blinded with brains. (167–68)

As with the general picture of seafaring life, Smollett's treatment of the Cartagena battle and other naval engagements was designed to create the harsh surroundings in which the picaro's struggle for survival takes place. If it was beneficial for him to have experienced the brutalities and cruelties of naval life in order to create his fiction, it was hardly necessary for him to pur- sue autobiographical fidelity to make his point. It was, after all, not Smollett who lay brain-splattered upon the deck during a battle, but Roderick the picaro who was being impressed with the fact that human life seems of small concern in the world's values.

Use of the Picaresque

But not only the naval scenes are tied to Smollett's picaresque plan; as the summary of *Roderick Random* suggests, Smollett's novel attempts to view the vast panorama of eighteenth-century life from the picaro's perspective. Smollett's commitment to the picaresque tradition stands clearly enough in his Preface, in which he acknowledges his indebtedness to Le Sage's *Adven- tures of Gil Blas*. To be sure, like other neoclassical writers, he was not inclined to slavishly follow his model; rather, he adapted the picaresque techniques to his own purposes. Unlike Le Sage, Smollett stresses didactic purpose. He alters his circumstances to achieve, with whatever success, greater "probability" and to arouse his readers—as he felt Le Sage had not—"against the sordid and vicious disposition of the world."

In the view of Robert Alter, whose *Rogue's Progress* explores the tradition from its beginnings, *Roderick Random* marks the first genuine migration of the Continental picaro to England; and Smollett himself, of all eighteenth-century novelists, is the one committed deliberately to conveying that alien tradition of the picaresque to his countrymen. Alter's definition of the genre goes beyond identifying it with an episodic structure, a journey motif, and a criminally inclined vagabond hero. The picaresque belongs to the "literature of learning . . . [and] experience"; its use of the servant-master relationship is satiric. Alter's description of the type fits precisely the characteristics of Smollett's first novel: "the adventurous story of a rogue's life, usually told in the first person; [which through] its episodic account of wanderings, adversity, and ingenious role-playing incorporates a satiric view of society."[26]

Of the two kinds of traditional picaros, Smollett chose to cast Roderick as "the butt of fortune, [who suffers] many adversities [and] vicissitudes," rather than as the antihero who controls his own fate and is "jack-of-all-trades, skilled manipulator, adept deceiver, artist of disguises, adaptable."[27] The fact that a choice between two types existed in the traditional picaresque suggests that the tradition itself was not static and allowed for change. Indeed, the possibilities for transformation present in the genre led to important differences between the Continental and English eighteenth-century picaresques; and two of these differences hold particular significance for *Roderick Random*. Departing from the Spanish tradition, the English rogue-novels stressed the picaro's ingenuity rather than his mere struggle for survival; and, at the same time, they developed the individual personality of the antihero, emphasizing the man rather than his adventures.

While Alter, with historical perspective and defined limits in his approach—limits perhaps too strictly drawn—considers Smollett's first novel to be a genuine picaresque, some other critics have argued against the dominance of the picaresque in *Roderick Random*. One goes so far as to describe the hero as an antipicaro.[28] Another terms the novel itself an attempted modification of the genre that illustrates the manner in which the picaresque died.[29] And yet another regards it as a failure to realize the structural and moral possibilities of the form.[30] Ranging from comments on the inconsistency of Roderick's character as a picaro—his greater perception, his more human and decent qualities, his maturation—to remarks on the structural differences between the novel and the genre, such criticism has placed Smollett's work outside the mainstream of the Continental tradition, and it requires some explanation and evaluation. Better than most critics, Philip Stevick recognizes how Smollett's novels, particularly *Roderick Random,* modify the picaresque for his own purposes and where the work stands in the tradition of the genre—how "from our point of view in the twentieth century, Smollett appears to link the end of one tradition, the great tradition of classic picaresque, with the beginning of another tradition of related and derivative works, such as, in our century, *Felix Krull* and *Invisible Man.*"[31]

Arguments that Roderick's picaresque character at the outset alters as he "becomes much more human and decent" while at sea or that he "is chiefly an adventurer," the kind of "person to whom things happen," do not accord with the facts.[32] Prior to going to sea, Smollett's hero evidences his fundamental qualities of decency and humaneness in the episode with Miss Williams, the prostitute. With nothing to gain from his kindness to her, he nevertheless offers her what little he has. In no sense, either, can Roderick be described as merely an adventurer or a passive agent. He involves himself in the struggle for existence; his very anger and indignation—noted by some critics as examples of unpicaresque behavior[33]—lead him to initiate action, and he displays "ingenuity and cunning, [and participates] in cruel hoaxes and [operates for] acquisitiveness" like a genuine picaro, although these points, too, have been denied him.[34]

Although the circumstances of Roderick's birth—as Ronald Paulson notes in his argument for the character as satirist rather than as picaro and for the novel as formal Roman satire rather than as picaresque[35]—alter such things as the service-of-masters theme and the survival concept in the novel, they do not destroy them. And Paulson seriously underrates Roderick's use of cunning and his fits of madness, just as he misleads when he declares Roderick to be apart from "the foolishness and knavery." What does such a final judgment do to Roderick's many schemes of vengeance, to his brutal treatment of his schoolmaster, to his use of Strap, and to countless other details in the novel? Surely, to call Roderick "a satiric observer ['outside the object of satiric attack'] who recognizes and rebukes" is to give him an objectivity and philosophical detachment remote from Smollett's portrait. Recognizing that those adventures in which Roderick is duped weaken his argument, Paulson does little more than set them aside.

As for the structure of *Roderick Random,* it is fundamentally picaresque. Episodic, using the journey motif, it ties together locale and experience, allowing the novelist to lay bare a society and to reveal his picaro's character through his adventures. To be sure, the influence of the Greek romances, particularly on the last section of the novel, cannot be denied;[36] but this proves suitable to what Alter has called "a post-picaresque coda in which [the writer] can get the hero settled down happily and comfortably."[37] Smollett, unfortunately, has handled his final material at too great length, shifted his tone to sentimentality, permitted himself too much freedom with the deus ex machina; but these qualities merely reflect bad writing, not a denial of the major overall picaresque manner.

To argue, as M. A. Goldberg does in a thesis that finds the novelist balancing between two extremes of thought, that, because *Roderick Random* offers a structural effectiveness not generally associated with the genre, it is therefore not picaresque,[38] merely repeats critical lack of comprehension of what means such writers as Le Sage and Smollett used to provide unity for their fiction—that unity upon which all good art depends for its verisimilitude. For too long critics have identified the episodic plots of the picaresque with the derogatory term "amorphous." Yet no novelist could hope to create a sense of a fictional world—with what Dorothy Van Ghent has described as its own reality and system of values and relationships[39]—unless he provides some structural unity that allows his readers to indulge their imaginations within its limits.

The picaresque writer, concerned with some satiric purpose or some social comment, cannot afford any more than other serious novelists to present a world of disparate parts and unrelated incidents. However broad his coverage or vast his plan, he must find the means for bringing his fictional elements under one cover, for linking his earliest episodes with his latest, and for deepening the understanding of the world he presents.

Smollett clearly recognized this fact, and some of his recognition is apparent in the way his novel makes later points of return to places and material described in earlier sections. When Roderick returns to London, Smollett's method effects a recall of his previous treatment; but it also deepens an insight into his material by satirizing town life on "a higher level than before."[40] Even in what might appear an obvious disregard for structural unity—the insets concerned with Melopoyn and Miss Williams—Smollett discloses an interest in keeping the parts of his work related to the whole. Paul-Gabriel Boucé has demonstrated the moral connections between their characters and situations and those of Roderick and argues that both are important for the moral evolution of the hero.[41] But as Roderick's subsequent conduct indicates, he has learned little from the experiences of Melopoyn. Miss Williams's experiences and her vision of the world provide Roderick with some insights into actuality and should forewarn him. The fact that they do not suggests the general character of the picaro, who learns only through his own experience and not through the lessons of others.

Characterization

But Smollett's most important means for holding his novel together is in line with the traditional device common to the genre. No less than other novelists, he uses rhythm as his primary device—rhythm through characterization, point of view, and theme. Rhythm, as defined by E. M. Forster and E. K. Brown,[42] consists of repetition and progression. It relates to any fictional element, and in *Roderick Random* it is perhaps easiest to perceive first through characterization.

Although Smollett's resources in characterization are limited primarily to caricature, he uses that technique as effectively as any other English novelist, with the exception of Charles Dickens. From Smollett, in fact, Dickens learned his technique of giving life to the grotesque by emphasizing the physical details of his eccentric characters, and of indicating his attitude toward them through the selection of specific bodily and facial characteristics.

One example should suffice to demonstrate the relationship between Smollett's methods and those of his Victorian admirer—the introduction to the detestable surgeon, Mr. Launcelot Crab, a man neither to be admired nor trusted: "This member of the faculty was aged fifty, about five foot high, and ten round the belly; his face was capacious as a full moon, and much of the complexion of a mulberry: his nose, resembling a powder-horn, was swelled to an enormous size, and studded all over with carbuncles; and his little gray eyes reflected the rays in such an oblique manner, that while he looked a person full in the face, one would have imagined he was admiring the buckle of his shoe" (26). Without question Smollett's fictional creation would be in place among the gallery of Dickens's rogues whose physical deformities are intended to suggest the corruption of their souls.

By insisting on the grotesqueries and idiosyncrasies of his characters Smollett provides a consistency in the environment of his picaresque world. The use of caricature is itself an example of rhythm in his novel. The first time it is presented the reader can only accept it for what it is at that point. Roderick's grandfather, in other words, may seem an exaggeration of certain traits; but he cannot, at the beginning of the novel, be classified as constituting the characteristic element of the world around the picaro. Yet with the repeated occurrence of caricature in one figure after another, from Strap to Bowling to the London and shipboard characters, it becomes apparent that this is a particular view of the world that the reader is being offered.

Were that the extent of Smollett's use of caricature, however, the result would be appalling, the monotony inescapable. Instead, Smollett varies his caricature from personality to personality; and, each time the device is employed, it not only reminds the reader of the consistency of the picaro's world, but enlarges his notions of the *kinds* of absurdities and exaggerations present within it.

It is incorrect to describe Smollett's use of caricature either as static or as without significance. In *Roderick,* for example, he employs "racial antipathies" to stir action and to get immediate satiric responses.[43] His audience was prepared to react to Mackshane's Irish papistry, to Morgan's Welsh loyalty, or even to Roderick's own Scottish temper and temperament. Merely bringing these national types together readied the reader for conflict since he had been trained by stage tradition in what to expect. In the same way, the easily recognizable portrait of the intellectual female in the character of Narcissa's aunt made immediate appeal to Smollett's audience. If her character is, as has been asserted,[44] incredible, that too is the novelist's comment on such behavior. When Smollett desires to make the bizarre believable, he knows how to do it; and, for all the oddity of a Tom Bowling, he emerges a genuine "human being."[45]

Moreover, Smollett's "grotesque" comic characters gain variety through his treatment of them.[46] At their simplest they are "mere humors" in the Jonsonian tradition, functioning as determinants of the main narrative action. Their grotesqueness may be rooted either in some trait of personality or in some physical characteristic. In their more complex forms, in figures like Morgan or Miss Snapper, they combine the two. At all events, these caricatured comic types are ideally suited as foils for Smollett's hero to use in his discovery of the world of folly and fraud.

At the other extreme from these humorous portrayals stand Smollett's heroines, stock figures with no intrinsically satiric purpose. Maligned though they have been,[47] characters like Narcissa *do* function in his novels. They are representatives of an eighteenth-century "norm," bearers of "virtue and discretion," images of "delicacy, elegance," objects of "soft and feminine grace."[48] In them breeding and wealth combine to make up their attractiveness. These so-called "milliners' dummies" are idealized womanhood in Smollett's novels; they are the goals of respectability toward which the hero strives, and their stability—the very absence of flaws in their makeup—serves to contrast them with the grotesque and unstable values of the picaresque world. Moreover, their presence gives some direction to the narrative. Throughout Roderick's picaresque adventures after he has met Narcissa, the suggestion of her existence provides some normal guidelines for the adventurer; and, with her return to the story, Smollett is able to terminate the action.

Roderick's Character

While the recurring contrasts between the idealized Narcissa and the corrupt picaresque world provide another example of rhythm in the novel, rhythm in characterization functions most importantly in *Roderick Random* through the picaro himself. As Alter describes it, the "I" in the novel becomes the center of a world that could not otherwise hold together within the rambling narrative framework of the picaresque.[49] But the particular "I" and the way it is developed are essential to an understanding of how the particular novel is held together.

Roderick's character is established almost immediately with the description of his red hair and his Scottish origins. He is the stereotype of the easily aroused, tempestuous, yet fundamentally good-natured character. The key words in the novel are *pride* and *revenge;* touch the one, and the other follows; and Smollett makes this clear at the very start. "This brutal behaviour," the narrator explains in the earliest episodes, "added to the sufferings I had formerly undergone, made me think it high time to be revenged of this insolent pedagogue" (16). An entire book and an almost uncountable number of adventures later, the tone and the message have not changed. Describing an attempt by Potion and his wife to gain the friendship of the now-affluent hero, he is unforgiving of past slights:

Mr. Potion and his wife hearing of our arrival, had the assurance to come to the inn where we lodged, and send up their names, with a desire of being permitted to pay their respects to my father and me: But their sordid behaviour towards me, when I was an orphan, had made too deep an impression on my mind, to be effaced by this mean mercenary piece of condescension; I therefore rejected their message with disdain, and bid Strap tell them, that my father and I desired to have no communication with such low-minded wretches as they were. (433)

From Roderick's savage beating of the schoolmaster, through his shipboard antagonisms, to his colonial, French, London, and Bath experiences, his motivation starts with pride and ends in a violence or rebuff that responds to some affront to his sense of self.

Again, if there were no more to it than that, the novel would prove an exercise in dullness. Indeed, it is not easy to escape the static in the picaresque; for, as Alter has remarked, one of the conventions of the genre is "that experience should never substantially alter the given character of the hero"; although he may learn, "he does not change."[50] But, to begin with, Smollett *did* deviate from the traditional in his characterization of Roderick, who proves a more committed character than the customary picaro; for *pride,* one of the Seven Deadly Sins to which the picaro supposedly does not respond, and *anger,* a luxury he cannot afford,[51] dominate Roderick's personality.

Yet the key to Alter's statement comes in the word "substantially." Roderick's character throughout the novel, as Goldberg has noted,[52] runs in a conflict between passion and reason. Goldberg regards Roderick as changing finally because of his knowledge that "only feelings controlled by reason, emotions reined by the understanding can be productive of the happiness and success he seeks."[53] But Goldberg seems to go too far; for what *has* changed at the end of the novel are the circumstances that Roderick is in rather than the character of the hero. The variety of the characterization does come, however, in the fluctuation of circumstances themselves.

Smollett achieves this necessary variety in the rhythmic pattern of Roderick's character by playing it against the shifting setting of the picaresque world and by deepening the reader's realization of the true nature of his character. Not merely movement but increased seriousness provides the setting for a display of Roderick's character. For an altogether different purpose from demonstrating the picaresque characteristics in the novel, Goldberg has shown how the repeated catastrophes in Roderick's experiences progress from the fairly incidental to those of greater moral consequence.[54]

However, it is not this increasing gravity of situations alone that is important. It functions together with Roderick's characteristic picaresque response to repeated assaults on what Alter has regarded as his fundamental decency and sympathy for others.[55] The repetition comes through Roderick's willingness to start over again after each rebuke; the variety or progression evolves through the changes in circumstances, the deepening significance of each affair. Roderick, contrary to William Piper's view of what Smollett's heroes are[56]—characters without "lasting peculiarities of character"—remains substantially the same throughout the novel. The many role changes—English sailor, French soldier, servant satirist, and the like[57]—are merely examples of Smollett's use of the picaresque tradition. Roderick's versatility and adaptability permit Smollett to show his character under a variety of circumstances and in a multiplicity of situations—all of which, together, underscore his hero's fundamental character, which in itself remains fairly static. The reader thus cannot judge the depth of Roderick's passionate pride or his fundamental kindness from any individual episode, but from the total accrual of incidents.

In another way, the character of Roderick functions rhythmically in the novel. The repeated picaresque vision of Roderick as narrator provides for unity and development, or—put in another way—point of view serves also to create the necessary rhythm. Two passages illustrate the manner in which point of view achieves its rhythmic function.[58] In the first, Roderick describes his earliest experiences, which are also characteristic of his later adventures:

I was often inhumanly scourged for crimes I did not commit, because having the character of a vagabond in the village, every piece of mischief, whose author lay unknown, was charged upon me.—I have been found guilty of robbing orchards I never entered, of killing cats I never hurted, or stealing gingerbread I never touched, and of abusing old women I never saw. . . . I was flogged for having narrowly escaped drowning, by the sinking of a ferry-boat in which I was passenger.—Another time for having recovered of a bruise occasioned by a horse and cart running over me.—A third time for being bit by a baker's dog. (6)

The other passage occurs considerably later in the novel. The incidents have become more serious and Roderick reflects on them and their significance:

I had endured hardships, 'tis true; my whole life had been a series of such, and when I looked forward, the prospect was not much bettered—but then, they were become habitual to me, and consequently I could bear them with less difficulty—If one scheme of life should not succeed, I could have recourse to another, and so to a third, veering about to a thousand different shifts, according to the emergencies of my fate, without forfeiting the dignity of my character, beyond a power of retrieving it, or subjecting myself wholly to the caprice and barbarity of the world. (136-37)

The speaker is the same as earlier—and as in the general observations throughout the novel. Point of view conveys the picaresque vision of a world of experience that is hard on the narrator, one that recognizes that justice has small role in his affairs, and that hardship is the common factor in his experience. So much, then, is the repetition characteristic of rhythm; but there are also subtle differences, increments of change that offer some progression in the point of view. In the very acknowledgment—an awareness shared certainly by the reader—that the pattern has "become habitual," Roderick indicates an advance beyond the earlier perception. While the first observation suggests a shock at the world's injustices, the second marks the narrator's increased knowledge of how to respond to them. He is no longer surprised by the rebuffs of fortune; prepared to meet them, to rebound as he has done before, he advances a slightly altered appraisal. The world, the circumstances, may be the same; the manner of looking at them has been somewhat revised. Point of view continues to represent the picaresque vision of experience, but it has been enhanced by the increased understanding of the narrator.

To some extent the point of view changes in the final portions of the novel. Whatever the justifications for Smollett's shift to romance in the last third of the book, however much it may be excused in terms of the "coda" sometimes affixed to the picaresque, the result does prove somewhat jarring. Point of view *is* affected by the romantic turn, for sentiment is inconsistent with the picaresque's mode of representing reality.[59] It does not seem to be quite the same Roderick who describes his situation at the close of the story: "If there be such a thing as true happiness on earth, I enjoy it.—The impetuous transports of my passion are now settled and mellowed into endearing fondness and tranquillity of love. . . . Fortune seems determined to make ample amends for her former cruelty" (435). Yet even here the first-person narrator has not lost the picaro's distrust of "true happiness on earth." Nor has he yielded altogether to sentiment in these closing pages as he describes with relish his rejection of the advances of Potion and his wife and the female cousin, all of whom had formerly mistreated him and now seek to gain the benefits of his improved status. Roderick's fundamental character has not changed despite the alteration of his circumstances. As Bouce has argued, the hero maintains his desire for revenge and still expresses his old vanity in his pride about his wife's appearance and his own sartorial splendor.[60] It is still the picaro's satiric view that comes through even in the long passages of romance.

In lesser ways, too, point of view provides rhythm for this picaresque novel. The narrator of *Roderick,* characteristically picaresque, "is no philosophical prober."[61] He relates occurrences without offering much in the way of analysis. Not only does he stay out of the minds of others; he rarely suggests what is taking place in his own. Were it not for the rhythmical function of point of view, which accustoms the reader to the surface depiction of events rather than to the psychological plumbing of Roderick's character, the character might come through as callous and unfeeling. Instead, the manner of repetition through which things are related allows the reader to make adjustments to the material itself. He is not stunned to discover that somewhere in Roderick's mind Narcissa has continued to exist despite the long absence of any mention of her. The reader has seen repeatedly that point of view is focused upon the experiential rather than the contemplative, and he comes to know that the very repetitiveness—whether related to trivial or consequential matters—reflects a concern for some satiric social purpose of the novel rather than for a view of some idiosyncratic characterizations.

Satire

Everything in the novel—characterization, point of view, plot, and tone—directs the attention to the satire, which also in itself performs a rhythmic function in *Roderick Random*. In the very first sentence of his Preface Smollett makes clear his purpose. His brief historical sketch of the genre, his statement of differences from Le Sage, his "Apologue," all show his satiric intent, his loyalty to the picaresque. After he proclaims his allegiance to Le Sage, Smollett goes on to explain that he has taken "the liberty . . . to differ from him in the execution," but that difference clearly enough relates to the novelist's attempt to achieve greater verisimilitude and appeal to national feelings, and not to shift the purpose of his narration or his commitment to picaresque satire.[62]

In characteristic picaresque fashion[63] Smollett allows his journey motif and the servant-master relationships to provide the vehicle for his satiric attacks. The Scottish scenes excoriate the petty tyrannies of village squires and local schoolmasters. Experiences with apothecaries lay bare the deceptions of the trade. Romantic intrigues expose the basest hypocritical personal relationships. In Roderick's journey to London, Smollett satirizes the pretensions of social climbers and the greedy practices of innkeepers. London itself provides opportunities for satiric thrusts against sharpsters and grafters. And on it goes: wherever Roderick travels, whatever Roderick does, Smollett chooses targets for picaresque satire. French and English military life, medical and legal practitioners, the abject prison society and London high society—all become objects of satire through Roderick's presence, through Roderick's experience. Dialect and nationality, literary and theatrical fashions suffer Smollett's satiric scorn.

How Smollett delights in the picaresque exposure of the deceptions of various professions. Miss Williams, suffering the ravages of venereal disease, has entrusted herself to a "physician." With what result?

. . . when she resolved to retire to some obscure corner, where she might be cured with as little noise and expense as possible; . . . she had accordingly chosen this place of retreat, and put herself into the hands of an advertising doctor, who having fleeced her of all the money she had, or could procure, left her three days ago in a worse condition than that in which he found her; that, except the clothes on her back, she had pawned or sold everything that belonged to her, to satisfy that rapacious quack. . . (116)

Smollett knew firsthand these medical quacks, men like Dr. John Hill, whom he despised; but he was not attacking a particular individual. Instead, he was applying himself to remedying the abuses that his picaro found in society. The same is true for his portrait of corrupt legal practices, and Roderick the picaro, like the hero of Le Sage, discovers that what makes possible the practices of prostitution are the law enforcement agencies that willingly turn their eyes away from the evil for the sake of some "contribution quarterly [paid] for protection" (90).

The picaro explores, as well, the vagaries of politicians. For assistance in gaining a naval berth, Roderick must attend the levees of the dispensers of patronage, whose least demands are servitude of the spirit. He learns the commonplace of a politician's morality, "that there was nothing to be done with a m-b-r of p-m-t without a bribe . . ." (73). In the great bureaucracy of the political state the list of those who must be "rewarded" for services extends from the most menial clerks and butlers to secretaries and ministers, the great men themselves.

In order to uncover the vastness of this corruption, in order to satirize the vices and abuses of mankind, the picaresque must move through a variety of incidents, must make rapid transitions from one point to another. It is likely to seem to many observers that such a structure merely reflects narrative chaos. Indeed, for those who generally argue the looseness of the episodic structure, there is only disunity to be found in *Roderick Random*. Ronald Paulson, for example, sees the novel as disjointed episodes, individual scenes too developed in separate satiric frames to come together as a single whole. According to Paulson, the "failure" results from Smollett's use of the picaresque for satire and of the formal verse satirists for his models, a mixture of incongruous forms.[64]

But the scenes are not separate, and the effect of the novel is indeed unified. In addition to the means already described for bringing them together, the satiric vision itself serves as a joining force. To be sure, as Paulson points out, no episode in itself is indispensable; and "there is always room for one more example in Smollett's bulging novels."[65] However, the repeated satire builds from its individual points a satiric effect that is achieved only from the whole. Each episode recalls the earlier satire and adds finally to a general satirical comment that is greater than the individual parts and becomes, as Smollett later declared, a satire on mankind.[66]

Perhaps the best comparison that can be made is with the pictorial narratives of his contemporary and friend, William Hogarth. The study of a series of engravings like *The Harlot's Progress* produces an effect resembling that of *Roderick Random*. Each scene carries its own satiric interest; each one brims with details important for the particular episode; and yet the genuine impact comes through the relationship of the satiric intelligence that informs the se-

ries in its entirety. Repetition assures us that the vision is unified; and the accrual of details, the broadening of the range that takes in more and more of
the society, provides for a progression essential to the proper uses of rhythm.
As Paulson himself recognizes, the miniature satires in Smollett's novel "deal
with one general subject," that pointed out in Smollett's Preface: "the selfishness, envy, malice, and base indifference of mankind."[67] For all its seemingly
episodic character, *Roderick Random* presents a sustained and unified attack
on a "world of arbitrary power and moral anarchy."[68]

Comparison with Hogarth serves to underscore other characteristics of
Smollett's world as it is presented in his first novel. The crudities of chamber-
pot humor, the violence, and the coarseness are part of a realistic view of
eighteenth-century England. Even Alter, whose criticism of *Roderick Random*
is quite favorable, remarks that Smollett's satire offers "violence . . . often too
harsh for any imaginable satiric purpose and it is too generalized: it pervades
the novel and never seems fully under the author's control."[69] For this violence and harshness one of Smollett's female contemporaries provides the
best explanation. Objecting to critical approaches that failed to connect the
low scenes, the savage and brutal detail in his novel, with its generally ap-
proved "fidelity to life," she stresses the necessary relationship of the two.[70]
That realism in Smollett's work represents, as Alter himself recognizes,[71] a
picaresque concern for "ordinary life."

Moreover, as the historical actuality behind the naval scenes in *Roderick*
suggests, Smollett did not always have to exaggerate the true conditions he
was dealing with. The injustices of naval life, its cruelties, inefficiencies, and
callousness needed little heightening for satire. Characters like Captain
Whiffle in positions of authority and conditions like those in the sick bay of
the *Thunder* stand up before documentary evidence.[72]

Like Hogarth, Smollett portrays sordidness in detail; like Hogarth, he de-
picts the corruption in the hearts of his characters as it manifests itself in their
conduct, as it marks even their facial characteristics. Tying together his picaresque narrative with an appropriate realism, he offers the most scarifying
material with the avowed purpose of "animating the reader against the sordid
and vicious disposition of the world."

Moreover, Smollett depends on scatological detail to achieve verisimilitude. Along with Swift he believed that noxious odors or disgusting physical
detail could convince the most adamant skeptics and sustain the probability
of the most improbable circumstances. Whatever the implausibilities of the
episode in which Strap mistakes his sleeping quarters at the inn, the presentation makes it difficult to reject them:

About midnight, my companion's bowels being disordered, he [Strap] got up, in order to go backward; in his return, mistaking one door for another, entered [Captain] Weazel's chamber, and without any hesitation, went to bed to his wife, who was fast asleep; the captain being at another end of the room, groping for some empty vessel, his own chamber-pot being leaky. As he did not perceive Strap coming in, he went toward his own bed, after having found a convenience; but no sooner did he feel a rough head with a cotton night-cap on it, than it came into his mind, that he had got to miss Jenny's bed instead of his own, and that the head he felt, was that of some gallant, with whom she had made an assignation.—Full of this conjecture, and scandalized at the prostitution of his apartment, he snatched up the vessel he had just before filled, and emptied it at once on the astonished barber [Strap] and his own wife, who waking at that instant, broke forth into lamentable cries, which not only alarmed the husband beyond measure, but frightened poor Strap almost out of his senses; for he verily believed himself bewitched; especially when the incensed captain seized him by the throat. . . . Mrs. Weazel, enraged . . . , got up in her shift, and with the heel of her shoe . . . belaboured the captain's bald pate. (51–52)

An incident as old as Chaucer's "Reeve's Tale" and one not unusual in eighteenth-century novels, the scene nevertheless remains typically Smollettian; it is full of the circumstantial, violent, and coarse detail that gives it fictional life and plausibility.

All this vision of life is conveyed in such manner that even a detractor, writing more than two hundred years after Smollett's first novel, could speak of "the robustness and verve of style which most readers of Smollett will rightly consider to be peculiarly his."[73] Whatever the limitations of *Roderick Random,* it was the first example of the narrative power that was to place Smollett among the great writers of his century.

Chapter Three

Peregrine Pickle:
The Rogue in High Society

In late February 1751 Smollett published the first edition of *The Adventures of Peregrine Pickle,* his second novel. Started prior to his Parisian trip during the middle of the previous year, its composition was not completed until after his return; and a sizable number of its incidents reflect some of his European experiences. Yet the immediate, although temporary, success that the novel enjoyed owed little to such material or even to whatever general literary merits the novel possessed. Attention focused mainly upon his inclusion of *The Memoirs of a Lady of Quality,* a long inset based on the marital and extramarital sexual activities of Frances Viscount Vane. Moreover, Smollett also fed the taste for scandal and topicality in his now almost infamous attack on such contemporaries as Henry Fielding, Lord Lyttelton, Mark Akenside, James Quin, and David Garrick, as well as in his partisan defense of Daniel MacKercher's role in the famous Annesley case.[1]

Time has eclipsed the kind of interest these matters once had. To be sure, their importance remains in any consideration of how they contribute to or detract from the literary merits of the novel. Their significance relates, as well, to the important distinctions between the original work and Smollett's revision for his second edition in 1758. They also reflect, to some degree, Smollett's temperament and personality; and they pose questions that continue to plague his biographers and bibliographers. Nevertheless, in any critical evaluation of the novel, these points of major concern to his contemporaries now play a subsidiary role.

Despite its appeal as a roman à clef, the novel ultimately did not stir quite as wide critical or popular interest as *Roderick Random* had done.[2] Perhaps the booksellers, aroused by Smollett's "reservation of the whole copyright," affected the sale. Perhaps Smollett's claim that enemies, terming the novel immoral and a libel, kept it from achieving genuine popularity, was not altogether unfounded.[3] Perhaps, too, the competition of John Hill's memoirs of a fictitious Lady Frail, with a more "sensuous appeal" than Lady Vane's *Memoirs,* undercut the sale of Smollett's novel.[4] More likely, however, its own literary qualities best account for its limited success. Almost twice the length of *Roderick Random, Peregrine Pickle* cannot escape a certain dullness through mere repetitiveness; and, for all its merits, it cannot but seem, at least superficially, no more than an imitation of his earlier work. Moreover, its own deficiencies provided easy targets for its earliest critics. Even its most favorable reviewers noted its coarseness and its abusiveness, and those less sympathetic to its merits were naturally more severe with its defects.[5] At any rate, a second edition was not forthcoming until seven years later, at which time Smollett's novel underwent considerable revision.

Comparison with *Roderick Random*

Part of the immediate interest in *Peregrine Pickle,* aside from the anticipation of scandalous revelations in Lady Vane's *Memoirs,* undoubtedly arose from the attention that Smollett had stirred with *Roderick Random.* It was only natural then, and remains so today, that the second novel should invite comparison with the first. What makes such a comparison an appropriate starting point in this instance are the obvious resemblances between the two works. Ever since the earliest modern criticism, they have been compared. Perry has been called "a cruder and more insufferable Roderick";[6] and Pipes's relation to Perry has been described as a counterpart of Strap's to Roderick. Although created at greater length and with finer craftsmanship, the figure of Commodore Trunnion has been equated with that of Lieutenant Tom Bowling, Roderick's uncle.[7] If Roderick may be considered as the "typical Scot," one critic reminds us, Peregrine "is projected as the typical Englishman."[8]

According to Alan McKillop, Smollett's second novel "extends the effects" of the first, offering similar heroes, practical jokes, final acquisition of fortune, and termination in happy marriage.[9] Although the satire in *Peregrine Pickle* proves heavier, more cruel, and more misanthropic than in Smollett's first novel, Knapp describes the work as an "extension and intensification of the materials and methods of *Roderick Random.*"[10] In achieving his comic effects in his new novel, Smollett in fact makes use of the techniques in his first, particularly that "contrast in characters [that] heightens the appeal of the incidents." The Francophile tutor Jolter is played off against the Anglophile Pallet, and both are pitted against the classical-minded physician.[11]

These points are well taken; but to evaluate them properly—to note the differences between the two works, and to consider the independent features of *Peregrine Pickle*—it is necessary to begin with a summary of the novel and, perhaps, to note that, although it ranks beneath its predecessor, it possesses sufficient merit of its own. The adventures of Peregrine, conducted on a continually higher social level than those of Roderick, move initially at a slower pace than the action in Smollett's first novel. In a long opening section that perhaps was modeled after *Tom Jones,*[12] but certainly might well have served as Sterne's model for parody in *Tristram Shandy,* Peregrine goes virtually unmentioned; his birth does not occur until Smollett has recounted the withdrawal of the hero's father from an active city life to a country retreat, where he is pressured into an unfortunate marriage by his elderly maiden sister, who then, after a falling out with his wife, herself marries an idiosyncratic retired commodore.

This preparation is indeed a lengthy one for the hero's emergence, but it contains some of the novel's finest comic scenes, some of those intensive caricatures whose very exaggerated qualities give them a sense of incredible credibility. Perhaps Smollett's finest achievement in *Peregrine Pickle* comes in this gallery of characters, for "as a creator of vivid eccentric types [one critic notes] Smollett is unsurpassed."[13] Gamaliel Pickle, the hero's father, develops as the paradigm of the henpecked husband; his sister Grizzle, as the model of the desperate, frustrated old maid; Commodore Trunnion, as the unforgettable, quixotic curmudgeon, irascible and kind, ludicrous and sympathetic. With Trunnion, especially, Smollett demonstrates his ability to give life to his bizarre characters. For all the Jonsonian-type characterizations, his eccentrics come alive; and there is with Trunnion that same kind of growth and development, indicating the author's increasing admiration, that Cervantes achieves with Quixote and Dickens with Pickwick.[14] The comic takes on other dimensions and becomes in turn a commentary on human values.

Nowhere in *Roderick Random* does Smollett's inventiveness match his creation of these early scenes. There are Grizzle's carrying out the labors of Hercules to placate her pregnant sister-in-law, her wily entrapment of the unwilling Trunnion, her misguided view that she is carrying a child—only to have her ego deflated along with the gaseous protrusion of her stomach. Whatever the living model for Trunnion,[15] Smollett imaginatively turns him into one of the great comic figures of fiction: Trunnion, the landlocked sailor, maintaining a garrison with all the paraphernalia of his former nautical existence; attended by his faithful exshipmates Tom Pipes and Jack Hatchway; living with shipboard routines and conditions, firing salvos, swinging in hammocks. Like Don Quixote roaming the countryside, Trunnion stands as a figure at odds with reality, humorous and sympathetic. The Don tilting at windmills is not funnier than Trunnion proceeding—a sailor on horseback—to his wedding ceremony, carried away from his destination by ill winds and a self-willed animal. Quixote in his wildest adventures does not surpass the Commodore on his marriage night, with hammocks falling and beds replacing them on the following morning.

In its opening pages, at least, *Peregrine Pickle* gives promise of achievement superior to Smollett's first novel. Once Peregrine is born, however, although the narrative pace quickens, the plot follows a pattern too similar to that of *Roderick Random*. Despite differences in detail, Perry's childhood resembles that of Roderick. Unnatural family behavior—Perry's mother rejects him as Roderick's grandfather had Roderick[16]—poses the hero's difficulties; and they are to be resolved somewhat through the beneficence of Trunnion, who behaves like Tom Bowling. Perry's educational experiences, made possible by Trunnion, prove more complex than, but not distinct from, those of Roderick. He emerges more slowly but not less brilliantly than Smollett's first hero; physical brutality, horseplay, and revenge balance those of the earlier novel. Although the heroine, Emilia, appears earlier than Narcissa had in *Roderick Random,* her idealization rivals her fictional sister's. Complications besetting the romance and alterations in Perry's conduct toward her go beyond anything offered in the first novel; but the outcome, the happy marriage, seems no less assured after their initial meeting.

While Smollett's treatment of Peregrine's first experiences in London differs from that in *Roderick Random,* the difference results from distinction in characters rather than from the incidents themselves. Perry, an Englishman, stands as a less likely target for the city's marksmen. He serves as an initiator rather than as a recipient of satire. Yet the various narrative details correspond with those of the earlier novel; and, after all, Roderick, once involved in an action, is no mere passive agent.

With the subsequent Continental adventures of the hero, the second novel expands considerably on the first. While Roderick affords Smollett some small opportunity for satiric thrusts against the French, Peregrine's journey provides a large-scale satire on the Grand Tour taken by Englishmen in the eighteenth century. Some of the European material admittedly does not differ markedly from the satire elsewhere in this novel or in the earlier work. Illicit liaisons, frustrated amours, roadside escapades full of slapstick comedy suggest little variation despite scenic changes. Yet the attack on French customs in *Peregrine Pickle,* striking at the system of justice and institutional practices, goes deeper than anything in *Roderick.*

Moreover, with the introduction of Pallet, an English painter, pretentious and ignorant, and an unnamed physician, pedantic and pompous, Smollett achieves comic invention equal to his best writing. The pair—one has recently been reputed to be William Hogarth; the other is certainly the poet Mark Akenside[17]—provide highly humorous subject matter in a satire on false taste and empty learning, highlighted with a mock-ancient feast in imitation of that of Trimalchio in Petronius's *Satyricon*. Involved in Smollett's satire is comment on some of the gross inanities in the old ancients-versus-moderns controversy that is reminiscent of Swift's manner in *A Tale of a Tub*.

After some additional satire on the Grand Tour with the location moved to Holland, Perry returns to England. Smollett's manner moves effectively in the scene of Trunnion's death, combining humor with tragedy in Shakespearean fashion.[18] From that point on, however, the novel slips into the mood and method of *Roderick;* and for too much of the remainder of the book, the action, superficially, appears merely repetitious, and the episodes seem redundant. Scenes in which Perry joins with the misanthropic Cadwallader Crabtree to uncover the vices of high society, like the earliest accounts of Perry's "pranks," have the tone and effect of a series of practical jokes. Episodes at Bath bear striking resemblances to those in *Roderick*. If the subsequent long inset of Lady Vane's *Memoirs*—more than one-eighth of the book—begins with some distinction, it palls before long in the monotony of that lady's protestations of her honor and her excuses for her misconduct.

With the action returned to Perry, the satire turns upon politics and the falsity of politicians. Perry, hitherto wary of sharpsters and intent upon their destruction, falls prey to this particular breed. Then, out of necessity, he turns to authorship, allowing Smollett sharp humor at the expense of the myrmidons of Grub Street. Finally, however, extravagance and imprudence bring Perry to the disgrace of Fleet Street Prison, where he undergoes the crisis of soul common to eighteenth-century adventurers, including Roderick and Fielding's Tom Jones.

Smollett handles the episode well, permitting despair to grow in Peregrine, prefacing the breakdown of hope with the long inset about Daniel MacKercher and the injustice done to the Annesley claimant. Throughout the experience Perry retains his ferocious pride, rejecting the aid of Hatchway; of Pipes; Emilia's brother; and of the young lady herself, who, for all her ill treatment at his hands, continues to love him. His release comes through a set of fortuitous circumstances—if the death of his father, intestate, may be so considered. Perry's fortunes rise, as well, with the rather miraculous return of his earlier investments; and he comes to a marriage with Emilia in all the glory that brought about Roderick's union with his Narcissa.

Even from this sketchy summary of its plot, *Peregrine Pickle* can be seen as operating in the same general picaresque mode as *Roderick Random*. To be sure, there are variations from that mode; but, while the work offers a combination of satire, realism, and melodrama,[19] the same may be said of Smollett's first novel.

Boucé has demonstrated the effect of Smollett's shifting from the first person of *Roderick Random* to the omniscient point of view of *Peregrine Pickle*. The expanded "vision is so wide that it enables him to include his hero's past, present and future at every turn [and his] definitely pronounced judgments . . . enable the reader to see in what moral direction he is inflecting the story."[20] The result is a clearer moral statement than that of *Roderick Random*, the presentation of a more direct confrontation of good and evil. Yet however modified the picaresque, John Cleland, in the contemporary *Monthly Review*, could excuse *Peregrine*'s crudeness as a natural part of that tradition.[21] Smollett never simply adopted the genre: his view that "life is at best a paltry province" belongs more to his own sense of values than to the genre. Yet in what proves "most essential in the career of a picaroon: the endless wanderings, the untiring assumption of new roles, the peaks and plunges of capricious fortune,"[22] Peregrine, like all of Smollett's heroes, belongs to the genre of Le Sage's *Gil Blas* and of *Lazarillo de Tormes*.

Picaresque Structure

The very structure of *Peregrine Pickle* is fundamentally picaresque. In earlier criticism, indeed, its form was attacked as being its weakest point, an attitude characteristic of the general view that the picaresque lacks unity and simply builds episode upon episode with no real design.[23] Even recently, Alan D. McKillop has repeated that point.[24] But such objections, as the earlier discussion of *Roderick Random* indicated, reflect a failure to recognize how the picaresque achieves its necessary artistic unity, the way in which the picaro and the persistent satiric view of the world function rhythmically to hold the structure together.

Even critics who have defended the form in *Peregrine Pickle* ascribe it to something other than the picaresque.[25] Boucé, who recognizes the function of Peregrine in the novel's thematic design, disdains all reference to the picaresque.[26] Other critics focus properly enough on the role of Peregrine as a unifying force, see how the theme as well as the plot centers upon him, and even note how the two long interpolations in the novel relate to the hero's own experience. But to give the novel its justifiable claim to unified form, they go outside the character proper to impose an external design. They see Smollett shaping his plot from either the grand model of the classical epic or the dialectic of the school of Scottish Common Sense philosophy. It is not, however, a plot superimposed upon the hero that accounts for the novel's form; instead, Smollett, following the picaresque tradition, allows the plot to grow organically through the figure of Peregrine cast in his role as a rogue.

As Rufus Putney, one of these critics, recognizes, a portrait of eighteenth-century society emerges from Perry's experiences.[27] Putney lists education, the Grand Tour, philanthropy, gaming, and dueling among the topics brought forth through Perry's activities. He notes the manner in which Smollett's hero ties together the "upper and under worlds," the way in which he explores political corruption and Grub Street practices. Yet these are not presented through some grand scheme, but rather from the natural movements of a picaro through society. To be sure, Smollett has modified the picaresque, but—for all its greater sweep of society than in *Roderick Random*— *Peregrine Pickle* continues in a line of English rogue adventures.

The Picaresque Hero

The main device for any picaresque unity is the character of the picaro, and Perry bears striking resemblances to Roderick, not only in his personality, but in his function.[28] Like Roderick, Perry displays a fierce pride, a ruling vanity, which, when assaulted, leads to revenge and to the violent action common to the picaresque. Perhaps Perry's pride, as Ian Ross suggests, reflects Smollett's ideological bias, his assertion of a country party philosophy derived from Lord Bolingbroke's opposition politics.[29] At any rate, nothing holds the novel more firmly together than this rhythmic use of Peregrine's character.

As with Roderick and his other picaros, Smollett establishes his character early in the novel. Even in his first educational experiences, Perry displays his ferocious pride that will accept no affront and that will stir him to action both brutal and violent: ". . . now that he had won the palm of victory from his rivals in point of scholarship, his ambition dilated, and he was seized with the desire of subjecting the whole school by the valour of his arm. . . . At length . . . he accomplished his aim; his adversaries were subdued, his prowess acknowledged, and he obtained the laurel in war as well as wit. Thus triumphant, he was intoxicated with success. His pride rose in proportion to his power" (56).[30]

There appears to be little difference between this first real insight into his character and the one in a final scene, when Perry, after a multitude of experiences through which he has finally come to glory, confronts those who have hurt his pride:

Many persons of consequence, who had dropped the acquaintance of Peregrine, in the beginning of his decline, now made open efforts to cultivate his friendship anew: but he discouraged all these advances with the most mortifying disdain; and one day, when the nobleman, whom he had formerly obliged, came up to him . . . , with the salutation of "Your servant, Mr. Pickle," he eyed him with a look of ineffable contempt, saying, "I suppose your lordship is mistaken in your man," and turned his head another way. (780)

This last portrait of Perry, like the first, shows his pride and determined superiority. The difference between them, however, comes through the effect of the accrued experiences on the reader. Where Perry the schoolboy has no cause to excuse his conduct, the man has been through the rigors of social hypocrisy and hardship; and his resultant pride has something admirable about it.

Like a genuine picaro, Perry does not change fundamentally in his character. As with Roderick, Smollett achieves unity through repetition of Peregrine's character traits; but, at the same time, he gains variety through shifting circumstances, through increased gravity in the situations. Even at the beginning of his romance with Emilia, the hero finds her lack of a fortune an alarm to his pride. He can, shortly after, ignore her kind words in a letter because "his imagination was engrossed by conquests that more agreeably flattered his ambition," and "his vanity had, by this time, disapproved of the engagement he had contracted" (217–18). It is not his "attachment to Emilia" but his "ambition" that keeps him from being "satisfied with the conquest of any female he beheld at Bath" (380). When he sits with her in a box at the playhouse, he would willingly sacrifice her reputation to those who might look upon his connection as "an affair of gallantry, and of consequence give him credit for the intrigue" (398). His very assault upon her honor emanates from his inordinate pride that makes even his passions subordinate to its designs. In each of these scenes Smollett repeats Perry's characteristic trait; but repetition deepens the significance of this pride; and varied situations show its intensity and pervasiveness.

But Smollett learned something from the composition of *Roderick Random*. His earlier hero has no real buffer to his pride; and, while its variation and repetition create unity in that novel, it fails to produce any sufficient dramatic tension in the narrative. Now, in *Peregrine Pickle,* Smollett sets his hero's pride against that of the heroine. Emilia may be an idealized Narcissa, may stand, too, as the final object of the picaro's quest; but she offers functional characteristics absent in the earlier heroine. If Perry's pride motivates him, Emilia's defends her. Attacked by his "artillery of sighs, vows, prayers and tears," she "was deterred [from yielding] partly by pride" (403). Whatever his imprecations against "the cruelty of her unjustifiable pride" (595), it is her sole means of protection against his baseness.

By no means do these examples exhaust Smollett's use of Peregrine's pride as a device for creating the necessary unity through rhythm in the novel. He overrates an easy amorous conquest by attributing the lady's submission to "his own qualifications" (283); he can dismiss his discovery of a woman's deceit by satisfying himself with the vanity "of manifesting his indifference" (428). What, after all, permits him to enter into disastrous financial and political ventures? His pride, or his vanity, deludes him into thinking himself virtually omnipotent.

Yet if pride is a source of weakness, Perry's also characterizes his greatest strength. It enables him to withstand misfortune and adversity. Even when he is imprisoned and despondent, he will not yield. Regardless of the lack of wisdom in his rejecting aid from such friends as Hatchway, Pipes, and Gauntlet, and particularly from Emilia, his conduct has something quite admirable about it. Pride and vanity, vanity and pride, constantly recurring, engrossing most of Perry's adventures, including the conduct of his prospective brother-in-law, Gauntlet, his wretched brother Gam, and a host of other characters, become not only the theme of the novel, but the device for achieving unity in the far-flung, seemingly disparate actions of *Peregrine Pickle*.

Satire

Pride and vanity are, of course, the natural subjects for satire; and the satire, which is the prevailing vision of Smollett's second novel, serves as in *Roderick Random* to create unity. It operates rhythmically throughout the novel; but, for it to do so, Smollett must provide a proper climate in which it can flourish: the violence, cruelty, and brutality for which satire seems an appropriate form. For Smollett, given to physical detail in his description and unsqueamish in presenting the rawest side of life, the task proved uncomplicated.

Although Cleland in the *Monthly Review* defended vulgarity in the novel as appropriate to the picaresque, subsequent critics have balked at some of the indelicate material. In particular, they have objected to Smollett's personal attacks on Lyttelton and Fielding, as well as to the attempted seduction of Emilia.[31] Among Smollett's supporters there has been praise for "the spirit of truth" in his writing;[32] but the chief defense comes from Putney, who attributes Smollett's satiric technique to his moral purpose.[33] If Putney has any reservations, they concern only those points at which "violence obscures at times his satiric intent, and [where] sometimes like Cervantes he contented himself with horseplay." But these are exceptions, and Putney finds few "mere escapades" in the novel; Smollett's "practical satire" proves generally a "prank with a purpose," and the technique lends "gusto" to his style.[34]

Although Smollett revised and modified *Peregrine Pickle,* he would not altogether acknowledge the justice of the charges against it;[35] and, considering the satiric intent of the novel, it is difficult to see how he could have accomplished his purposes without the generally vulgar and brutal background in his picaresque world. Satire requires exaggeration, and somehow the novelist must convince his reader of the reality of his grotesque world. Smollett does it, as has been noted, by emphasizing the malodorous, the indecorous, the physically abhorrent. However unbelievably ludicrous the character of Grizzle Pickle, she cannot be denied existence as the contents of her perforated chamber pot fairly submerge the innocent, bizarre, and equally incredible Trunnion. To bring credence to the absurd feast prepared in a classical manner by the obsessed physician, Smollett has need of the revolting details attendant upon its participants—their anal and oral evacuations seem undeniable affirmations of reality. Again and again, the whippings, the beatings, the chamber pots, and the cooking odors become part of the realistic world in which the picaro must travel.

The satire itself in *Peregrine Pickle* encompasses far more of society than that in *Roderick Random*. Its purpose is apparent in Putney's comment, in which he describes the relationship of the picaresque hero and the reader: as Peregrine learns through his experiences, the reader does too.[36] In his criticism of the novel Paulson notes the quality of "portraits and tableaux" in the individual satiric scene; but he complains that even the best "do not lead anywhere."[37] In a purely narrative sense perhaps those individual satiric views do not appear to have direction, but the repeated satire and the increasing intensity of purpose do finally convey a progression toward a panoramic impression of the picaro's world and its significance.

Smollett, who leaves few areas of eighteenth-century society outside his scope, permits no doubt that what he offers is a synecdochical image of the rest of society. Describing Perry's attractiveness, Smollett says, "He inspired love and emulation wherever he appeared; envy and jealous rage followed of course" (93). This comment is not merely on the hero's situation but on the ways of men. Again, particularizing the effect of Emilia's beauty on an assembly of ladies, Smollett concludes: "in short, there was not a beauty in her whole composition, which the glass of envy did not pervert into a blemish" (94). A given assemblage of ladies ceases to concern Smollett and becomes, instead, the subject of mankind's perversity when confronted by the desirable that belongs to another.

But Smollett reenforces his general satiric observations by particulars, especially those of the corruptions of his own age. If Perry is embarrassed to acknowledge his acts of generosity, it is "because he was ashamed of being detected in such an awkward unfashionable practice, by the censorious observers of this humane generation" (611). How else could the Galatea that Smollett's hero creates from a bedraggled human wretch fool the best society, unless its conduct was artifice without substance? Just as George Bernard Shaw's Eliza Doolittle in *Pygmalion* notes that the difference between a lady and a flower girl is in the way she is treated, Smollett observes that polite company differs from the lower classes of mankind merely in "the form of an education, which the meanest capacity can acquire, without much study or application" (599).

The view of the society emerges most clearly in the practical jokes played upon it by Perry and Cadwallader Crabtree, disguised as a fortune-teller. "It would," Smollett summarizes, "be an endless task to recount every individual response which our magician delivered, in the course of his conjuration" (568). But Smollett tries; and, parading their problems before the bogus seer, the consultants reveal the depth and extent of contemporary hypocrisy, deceit, avarice, and immorality that hide behind the façade of respectability.

Some of Smollett's targets are the customary objects of ridicule in the picaresque: the malpractices in law, medicine, politics, and religion. Commodore Trunnion despises lawyers and their methods not so much because of his own eccentricity as because of the despicable character of the legal profession. Perry shares the old man's antipathy; and, when he discovers himself in the hands of those practitioners who seek extended litigation for the profit they can make, his dislike seems justified. Perry, involved in a lawsuit, finds—in a kind of anticipation of Dickens's lesson in *Bleak House*—that lawyers alone profit before the bar of justice. Like shrewd parasites, they fix themselves upon the parent body and sap it of all its life: "The lawyers, indeed, continued to drain [Perry's] pocket of money, while they filled his brain with unsubstantial hope" (666).

Satire on medical practices receives even more treatment in *Peregrine Pickle*. That Smollett was a doctor heightened his contempt for colleagues who abused their trust or for charlatans whose only knowledge consisted in means for mulcting the public. In the portrait of the pedantic doctor that Peregrine meets on the Grand Tour, the satire concerns itself more with personality than with specific professional incompetence. However, an example of the latter provides for some bright comedy in the novel. Confronted by the peculiar behavior of his painter-friend, the doctor describes it as hydrophobia, brought on not by the bite of a mad animal but through "the violent frights he had lately undergone" (302). As diagnosis it ranks with the maddest flights of "invention," the kind of speculative medical theory that Smollett, like Swift, regarded as lunacy. The doctor ascribes the illness to "the effects of fear upon a loose system of nerves," and he goes on to demonstrate "the modus in which the animal spirits operate upon the idea and power of imagination." Losing himself in his own oratory, he almost forgets about the patient, which might have been just as well for the painter, who finally suffers, by way of prescription, a dousing from a chamber pot; and he is saved from further ignominy only by taking his sword in hand.

Smollett was familiar with these fanciful medical notions and remedies, both through his own experiences and from the numerous accounts of experiments, case histories, and various nostrums that filled the pages of such publications as the *Philosophical Transactions of the Royal Society*. He was equally aware of the enormity of impositions and deceits practiced upon a gullible public at such health resorts as Bath. In a chapter devoted to this subject, Smollett uses the picaresque character of Peregrine to expose and avenge the malpractices of physicians who prey upon the unsuspecting public. His exposition of their assorted methods of operation speaks in purest picaresque prose about the picaro's knowledge of deceptive means, in a tone that justifies satirical treatment, and provides a sweeping denunciation of corrupt practices within a large class of society.

No less picaresque is Smollett's treatment of political chicanery, graft, and corruption. Although he viewed government conservatively and feared tampering with its established structure, Smollett, like the Augustan satirists, recognized that one of the great dangers to the state lay in corruptions within the body politic. In using satire as a corrective, therefore, he was acting in defense of, rather than in opposition to, the political order. Again, Peregrine as picaro serves as his means of satirizing the abuses of the governmental system.

Perry learns early in his Oxford career to regard scornfully the fripperies of light-headed politics. The little political club he joins for some amusement "resolved [its] schemes for the reformation of the state" in such a condition of literal intoxication, toasting well in advance the "accomplishment of [its] plans," that the members lost their patriotism in the gaiety of drink. For Perry, an attachment to these "wrong-headed enthusiasts" has the appeal of a picaresque "subject for his ridicule" (114).

More seriously, the mature hero discovers the chicanery of office seeking, the cost of playing the political game, the required payment in cash, flattery, and general sycophancy to ministers who promise all and deliver nothing. He experiences the frustrations of depending upon the honor of dishonorable men; he suffers the embarrassments of attending gatherings where patronage is dispensed without regard for merit; he learns the sacrifice of pride that comes with sitting hat-in-hand, waiting upon his lordship's pleasure, only to be turned away with some flimsy pretense, some social lie, or some rude excuse. Through the misadventures of his own political ambitions Peregrine finds that parliamentary seats and political appointments are at the disposal of ministers and party chieftains concerned only with the acquisition of personal wealth and power.

Related to this political corruption was a deplorable system of military promotions that Smollett knew at first hand. The practice of purchasing commissions, offering advancement based on connections or wealth rather than merit, had placed tremendous burdens on the nation's military forces. At Cartagena, Smollett had seen the consequences of nepotism and favoritism. However eccentric Trunnion's language, the Commodore speaks only the truth when he damns the way in which others have risen to positions of importance in the service: "For my own part, d'ye see, I was none of your Guinea-pigs; I did not rise in the service by parliamenteering interest, or a handsome bitch of a wife. I was not hoisted over the bellies of better men nor strutted athwart the quarter-deck in a laced doublet and thingumbobs at the wrists" (9).

The language is more straightforward when Smollett describes Perry's reaction to the plight of Gauntlet, Emilia's brother, who for want of money has not been able to advance in rank: "Peregrine's generous heart was wrung with anguish, when he understood that this young gentleman, who was the only son of a distinguished officer, had carried arms for the space of five years, without being able to obtain a subaltern's commission, though he had always behaved with remarkable regularity and spirit, and acquired the friendship and esteem of all the officers under whom he had served" (152). It does not diminish the justice of these remarks that Smollett later has Perry purchase advancement for Gauntlet; for, while recognizing the evils around him, survival remains the picaro's concern.

The picaro naturally engages in action devoted to anti-ecclesiastical satire. Although Smollett himself regarded religion with fideistic conservatism, afraid to tamper with fundamental belief since religion was necessary to the proper functioning of a state, he did not hesitate to attack abuses in religious practices or religious scoundrels. Some of the most caustic commentary in his *Critical Review*, a few years later, concerned the infamous Archibald Bower, who opportunistically shifted back and forth between the Anglican Church and Roman Catholicism. In *Peregrine Pickle* itself Smollett directs some of his sharpest satire against the Roman Catholics, a favorite target of the picaresque and a group to whom Smollett owed no allegiance and whose practices he abhorred.

Peregrine's European journey provides Smollett with an opportunity for some very harsh treatment of the Roman Catholic clergy. One episode, an attack on the carnality of nuns, is so outlandish that Smollett omits it altogether from his second edition.[38] His assault on a Capuchin friar, however, appears, its savagery unabated, in both editions. In this episode Perry seeks an amour with a married traveling companion, and he enlists the aid of a Capuchin friar in whose charge she has been placed. For ten guineas the ecclesiastic showers benedictions upon the soul of the conspirator. Learning that the hero has planned an assignation, the Capuchin keeps careful watch, not to protect his charge, but to insure his own financial interests, frightened that "the adventure should be atchieved [*sic*] without his knowledge; a circumstance that would deprive him of the profits he might expect from his privity and concurrence" (288). He delights to discover Perry's ruse for another attempt on the lady's chastity, after the first has been frustrated, since a continuance offers the likelihood of additional profit.

Smollett's satire aimed at Catholicism in *Peregrine Pickle* goes beyond the customary picaresque anti-ecclesiasticism, however. Not only abuses of religious practices suffer ridicule; Catholic doctrine itself becomes a satiric target. While using the dispute between the Deistical physician and the Capuchin to level the pretenses of freethinkers and skeptics, Smollett takes occasion to score "the points of belief in which the Roman Catholics differ from the rest of the world" (284). To be sure, the argument of the physician receives no endorsement from Smollett; but the Capuchin's exaltation of the Virgin above the doctrine of the Trinity clearly is intended as a ludicrous point, particularly when, for the protection of that figure of mercy and charity, the friar threatens the worst inquisitional tortures. Similarly, the Capuchin's later attempts to cure Pallet with the help of relics provide a means for Smollett to ridicule Catholic practices, which he clearly regards as madness and superstition. The friar's relics, supposedly the "parings of the nails belonging to those two madmen whom Jesus purged of the legion of devils that afterward entered the swine," prove to be no more than "the parings of an horse's hoof" (304).

Satire in *Peregrine Pickle* is not limited to the traditional subjects of the genre, but the picaresque structure, covering as it does enormous ground, allows for opportunities to lampoon a variety of related social, literary, and aesthetic practices, customs, and beliefs. The picaro, roaming about in the world, naturally comes upon characters and enters into situations suggestive of "national types" or stereotypes. Smollett displays a fondness for satire that plays upon exaggerated characteristics of nationality. In *Roderick Random* figures like Mackshane and Morgan demonstrate his use of stock representations of Irish and Welsh characters in crude stage comedy. Morgan himself reappears to the same effect in Peregrine's adventures. However, in this new novel the gross caricature of national types exceeds anything in Smollett's comparatively limited satire on the subject in his earlier work.

In what has been called Smollett's extended satire on the Grand Tour,[39] the French and Dutch particularly become the objects of caustic comment. Smollett's portrayal of the French throughout his work led Lord Shelburne, some years later, to reject him for appointment to a consulship at Nice, remarking, "The People would rise upon him and stone him in the Streets on his first Appearance."[40] The reasons stand clearly enough in *Peregrine Pickle*. After offering a few generous words on those men of "honour, profound sagacity, and the most liberal education" who abound in France, Smollett describes Perry's gratefulness "on his title to the privileges of a British subject" (210). To set the record straight for Britons who might envy their neighbors, he presents "a few specimens" of French government and justice to be compared with the British. What follows is a portrait of arbitrary judicial proceedings, tyrannous and nepotistic officialdom, inhumane social practices, unmitigated wanton treatment of the common people, and unparalleled licentiousness. French gallantry and manners are insufferably affected; gambling is a national vice, and cheating is an accepted financial practice. From *Roderick Random* through his famous *Travels* Smollett denigrated the French and their culture, and *Peregrine Pickle* does not fall outside the pattern.

The Dutch fare no better in the novel. Smollett leaves no doubt about his opinion of Dutch drama as he describes Peregrine's physical revulsion to the performance of a tragedy. Dutch morality and manners receive the same harsh treatment. According to the novel, it is through the "connivance of the magistrates" that Dutch taverns for illicit assignations thrive (350). Bawdy, Smollett claims, represents the height of Dutch achievement in the humorous arts.

By no means, however, does he limit his satire of national types to the French and the Dutch. In the pseudoclassical feast provided by the pedantic physician, the Italians, the Germans, and the English become subjects for caricature according to what Smollett considered to be national characteristics. In his portrait of a Jew traveling in company with Perry, Smollett employs the worst features of stereotyping, drawing heavily, as usual, upon contemporary drama for this kind of approach to his satire.

Autobiographical Material

Within the picaresque framework Smollett has ample opportunity to satirize literary and artistic tastes and practices, merging his personal antipathies and preferences with more general grievances. By far the most notorious personal satire in *Peregrine Pickle* concerns Smollett's relations with the London theater and its administrators. His experiences with *The Regicide* had roused him to a fury expressed in Melopoyn's adventures in *Roderick Random;* it remained undiminished in his second novel. In the first edition of *Peregrine Pickle* he recalled his animus against Fleetwood, Lacy, and Rich, the leading theater managers. He was not yet ready to forgive Quin or Garrick.

The attack upon Garrick, especially, stands forth as an example of Smollett's method. What proves most interesting is his technique. In Peregrine's discussion of the English stage with a Knight of Malta the hero entertains his companion with his opinions and his mimicry of the outstanding actors of the age. Perry, "like a good Englishman, made no scruple of giving the preference to the performers of his own country [above those of France]" (272). The Knight, "a man of letters and taste, and particularly well acquainted with the state of the English stage," responds in neither anger nor haste, judiciously praising an English actress before launching an assault against Britain's foremost actor. In this celebrated attack, therefore, Smollett has removed himself from personal responsibility by giving the words to someone other than the hero with whom the novelist might be expected to identify, and he has prepared for the judiciousness of the judgment by his appraisal of the speaker.

As the Knight attacks Garrick's portrayal of Richard III and Hamlet, dismissing the performances as "egregiously mistak[ing] the meaning" of Shakespeare (273), the effect is devastating. The Knight goes on to condemn Garrick's ranting, poor taste, lack of "feeling, judgment, and grace." For him, Garrick's "whole art is no other than a succession of frantic vociferation, such as I have heard in the cells of Bedlam, a slowness, hesitation and oppression of speech . . ., convulsive startings, and a ductility of features, suited to the most extravagant transitions" (273–74). Together with the defamation of Quin that follows—a caricature at once more vehement than any other attack and yet accurate in its portrayal of the actor performing in a dying tradition—it draws forth Peregrine's pique, but in a defense so weak as to underscore the Knight's victory.

Smollett carries on his vendetta against the stage managers in Crabtree's later refusal to give advice to a playwright about the prospects for seeing his play produced because such matters are "intirely regulated by the daemons of dissimulation, ignorance, and caprice" (568). In a ludicrous description of a "College of Authors" the attack continues; and Smollett squares accounts with Lord Chesterfield, a patron of unwilling patronage, in a passage that recalls Samuel Johnson's similar criticism of him.

In all this satiric comment Smollett pursues his personal grievances; but it has, as well, a larger significance for him. If his own experiences led to his account of unfair treatment of playwrights by theater managers and patrons, Smollett at least felt that the abuses were not limited to his own case. His satire receives its impetus from his violent temper and oversensitive nature, but he approaches it with a crusading spirit. In self-justification he writes scathingly, and rather tastelessly, about Fielding; for he believes him guilty of having plagiarized from *Roderick Random* for *Tom Jones* and because of his rival's friendship with Lord Lyttelton, by whom Smollett felt he had been mistreated.[42] Lyttelton himself is burlesqued in *Peregrine Pickle,* and, whatever the personal animus in Smollett's attack, the object of his satire—Lyttelton's publication of his *Monody*—has again some larger justification. The poet William Shenstone, in fact, writing to the novelist Richard Graves, describes Lyttelton's poem on the death of his wife as "too tender for the public ear" and suggests that it "should have been printed privately, and a number of copies dispersed only among their friends."[43] Smollett's burlesque ode makes the same point. However, there is satire on "the appearance and character of Lyttelton" that is largely personal.

Augustan Satire

Some of Smollett's funniest satire on the state of literature that is packed into his picaresque novel reads like a Popean *Dunciad.* In his riotous account of a "College of Authors" the ways and means of Grub Street stand exposed in all their naked wretchedness. The small group that Perry is introduced to has banded together "for their joint advantage and satisfaction, opposed to another assembly of the same kind, their avowed enemies and detractors" (638). In order "to assist and support each other in their productions" they practice all the arts of self and mutual praise through "epigrams, criticisms, and advertisements inserted in the public papers" (639). Smollett unmasks the means to gain attention of authors who arouse controversy by anonymously abusing their own work and then responding to their own abuse. With mock-epic irony he describes their appearance and affectations, the little cabals, the tiny gambits, the small conceits that rise from their petty minds. Out of this grand array, met in grand conclave, develops a battle, one naturally fought in mock-epic style. *"Blockhead, fool,* and *scoundrel"* become the battle cries as lyric bards, satirists, and epic poets engage in vulgar combat, suggesting what may be expected of their art (642).

There is more of the same on literature and art in the ample terrain of the picaresque: booksellers who prey upon "men of genius" and patrons who gain glory without giving aid (645). In presenting the adventures, opinions, and absurdities of Pallet, the English painter whom Perry meets on the Grand Tour, Smollett strikes at the false taste that responds to reputation rather than to the work of art. Pallet pretends to a love of Rubens; but, in the presence of an "excellent collection" of the artist, he remains unmoved, except to condemnation, because Perry has maliciously informed him "that there was not one performance of Rubens among the number" (333–34). Through the classical worship of the physician, unable to distinguish between genuine achievement and trivia, devoted to a pedantic acquisition of bits and pieces of knowledge and misinformation, Smollett ridicules the slavish imitation and nonsensical adoration of the ancients, although he himself was an ardent admirer of the classical tradition.

Throughout his satire on taste and learning, taking full advantage of the great range possible in the picaresque form, Smollett follows in the Augustan line of Pope and Swift. Like Swift, particularly, he scorned speculative, impractical schemes, experiments, and inventions. In *Peregrine Pickle* one of the most delightful satirical episodes concerns a society of such virtuosi who gather for breakfast at the home of a patron whose own vanity is satisfied by their fawning, simpering praise. Smollett, fully aware of the massive display of trivia in the *Philosophical Transactions of the Royal Society,* brings together some of the choicest nonsense that cluttered its pages. Profoundly, the company discusses the weather, requiring "all the barometers and thermometers that ever were invented," before concluding "that it was a chill morning" (662). Antiquarian interests in medals, involved and impractical "contrivance[s] for cutting cabbages," and a method for "the procreation of muck flies" are among the topics presented and discussed by these "adherents of knowledge and philosophy," who cannot distinguish between "the ruins of an English farthing" and an ancient coin (663–64).

Swiftian, too, is Smollett's attentiveness to abuses of the English language. His picaresque again gives him latitude enough to satirize dialects, jargon, and vapidity in language. Some of it, of course, merely reflects the dialect humor of the theater: the Dutch, Welsh, and country folk distortions. More interesting is Smollett's play upon pedantry as a schoolmaster, "proud of an opportunity to distinguish his talents" (104), turns Perry's simple love letter to Emilia into such fustian that the young lady believes she has been ridiculed. Having entrusted Pipes to deliver his note, and unaware that his courier has presented a substitute for the original which was accidentally destroyed, Perry has no idea why Emilia should be offended by the language of love.

If Smollett uses his play on language in Perry's letter as satire, he also manages to draw from it—as old medieval and Renaissance playwrights had done—material to complicate and advance his plot. His use of nautical terms and jargon in the speeches of such characters as Trunnion, Pipes, and Hatchway also serves a multiple purpose. Part of the richness in his characterizations derives from the peculiarities of their language. It was, for its time, strange and unusual and immediately gave new dimensions to his characters. Beyond that, the jargon permits Smollett to underscore the bawdiness of their expressions, while still getting across their spicy comments. Examples abound: Trunnion and Hatchway speaking about marriage and women repeatedly offer double meanings and puns with sexual connotations. Translation of Trunnionese into the common language shows that the charm and wit yield simple vulgarity:

He compared a woman to a great gun loaded with fire, brimstone and noise, which being violently heated, will bounce and fly, and play the devil, if you don't take special care of her breechings. He said she was like a hurricane that never blows from one quarter, but veers about to all points of the compass: he likened her to a painted galley curiously rigged, with a leak in her hold, which her husband would never be able to stop. He observed that her inclinations were like the Bay of Biscay; for why? because you may heave your deep sea lead long enough, without ever reaching bottom. (15)

In all his punning and double entendres Smollett displays a Joycean quality. Not until Winifred Jenkins in *Humphry Clinker* does he develop it fully, but *Peregrine Pickle* hints at the later success. When Deborah Hornbeck,[44] writing to Perry to further their amour, mistakes "meating" for "meeting" and "playsure" for "pleasure" and "hottail" for "hotel," she anticipates the illiteracies of Winifred's letters with their Joycean suggestions of subconscious sexual revelations (219).

So pervasive is the satire in the novel that, after all this discussion, the topic has not nearly been exhausted. Smollett's play upon Gothic interests, upon sentiment, and upon the ancient-modern controversy could provide material enough for several chapters. It seems sufficient, however, to point out that such material composes the fundamental vision of the novel and that its repetition in incident after incident, recalling each time what has gone before and constantly expanding its scope, serves rhythmically to give unity to the picaresque structure. At the same time the satiric intention of the novel justifies Smollett's methods of characterization and accounts for the coarseness, vulgarity, and violence of his world. David Evans aptly characterizes Smollett's work as a fictional experiment that attempts to combine the conventions of the novel with those of satire.[45]

Use of Insets

Perhaps some questions may be raised by the role played by the two long insets in the novel. How do they suit the picaresque character of the work? What relationship do they have to the whole? Both insets have frequently been regarded by early and recent critics as defects in the plan of the novel.[46] Both have been decried by one critic as dull,[47] and Lady Vane's *Memoirs* has been seen as characteristic of the "disharmonies of Smollett's neo-picaresque novel."[48] Yet the inset was no remarkable feature for eighteenth-century readers and certainly in itself was no unusual inclusion in the picaresque.

Of the two, Lady Vane's *Memoirs* poses the greater problem. To begin with, its very length seems inordinate. Moreover, there has always been the question of Smollett's responsibility for its authorship. Who wrote the original memoirs? Was Smollett paid for its inclusion? Was it, together with the MacKercher episode, merely intended to create popularity through notoriety and topicality? Perhaps some of these questions are unanswerable, but the evidence points to Smollett's at least having polished the material for inclusion in his novel.[49] Moreover, a case may be made for its appropriateness to the theme and to the picaresque character of *Peregrine Pickle*.

Even critics who have seen the insets as the "greatest impediments to narrative flow within this middle section" have acknowledged their appropriateness to the theme.[50] Although the tone of Lady Vane's narrative suggests the novel of sentiment and although she herself has some of the qualities of the sentimental heroine,[51] her story—in picaresque fashion—provides an exposé of the "vices and depravity of aristocratic society."[52] In her attachments to various lovers, in her movement from one locale to another, and in her revelations of the tricks, devices, and artifices used to subdue her or to rebuff her pursuers, Lady Vane plays the role of a picara.

Smollett leaves no doubt of the relationship between her *Memoirs* and the adventures of Perry. When she describes a lover who, graced with every advantage of appearance and manners, can overcome every female heart and make conquests while refusing to surrender his liberty in marriage, her description obliquely comments upon Perry and upon the kind of unfair advantage he has tried to take of Emilia. That Lady Vane's story parallels in her discoveries the experiences of the novel's hero becomes clear in her sympathy for him when she learns he is imprisoned and believes him to be mad: "She had seen him courted and cultivated in the sun-shine of his prosperity; but she knew from sad experience, how all those insect followers shrink away in the winter of distress" (673). What she has learned about the world through her picaresque experiences coincides with the knowledge that Perry as a

picaro has gained. To be sure, although Perry's fundamental character remains unchanged, the plots of Lady Vane's *Memoirs* and Peregrine's adventures, as David Jeffrey argues, lead to different conclusions. "Peregrine moves
from a grotesque to an ideal world, [while] Lady Vane resigns herself . . . to
the union with that comic grotesque her husband."[53] Nevertheless, as Jeffrey
acknowledges,[54] there are undeniable similarities between the two plots, and,
as a critic who finds fault with the structure of Smollett's novel recognizes,
both are examples of eighteenth-century developments of the picaresque.[55]

The MacKercher inset bears an even closer relationship to the main narrative. Once more the journey motif allows MacKercher to wander, investigate,
and experience in picaresque fashion. To be sure, it was propaganda for
MacKercher, who supported Annesley in his claim to the Anglesea title and
who was hurt as a consequence. Smollett was certainly concerned with accuracy in his details regarding Annesley's cause.[56] Nevertheless, the episode
functions in the novel through its attack on injustice and through its example
of how social forces can triumph over truth. Perry, already uneasy in prison,
responds to the tale of MacKercher's misfortunes by throwing himself into
despondency, by reaching his spiritual nadir; it serves as the climax of the
novel. Smollett leaves no doubt of the story's effect on Perry, who regards the
proceedings as evidence of "inhuman neglect" and characteristic human in-
gratitude (732).

Point of View

The insets, therefore, continue the picaresque examination of society,
maintaining a consistent satiric attitude toward the ways of the world. Everything in the novel contributes to Smollett's purpose, and only in one important respect does *Peregrine Pickle* make a major departure from the
picaresque and from *Roderick Random*. Instead of the customary first-person
point of view for the genre, Smollett's novel changes to an interpreting narrator. The effect, as may be seen from a few passages, lends a greater moral
quality, perhaps accounting for Putney's insistence—subsequently supported by Boucé—on the novel's essential morality.[57]

But not all the narrator's interpolations serve such purpose. Some have no
more significance than to explain that the novelist has dwelt upon a character
because of its importance to the story or to escape having to give an account of
material he chooses not to include or to offer some simple foreshadowing. Of
greater importance is Smollett's apparent fear that the unnatural behavior of
Perry's mother in rejecting her son would be difficult for the reader to accept.

Expressing his own shock, the novelist seeks to convince the reader that only fidelity to truth forces his inclusion of such material.

Yet the major effect of Smollett's interpretations is to gain a moral point of view absent in the first-person narration of *Roderick Random*. Through his omniscience he can comment directly on London high society in a way that Perry, involved in the action, would be unlikely to do. Perry, returning to London with letters of recommendation from Paris, is eagerly greeted. For him, of course, it must seem merely a reward for his charm; but Smollett, who knows better, explains that Perry's appeal is as "a young gentleman of fortune, who, far from standing in need of their countenance or assistance, would make an useful and creditable addition" to their company, just as the ladies delight in his extravagance at the gaming table (354).

Perry, youthful and high-spirited, full of pride, self-confidence, and self-righteousness, would be unlikely to observe his own conduct objectively. Roderick never does. But Smollett as narrator can point out the injustice of Perry's treatment of Hornbeck, a man he has cuckolded and then seeks to chastise. Smollett can account for his hero's covering his own guilt with brashness and arrogance. Let Perry dissimulate in his designs upon Emilia, and the author can condemn him—as at that point Perry would be unlikely to do—for "vanity and pride," for being concerned only with "self-gratification" (360). Smollett marks the path taken by his hero's conceit, leading ultimately to that spiritual crisis that stands at the novel's climax. "Vanity and whim," callousness and disdain characterize Perry's conduct; and the reader does not have to guess at the author's attitude toward them (371). When Perry makes his shameful assault upon Emilia's virtue, Smollett's language leaves small doubt of his disapproval of the way his hero's "guilty passion absorb'd his principles of honour, conscience, humanity" to pursue his "vicious design" (397). Nowhere in *Roderick Random* does Smollett comment in this way upon his hero's conduct. Revenge and violence go unrebuked in that novel; maltreatment of Strap, neglect of Narcissa remain uncensured. But in his second novel Smollett takes a slightly greater turn from the traditional picaresque; and its effect is to achieve a greater sense of morality.

Peregrine Pickle stands somewhat below both *Roderick Random* and *Humphry Clinker* in Smollett's canon. Like *Jonathan Wild* in relation to Fielding's *Joseph Andrews* and *Tom Jones,* it displays a great novelist's power without quite making the first rank as a novel. Yet it does not fall far short of those five or six works that gave the genre prominence in the eighteenth century, and as an example of the possibilities that the picaresque tradition had to offer, its significance is primary.

The 1758 Revision

In 1758 Smollett published his revised edition of *Peregrine Pickle*. Its changes, while numerous, do not materially affect the substance of the preceding discussion.[58] Instead of adding anything of great consequence, he deleted obscenities and removed his satiric portraits of Garrick, Fielding, and Lyttelton. No one will bemoan the reduction of the number of Perry's practical jokes, but to those who most admire Smollett's vigor, the deletions of the famous perforated chamber-pot incident, involving Grizzle Pickle and Trunnion, and the scandalous conduct of the lascivious nun are a loss. Even the elimination of some of Perry's erotic adventures seems less than compensated for by the greater artistic smoothness of the revision.

Major alterations in organization took place only in the *Memoirs of a Lady of Quality*. Authorship of the inset in the first edition has been variously ascribed to Lady Vane, the scurrilous Dr. John Shebbeare, Daniel MacKercher, as well as to Smollett; and both Shebbeare and Smollett have been named as responsible for editing the *Memoirs* in the 1751 text. By now, the truth seems hopelessly obscure; but, whatever Smollett's responsibility for writing and/or revising these in the first edition, little doubt remains that he had a considerable role in making the changes in the second. Like the most common changes in the rest of the novel, those in the *Memoirs* concentrated on sentence revision. Clarity of expression, the aim of much of the alteration in the inset, characterizes a major portion of the general revision. Beyond that, however, the revised *Memoirs* contains "amplifications and transpositions of passages" not characteristic of changes elsewhere in the second edition.

Overall, the improvements in Smollett's revision of *Peregrine Pickle* seem insignificant: some refinement of grammar and usage; some small heightening and intensification of the humor. The result does not substantially affect the merits of the novel, whose achievement stands in the manner in which it carried the picaresque tradition further into English literature and suggested some of the ways that the older conventions could be played upon in a new setting.

Chapter Four
Ferdinand Count Fathom: Smollett's Iago

Two years after the first edition of *Peregrine Pickle* Smollett published his third novel; but if, harassed by financial and legal difficulties in 1753, he had expected some solace from the publication of *The Adventures of Ferdinand Count Fathom,* "it is safe to assume," as his biographer writes, "that he was deeply disappointed."[1] The novel proved neither a commercial nor an artistic success; for, preoccupied with politics and with the mysterious and sensational events in the disappearance of one Miss Elizabeth Canning, the public virtually ignored the book, and the less than enthusiastic review in Griffiths' *Monthly* was unlikely to create much interest. Not until 1771 was there a second London edition—the poorest record for any of Smollett's performances—and critical opinion in the nineteenth and twentieth centuries did little to suggest that the fate of the novel was undeserved.[2]

In the canon of Smollett's work *Fathom* came to be regarded, in George Saintsbury's phrase, as his "least good novel."[3] It was criticized as a "curious mélange of incongruous fairy tale material and conventional Gothic claptrap."[4] Its credibility was assailed; its inventiveness, depreciated. Even Smollett's most sympathetic readers lamented his loss of the comic touch, his consciously literary and artificial approach, and his failure to sustain a consistent mood. They generally agreed that his division of characters into good and evil categories is mechanical, and they bemoaned the absence of even a single memorable figure in the work of a man who had produced a gallery of remarkable characters in his first two novels.[5] To use the rating scale provided by Ernest Baker, Smollett had descended from the brilliance of *Roderick Random* to the "more doubtful" accomplishment of *Peregrine* to the "laboured and jejune" performance in his third novel.[6]

Subsequent criticism has examined *Fathom* more closely and has emphasized its strengths and offered useful insights generally without greatly altering or even attempting to alter the traditional judgment of its place in the Smollett canon or its importance among eighteenth-century novels. In both his study of Smollett's style and his introduction to the Oxford English Novels edition of the work Damian Grant insists that "useful criticism of Smollett must end up talking about style, not structure." For Grant, "the formal intention of *Fathom* . . . is a mistake, and in so far as Smollett attempts to carry it out it involves him in all kinds of clumsiness and redundancy."[7] He praises "the brilliant episode, the local effect, despite the fragility of the total structure."[8] P. G. Boucé is equally disdainful of the technical structure of *Fathom,* rejects its "unfortunate incursion into the sentimental novel dominated by Richardson,"[9] recoils at the conventionality of its happy ending, but argues strongly and intelligently for a thematic structure wrought from Smollett's moral purpose. That moral purpose has been explored to good effect in T. O. Treadwell's study of the "didactic motive underlying the novel"[10] and the satiric method by which Smollett carries out his moral purpose. While Treadwell makes no direct statement about the position of *Fathom,* or an attempt to rank it, in Smollett's canon, he finds its interest "in its quality as a unique formal experiment."[11]

Robert Giddings, who discusses *Fathom* in a study of Smollett's fiction in the tradition of the English novel, is largely concerned with demonstrating how it marks a change from *Roderick Random* and *Peregrine Pickle.* Curiously, Giddings concludes that "the total effect of [the work] is certainly unsatisfying [because] it lacks a moral framework."[12] Giddings finds it difficult to read, unclear in its moral tone, and attributes its failure to Smollett's weariness with the picaresque. To some extent, Thomas R. Preston, in relating *Fathom* to the tradition of the novel of the man of feeling, seeks to rescue the work from its customary designation derived from Saintsbury's low opinion of it. Whatever the excesses of Preston's argument, he successfully demonstrates that the novel has too often been read as Smollett's attempt to imitate Fielding's *Jonathan Wild* and shows how *Fathom* "dramatizes the man of feeling in need of disenchantment with the pleasing appearance of the world."[13] In his recent essay also defending the merits of the work Jerry C. Beasley extends some of Grant's earlier arguments about the composition of *Fathom* and other than traditional elements that characterize its achievements. Beasley, of all these modern critics, provides the highest estimate of Smollett's accomplishments in *Fathom.* To be sure, he refrains from describing it as "a great novel or an unrecognized masterpiece" or even "Smollett's finest achievement."[14] Nevertheless, "despite its inadequacies," Beasley rates it above *Peregrine Pickle,* considers it "a very considerable achievement of its author's novelistic career, the most impressive and satisfying of his narratives after the superior performances of *Humphry Clinker* and *Roderick Random.*"[15]

Instead of considering at this point the literary merits of *Fathom,* it seems more important to begin by asking what Smollett was attempting to do and what was occurring in his artistic development. Two modern scholars—

Martz and Kahrl—have been most responsible for the current opinion that Smollett experienced a decline in his creative power after his second novel, that he grew disenchanted with his earlier methods of satire and his use of the picaresque, and that only by the discipline of his editorial work, the rigorous training in style, and finally a return to his own experiences was he able to emerge at full strength and in a new fashion in *Humphry Clinker*. For Martz, *Fathom,* then, is an indication of Smollett's first turning away from the picaresque, his "seeking new inspiration" in the "horror-tale," the "fairy-tale," the "Gothic," and "fantastic narrative"; for Kahrl, "Smollett was turning from his own experiences to the drama for character, incident, and setting."[17]

Admittedly, neither in effectiveness nor technique is *Fathom* identical with Smollett's earlier novels. But there is something wrong with the expectation that a novelist, because he works within a particular tradition, must either slavishly follow his pattern or relinquish all rights to the tradition itself. G. S. Rousseau, who recognizes Smollett's experimentalism, fails to see the character of his experiments and denies specifically his transformations of the picaresque.[18] Yet Smollett never ceases to use the picaresque—not in *Fathom,* not even in *Humphry Clinker.* Just as he presents variations on the form in *Peregrine* that make it distinct from *Roderick,* he now experiments with other possibilities in *Fathom.* The use of the drama—as Thomas Preston has demonstrated[19]—is nothing new for Smollett, but the innovations in its use are part of his attempt at artistic development.

Smollett's Intentions

To understand what Smollett is about, we should logically begin with his preface. E. A. Baker's biased comments that it is "not to be taken seriously" are themselves no longer to be taken seriously. They emerge from an unfounded belief that Smollett is neither "a thinker on life and art nor a serious novelist,"[20] a judgment that makes the production of two of the outstanding novels of the eighteenth century one of the miracles of literature. Modern criticism has come to see in this preface not only the most memorable part of *Fathom,* but a brilliance that describes, better than Fielding's more celebrated criticism, the "average eighteenth-century novel."[21] If McKillop has recently regarded the preface as a sign of Smollett's own uneasiness with his purpose,[22] it would be well to remember that Dryden has been praised for the very same practice of prefacing each new literary experiment with an exposition of his technique; and Smollett, after all, was taking the picaresque in a new direction. Moreover, whatever uncertainty Smollett expresses in the preface results more likely, as Knapp has indicated, from Smollett's personal

problems than from any queasiness in regard to his purpose. He was involved
in a legal battle with Peter Gordon, who had repaid his generosity by reneg-
ing on his debt. Angered, Smollett had engaged in an attack on Gordon and
his landlord, Edward Groom; and, at the time of *Fathom,* he was being sued
by both for a total of fifteen hundred pounds and accused of assault and tres-
pass. There is, then, in the preface a reflection of Smollett's "depressed and
romantically introspective mood."[23]

One of the important contributions of his prefatory remarks is that they
present a remarkable assessment of the novelist's evaluation of his own character. Addressed to the anonymous Doctor—, the dedication seems clearly
directed to himself, an exercise in self-analysis that accords well with objective
information available and that Smollett himself later used in great part for
the semiautobiographical portrait of Matt Bramble in *Humphry Clinker:*

> Know then, I can despise your pride, while I honour your integrity; and applaud
> your taste, while I am shocked at your ostentation—I have known you trifling, su-
> perficial, and obstinate in dispute; meanly jealous and aukwardly reserved; rash
> and haughty in your resentments; and coarse and lowly in your connexions—I have
> blushed at the weakness of your conversation, and trembled at the errors of your
> conduct,—Yet, as I own you possess certain good qualities, which over-balance
> these defects, and distinguish you on this occasion, as a person for whom I have the
> most perfect attachment and esteem, you have no cause to complain of the indeli-
> cacy with which your faults are reprehended: and as they are chiefly the excesses of
> a sanguine disposition and looseness of thought, impatient of caution or controul,
> you may, thus stimulated, watch over your own intemperance and infirmity with
> redoubled vigilance and consideration, and for the future profit by the severity of
> my reproof.(2)

A little harsh perhaps, but on his own weaknesses, especially—"pride, obstinacy, jealousy, impetuosity in taking offense, lack of emotional control," as
Knapp has summarized them—[24] Smollett is a reliable authority.

But far more important for critical purposes is what Smollett's preface
contributes to an understanding of his novel. If the novel is indeed a failure,
the reason is not to be found in his inability to carry out his plan, for *Fathom* is
in every way consistent with his stated objectives. The preface calls for a concerted attack on "malice, ignorance, and presumption"; it aims to "teach us to
relish the disgrace and discomfiture of vice" by leaving "a deep impression of
terror upon the minds of those who were not confirmed in the pursuit of morality and virtue." Using the drama as guide, Smollett argues that the villain
as hero is altogether appropriate to a work of instruction, that the audience
may learn morality from evil examples as well as from good.

At the same time Smollett reasons that a portrait of unrelieved evil may tire the mind and disgust the imagination. The very shifts in tone, the contrast in characterization between incarnate evil and angelic virtue, that have created critical censure, were deliberately planned by the novelist. Even the continuation of the picaresque tradition, under these somewhat altered circumstances, is prepared for:

A Novel is a large diffused picture, comprehending the characters of life, disposed in different groupes, and exhibited in various attitudes, for the purposes of an uniform plan, and general occurrence, to which every individual figure is subservient. But this plan cannot be executed with propriety, probability, or success, without a principal personage to attract the attention, unite the incidents, unwind the clue of the labyrinth, and at last close the scene by virtue of his own importance (2–3).

If the definition suggests the scenic situation of dramatic groupings or a kind of portraiture familiar in Hogarth's sequences, it also makes clear that what holds the work together and what gives it the necessary social scope and variety come straight from the picaresque techniques in characterization and plot development.

The Plot

For all its incidents, the plot itself remains simple; and a summary makes clear Smollett's continued use of the picaresque structure. Son of a camp follower who pilfers and robs the dead, Fathom is befriended and reared by the Austrian Count Melville, who mistakenly believes he owes his life to the generosity of the boy's mother. Fathom repays the kindness by stealing from his benefactor's household; by creating suspicions about Renaldo, the count's son; and by plotting the seduction and defrauding of the count's daughter. Through a variety of deceits, in a multiplicity of occupations, and against a constantly shifting setting, Fathom devotes himself to the cause of dishonesty. He cheats in Venice, Paris, Holland, and England. He plays the role of soldier, musician, aristocrat, jeweler, and physician. Learning the tricks of every trade, he preys upon the innocent and uses the greed of the disreputable to extort their own ill-gotten spoils. Not always is Fathom successful, but generally he turns his minor defeats into lessons for later use or opportunities for recouping his losses.

Then, at the point where his fortunes seem lowest, his prospects bleakest, he is rescued from jail by Renaldo. The young count, unaware of Fathom's despicable nature, introduces him to Monimia (Serafina), his sweetheart. Fathom plots her seduction and Renaldo's ruination, but is thwarted by circumstances miraculously contrived. Crushed by a lifetime's malice suddenly gathered like a gigantic boulder and sent hurtling at his evil being, Fathom repents. Where others who have suffered from his treachery might now take advantage of his defenselessness, Renaldo, generous to what many critics have called a fault, enables him to recover from his misfortunes and to live to regenerate himself as a human being.

Whatever the weaknesses of the plot—and it is, after all, no more farfetched than those of many successful eighteenth-century novels, including Smollett's own—it stands consistent with Smollett's announced aims in the preface and follows the normal pattern of the picaresque. The large, sprawling satire is designed to give as vast a picture of corrupt manners and morals as is possible within the framework of the novel. The picaresque—with its journey motif as well as its loose, episodic structure—is an appropriate technical device. In the same way, the picaresque character of Fathom easily "attracts the attention," serves to "unite the incidents," and helps to "unwind the clue of the labyrinth," without diverting "the purpose of the plan" to which all else in the narrative is subservient. Fathom's movements in a variety of settings give Smollett the opportunity to present a diversity of characters "in various attitudes" for the purpose of unfolding his satirist's art.

The extent of Smollett's commitment to the picaresque becomes apparent when the plot elements and the central character are examined in some detail. The continual shift in setting makes little attempt to relate one incident to another, and the episodes themselves might be reversed or omitted without doing any real damage to the plot itself. To be sure, there is some superficial link between events, as Smollett logically accounts for Fathom's moving to Vienna to accompany the "untrustworthy" (in his family's eyes) Renaldo in his training, or as he leaves Vienna to become a soldier, or departs for France because of his cowardice. But the circumstances in each place are complete in themselves, and Smollett is merely making excuses for putting Fathom into situations where he can conduct those picaresque adventures that will satirize folly, ignorance, false taste, and hypocrisy. The novelist seeks opportunities to display Fathom's talents for uncovering the deceptions of professions like the law and medicine, or business practices, and fashionable life.

Character of Fathom

That Fathom is a picaro is obvious from Smollett's earliest description of him:

. . . the sole study, or at least the chief aim of Ferdinand, was to make himself necessary and agreeable to those on whom his dependence was placed. [He was guided by] a most insidious principle of self-love, that grew up with him from the cradle, and left no room in his heart for the least particle of social virtue. This last, however, he knew so well how to counterfeit, by means of a large share of ductility and dissimulation, that, surely, he was calculated by nature, to dupe even the most cautious, and gratify his appetites, by levying contributions on all mankind.(19–20)

It proves to be not merely the gift of nature, but also the product of singular application by one whose practice is to dive "into the characters of mankind" (28). Even adversity serves to instruct him so that, when he falls prey to a confederate in crime, "instead of beating his head against the wall, tearing his hair, imprecating vain curses upon himself, or betraying other frantic symptoms of despair, he resolved to accommodate himself to his fate, and profit by the lesson he had so dearly bought" (107). Defeat serves to reinforce his caution and instructs him in the art of suppressing "the dictates of his avarice and ambition" (108). In this respect, he is far more the picaro than those intemperate and emotional heroes, Roderick and Perry.

Like most picaresque novels, moreover, *Fathom* achieves its unity through the character of its picaro and the idea of its concerted satiric attack. From the earliest criticism, the character of the antihero in Smollett's story has been regarded as an incarnate fiend; and no doubt the text verifies such judgment. But more important, Smollett uses this diabolism—at first only implied, but later expressed in no uncertain terms—to link episodes together in a way that the narrative technique fails to do other than superficially.

From the outset, in Fathom's conduct and in the narrator's comments, Smollett suggests that his antihero is spiritual heir to Shakespeare's Iago. But Smollett's character has none of the stature of Shakespeare's villain; for Fathom, a character in a melodrama intended to convey the effect of a moral fable, is a caricature of Iago. Yet Fathom has Iago's ability to probe into the minds and hearts of those around him, to discover their weaknesses, even to make use of their jealousy. Trying to win Renaldo's sister, he recognizes that he must beware of behaving with precipitation, "in order to undermine those bulwarks of haughtiness or discretion, which otherwise might have rendered his approaches to her impracticable" (24).

Like Iago, he knows how to enlist the aid of confederates and to instruct them in the devices he himself employs. When he learns of the affection of the maid Teresa, he deftly turns it to his own purpose, the conquest of her mistress, Renaldo's sister. Watching her carefully, assessing her correctly, he appeals to her sense of self-importance and makes her believe that their future happiness depends on "the execution of a plan, which he had projected for their reciprocal convenience" (29). Only then, at the proper moment, does he disclose his plot. There is, in fact, something uncanny in his ability to perceive the qualities of other people, to know upon whom he may count for the successful pursuit of his villainy. Only with the greatest caution has he approached Teresa, but instinctively he knows that she may serve as a devil's agent. In *Fathom* Smollett consciously merges his picaresque with moral allegory for a confrontation between the forces of good and evil.

Fathom's stock-in-trade is insinuation, a talent upon which he confidently depends; and these insinuations are ascribed as the novel develops to something more than maliciousness. Fathom is not content, as picaros generally are, to prey upon others for the sake of his own survival. For him nothing satisfies so much as the art of despoiling; he is never so happy as when he has completely defiled his victims, taken what was most virtuous and then discarded it when he has made it thoroughly worthless. Not only the innocent dupe of one of his adventures comes to regard him as "surely something supernatural," working upon her very soul, but the author himself declares Fathom to be something other than human, to be devoid of compassion and benevolence. Fathom, utterly unable to comprehend good instincts in others, attributes them to some subtle, subversive purpose. From every side the comments of narrator and characters label Fathom a devil's disciple, "abandoned by principle and humanity." He is a "devil incarnate," an "artful serpent," a "Monster! fiend!" Renaldo calls him "monstrous and unnatural"; his artifices and plans are "infernal"; his insinuations, "diabolical"; his genius, "evil."[25]

His contest with Monimia is put in terms of the devil's struggle to win over a virtuous soul, and his failure results from the perfection of her being and heaven's intervention. After his "artful temptations" have failed to seduce Monimia, Fathom resorts to force. He himself recognizes that her resistance has the power of "something supernatural," as she strikes out at him, not merely with physical fury, but also with the threat that "the vengeance of Heaven shall not be frustrated." Heaven, indeed, comes to rescue her honor, as Smollett's chapter heading informs the reader. In the agony of the aftermath of his attack, Monimia seeks the solace of the church. Although Smollett describes the general inhospitability of English churches to strangers, Monimia is not forsaken; heaven's intercession comes in the form of the aptly named Madame Clement, who succeeds in protecting her from the wiliness of Smollett's "perfidious wretch" (242).

The characterization of Fathom as fiend carries through the bulk of the novel; and, even when Monimia, after all the distress he has caused her, pleads to others for mercy toward him, she describes him in terms that recall theological arguments to explain evil as part of heaven's plan. "Heaven," she says, "perhaps hath made him the involuntary instrument for bringing our constancy and virtue to the test" (341).

Partly through this consistency in Fathom's character, Smollett imposes a sense of unity on the loose, episodic narrative structure of the picaresque. Eighteenth-century critical theory made easier his task, for the obsessive features of the characterization are consistent with the view that a character is driven by a ruling passion, a "hobby horse," as his contemporary Laurence Sterne puts it. Yet it is important to note that, for all the repetitiveness of its detail, Smollett's depiction of Fathom is kept from monotony by the rhythmic device that combines repetition with some kind of progression.

Whatever the consistency in Fathom's malignity, his character does not remain static. Only gradually does it become clear that his ruthlessness corresponds to some supernatural concept of evil. The multiplicity of picaresque experiences, piled one upon the other, convinces the reader that Fathom is the satanic influence that Monimia describes at the end of the novel. Regarded in this light, the function of the conclusion becomes more obvious; and the type of characterization used for Renaldo and Monimia seems more plausible. To effect a change in the diabolical Fathom requires a truly miraculous force, the power of God's own angels. Not only is the fallen woman Elinor, whom he has debauched, suggestive of Mary Magdalen, but Monimia serves as a kind of Virgin Mary, interceding for the most hopeless criminal; and Renaldo— innocent and noble throughout—ultimately has the Christlike power to provide for Fathom's redemption.

To understand properly Smollett's use of rhythm in presenting Fathom's character, it may help to isolate some passages dealing with his antihero's primary flaw. Albrecht Strauss has commented upon Smollett's use of repeated phrases, noting that, in their repetition, they are merely rearranged; and he attributes this to a failure in "Smollett's stylistic equipment."[26]. These passages relating Fathom's weakness suggest, however, Smollett's conscious use of repetition to gain unity and plausibility and show, too, his ability to take advantage of the reader's accrued experiences to escape the charge of monotony.

When Fathom's lack of self-restraint is first mentioned, Smollett submerges the point in the interest of the episode. Fathom has been accustomed to copying Latin assignments from Renaldo, altering them slightly, and submitting them as his own. On one occasion, "having spent the night in more effeminate amusements" (20), he neglects to make the variations. Although he escapes punishment and although Renaldo is accused instead because of the master's stupidity, the incident reveals Fathom's self-indulgence which ultimately leads to his fall.

After a variety of experiences that expose the same weakness in sundry ways, Smollett calls it to the attention of his readers by underscoring the point that Fathom "had a weak side" and by then immediately illustrating it. This time, to be sure, it is no mere "effeminate amusements" that Smollett describes (172), but the particular sin of covetousness. Yet the point of origin for the two is the same: Fathom's lack of restraint, his yielding to excesses to satisfy his self-love.

If there is any doubt that Smollett's use of the technique is conscious, he dispels it in later references. Again what he counts on is the reader's acknowledgment of the clarity in his pattern. At the same time he makes clear that he has attempted to develop consistency without yielding to monotony: "We have already recorded divers instances of his conduct, to prove that there was an intemperance in his blood, which often interfered with his caution; and although he had found means to render this heat sometimes subservient to his interest . . . Heaven mingled the ingredient in his constitution, on purpose to counteract his consummate craft . . ., and, at last, expose him to the justice of the law, and the contempt of his fellow-creatures" (201). It should not go unnoted that while Smollett uses the passage to summarize what he has been developing, even here he includes some forward movement: the introduction of supernatural forces at work.

Finally, at the very climax of his narrative, Smollett offers a summary view of Fathom's self-love in yet another guise: "We have formerly descanted upon that venereal appetite, which glowed in the constitution of our adventurer, and which all his philosophy and caution could hardly keep within bounds: the reader, therefore, will not be much surprised [at the following adventure]" (264).

Satire

While these passages suggest the way in which Smollett sought unity in his picaresque novel through rhythmic devices applied to his central character, it was, of course, not his only means. The picaresque always has gained a sense of unity by its overall satiric intent. *Fathom,* although criticized for its inconsistent tone—its use of sentimental, Gothic, and didactic materials—is no less a complete satire than his earlier novels. For, in his very first chapter, although maintaining a comic air, Smollett places his work in the satiric tradition extending from classical antiquity through the masters of the picaresque to the English Augustans, Swift and Pope. With sharp scorn, he strikes at those critics "who applaud Catullus, Juvenal, Persius and Lucan, for their spirit in lashing the greatest names of antiquity; yet, when a British satirist, of this generation, has courage enough to call in question the talents of a Pseudo-patron in power, accuse him of insolence, rancour, and scurrility" (8).

Later he makes the satirist's customary excuses for having censured the clergy—pointing out that not the profession but abuses within it have been attacked. And, finally, in an apostrophe to Fathom, he explains why he has undertaken the satirist's role: "such monsters ought to be exhibited to public view, that mankind may be upon their guard against imposture; that the world may see how fraud is apt to overshoot itself; and that, as virtue, though it may suffer for a while, will triumph in the end; so iniquity, though it may prosper for a season, will at last be overtaken by that punishment and disgrace which are its due" (242). Smollett is speaking in the third voice of Horatian satire—the great public defender in the form of satirist.

In the public defense Smollett presses a far-reaching, scattergun attack. Because of its general similarity to *Jonathan Wild, Fathom* has been criticized as having none of the concentrated direction of Fielding's work;[27] it has been abused for its inconsistent tone—though it will be seen, in relation to the Gothic, sentimental, and various other material, not to lose its fundamentally satiric intentions. Even allowing for such "inconsistency," however, Paulson has pointed out that the rambling quality itself gives "a greater illusion of reality than do the over ordering, the selectivity, the complete consistency, of satires like *Jonathan Wild.*"[28] Moreover, Smollett does not aim at a single target, a particular person, as Fielding does in his attack on Sir Robert Walpole. Indeed, the satire in *Fathom,* as Knapp has noted, stands "quite free from recognizably personal satire, [but instead] Smollett's indignation against certain groups is vigorously exhibited."[29]

Like the earliest picaresque writers and as in his previous and subsequent novels, Smollett is particularly concerned with medical, legal, and religious practices; and he in general is worried about public morality. His attack on medical quackery is especially well aimed, for Smollett spaces it judiciously throughout the novel and finally uses it neatly as a part of his plot development. His first sally is made when Fathom feigns illness to win the sympathy of the count's daughter. With all the irony of innocence the narrator describes the situation in which the attending physician, "like a true graduate, had an eye to the apothecary, in his prescriptions; and such was the concern and scrupulous care with which our hero was attended, that the orders of the faculty were performed with the utmost punctuality." Fathom receives the full treatment, until his imaginary ailment gives way to genuine sickness; and "unable to cope with two such formidable antagonists as the doctor, and the disease he had conjured up," Fathom becomes genuinely ill (26).

When Smollett returns next to the topic, he treats an area well known to him: the spas and health resorts that attracted the most notorious quacks. Fathom, now an amateur practitioner, impresses with his bombast and wild theorizing; and he gains a reputation from a victory over a tired old doctor. With ridiculous arguments, reminiscent of those in the third book of *Gulliver* and akin to the nonsense appearing in contemporary pamphlets, he advocates a theory "that fire was the sole vivifying principle that pervaded all nature." But Smollett directs his comments less against medical malpractices than against the public willingness to be duped which he attributes to ignorant delight in abuse of genuine learning. Given the chance to choose between knowledge and ignorance in medical matters, Smollett declares, the public favors the latter: "On all such occasions, the stream of prejudice runs against the [knowledgeable] physician" (166).

Later, as Fathom, through necessity, turns to the profession of medicine, Smollett outlines the procedures of medical fakes. If he is caustic about fee-splitting, profit-sharing practices of doctors and their waiting-women, apothecaries, and midwives, he is again no less severe on the victims whose vanity and gullibility permit the deceits. He details the way in which the pseudo-physician goes about building up a practice, the ostentatious appearance of affluence, the false impression of busyness, the airs of gravity, and the fraudulent puffs in newspaper articles.

Having outlined these matters before Fathom's success, Smollett, in a neat plot device, uses them as signs of his character's fortunes at the end of the episode. It is apparent that Fathom is slipping from power when he can no longer afford the pretense, and the terms of reversing his fortunes depend for their complete understanding upon this earlier information. Once more within the framework of the rambling narrative structure of the picaresque, Smollett indicates his concern for devices that help to achieve unity and verisimilitude.

In *Fathom* Smollett's satire on the operatives of the law proves less wide-ranging than his assault on the medical profession. Some years later, in *Launcelot Greaves,* he presents a severe case against the legal profession; but in *Fathom,* written under similar circumstances of personal legal difficulties, he manages to keep his personal animus somewhat in check. Not that he is gentle in his treatment! He simply restricts his attack to a few sharp instances and gives no sense of personal involvement. Nevertheless, what he includes is devastating, whether he is ridiculing the pomposity of templars or justices of the peace, or exposing the lawyers' methods of delaying a case until the clients' funds are exhausted. This practice is developed at length when Fathom runs afoul of the law and discovers that his solicitor must be "supplied with one hundred pounds after another, to answer the expense of secret service." The suit continues so long as the attorney can find means for profitable postponement; Fathom is held to account for chance meetings with him "in the park, the coffee-house, or the street, provided they had exchanged the common salutation; and [Fathom] had good reason to believe the sollicitor had often thrown himself in his way, with a view to swell this item of his account" (174).

More serious and more varied, although no more extensive, in *Fathom* is Smollett's satire on religious abuses. Out of his commonsense point of view, he comments ironically on the effect of cramming religion down the throats of children, who then "renounce it in their youth, among other absurd prejudices of education" (9). He ridicules the hypocrisy of a clergyman who forgives his wife's adultery with Fathom so long as he believes she is dying but, upon her recovery, repents his Christian generosity.

If the passage hints at Smollett's attitude toward Roman Catholic practices of confession, he attacks that religion in more direct ways in his novel. At the same time that he proclaims the noble aim of his satire to be directed at "the folly of particular members" and declares that the "worthy . . . shall always be sacred from my censure and ridicule," he scornfully describes the French abbés who look upon their church as the means for making a place for themselves in the world rather than as a spiritual calling (92). For the actual religious practices of the Roman Catholics in France, he uses as an example Cardinal Fleury, who under Louis XV wielded political power that subordinated all other considerations to his personal temporal control. Finally, when Smollett arranges the marriage of the Catholic Castilian Don Diego to an Englishwoman, it is the Don who renounces his religion.

Smollett's view of his own church was that it was necessary for maintenance of the social and political order; a threat to the Anglican establishment could not be tolerated; and Smollett's sharpest religious satire is directed, therefore, at the Methodists, those homebred religionists regarded by the Anglicans as most subversive of the state church. For Smollett, the Methodists are always enthusiastic madmen. In the character of Joshua, the beneficent Jew who aids Renaldo, Smollett propagandizes for the Jewish Naturalization Act; but there is no corresponding sympathy for the Methodists' "deranged" return to Hebraic studies as their instrument for discovering the true religion. Chiefly, Smollett casts his satire in the comic form of Sir Mungo Barebones, whom Fathom meets in jail. Sir Mungo, "representative of a very ancient family in the north," is in the saddest physical and mental condition. Once greatly respected and honored, he has through "his evil genius engaged . . . in the study of Hebrew, and the mysteries of the Jewish religion, which fairly disordered his brain, and rendered him incapable of managing his temporal affairs" (184–89).

Smollett also recalls the barrage of ridicule hurled at the Hutchesonians, Whitefieldites, and Wesleyites: "wrapt in visionary conferences with Moses on the Mount"; "settling the precise meaning of the word *Elohim*"; and extracting "from the Pentateuch, a system of chronology, which would ascertain the progress of time since the fourth day of creation to the present hour, with such exactness, that not one vibration of a pendulum should be lost" (189,191). For Smollett, as for Swift, these are the dangerous excesses, the deviations from the norm. They serve as a proper target for his ridicule and as a part of the overall satiric design that brings unity to his picaresque novel.

Part of that same design, and closely related to the religious satire, is Smollett's attack on contemporary morality, social values, and taste. What is it, after all, that makes possible Fathom's success? To begin with, superficial judgment so occupies itself with the appearance of things, with external form, that it never properly values that which is not a mere display of fashion, a glitter of manners. Even within the count's household Fathom is preferred to Renaldo because of "his genteel deportment and vivacity" (19), his airs learned from a dancing master, his assurance in conversation. In vain, Renaldo hopes to gain the respect of those who are concerned with "the mere exteriors and forms of life." If he behaves nobly, his doing so suggests some guilt because "nothing is more liable to misconstruction than an act of uncommon generosity; one half of the world mistake the motive, from want of ideas to conceive an instance of beneficence, that soars so high above the level of their own sentiments; and the rest suspect it of something sinister or selfish, from the suggestions of their own sordid and vicious inclinations" (22).

It is Fathom's strength that he can look into the minds and hearts of others and discover their abundant weaknesses. Recognizing the importance of money in gaining "respect, honour, or convenience . . . in life," aware that "wealth amply supplied the want of wit, merit, and pedigree," he knows what he must go after (225). He achieves his triumphs by exploiting the rage for novelty, the love of the fashionable, the desire for gambling—indeed, the complete decadence in public morality. He makes amorous conquests because he understands how to work the selfishness and vanity, the lust and concupiscence even within a single family group. France, as a "centre of pleasure and politeness," is an undefended country for the picaresque soldier of fortune (80). England, in its affluent softness and its smug complacency, equally invites his attack. Willing to take advantage of foreigners whom they regard as some sort of subhuman species—"chattering Frenchman, an Italian ape, a German hog, and a beastly Dutchman," not to mention their own "beggarly Scot, and an impudent Irish bog-trotter" (145)—the English are not only easy but deserving victims of those, like Fathom, who play upon their prejudices.

If Fathom pretends to be a connoisseur, a judge of diamonds, a student of music, he succeeds because those who are impressed are themselves intent upon impressing. He takes "a number of old crazy fiddles, which were thrown aside as lumber," falsifies their mark, and presents them as rare instruments. Various worthless objets d'art become valuable because he gives them his arbitrary approval. Indeed, "nothing was so wretched among the productions of art, that he could not impose upon the world as a capital performance, and so fascinated were the eyes of his admirers, he could easily have persuaded them that a barber's bason was an Etrurian Patera, and the cover of a copper pot, no other than the shield of Ancus Martius" (151).

Decadence in taste, morals, and manners is a part of the territory of picaresque satire—and Smollett includes his sallies against false, boisterous patriotism as well as his customary assault on abuses of the English language. But his satiric intent extends even into those areas that have been marked off as outside the bounds of his proper purpose: the new ground of Gothic and sentiment that was being discovered in the middle of the eighteenth century and that Smollett had satirized in *Roderick Random* and *Peregrine Pickle.*

Without minimizing the amount of digressive tonal elements in the novel which tend to weaken the original satiric purpose, it is possible to point out that most of what Smollett is doing with this material is consistent with his overall picaresque manner. His treatment of the Gothic—generally regarded as his capitulation to new fashions[30]—is particularly easy to fit into his satiric framework because he never simply yields to the devices of supernatural terror; indeed, he ridicules them even as he uses them.

Even the celebrated passage concerning Fathom's adventure in a hurricane is used to ridicule Gothic fears and the character's inordinate cowardice. Smollett begins the episode with an ironic comment on Fathom's courage. During the nightmarish experiences in a forest that has come to life with dreadful personifications of terror, the narrator deliberately recalls the distortion of "reason and philosophy" that is taking place; and he accounts in naturalistic terms for Fathom's legitimate dread of assassination, emphasizing the distance from "the habitations of men," mingled with the "dejection of [Fathom's] spirits," and the guide's tales of "travellers who had been robbed and murdered," to account for Fathom's fears (83). Here, in advance, Smollett offers the explanations for forthcoming events. Like the picaresque novelists before him, he presents not Gothic terror, but the natural turmoil of the mind and actual physical dangers—borne out by an attack on Fathom in his roadside "sanctuary"—as his adventure. If this is an early use of the Gothic in the English novel, it is one that takes little advantage of supernatural elements to harry the imagination.

Smollett's attitude toward the Gothic and those to whom it appeals is revealed when Fathom seduces the innocent, rather weak-minded Celinda. Here indeed are the materials later exploited by Ann Radcliffe: the mysterious music in the night, "the piteous groans," and the strange voices. But Smollett derides these by labeling them "enthusiastic terrors," which obviously can appeal only to one "credulous enough to believe the most improbable tale of superstition" (103).

In a way these two satiric attacks on Gothic illusion serve to undercut the terror in the one genuinely Gothic portion of the novel when Renaldo comes to what he believes to be the grave of Monimia and meets his suddenly "resurrected" sweetheart. For those readers too dull to recognize that the description of Monimia's "death" was verbally hedged beyond statement of fact, Smollett lays this new scene in a way to anticipate its false terror. Renaldo comes to it "wound up to the highest pitch of enthusiastic sorrow"; "his imagination began to be heated into an extasy of enthusiasm"; "reason shrunk before the thronging ideas of his fancy" (317, 323). It is all a language cast to set doubts on the authenticity of the horror; and, while Smollett gets the most out of the new taste for terror, he does it clearly with the touch of the satirist.

While *Fathom* offers some of the unrestrained sentimental language characteristic of the worst romances,[31] Smollett does not yield to the excesses of the sentimental novel and, for the most part, carries on his satiric purpose even here. His commonsense values stand evident in the character of Renaldo's sister, who presents an antithesis to the romantic heroines and who consequently thwarts Fathom's basest designs. Where a young lady is given to such excesses of feeling, Smollett shows scant sympathy for her; and she becomes a natural target for Fathom's wiles. For Smollett, there seems nothing more ludicrous than such clichés as those of the pastoral romance, nothing less attractive than the romantic primitive lure of a "bleak, inhospitable Greenland" (282).

Augustan Satire

With all this evidence of Smollett's continued use of the picaresque and its values, however, criticism has been insistent that the book represents his turning away from the old tradition. Two other elements affecting tone perhaps account for this general assessment, although upon examination they do not justify the conclusion. Smollett, in *Fathom,* adds two voices to the narrative: one, mock-heroic; the other, didactic. While these do not appear at once to be consistent with the picaresque, Smollett's technique certainly makes them so.

Since he regarded himself as a successor to Pope and Swift, it is not remarkable for Smollett to turn to the mock-heroic. If, as Putney suggests, Smollett uses the classical epic for satire in *Peregrine Pickle,* in *Fathom* there is a wonderful battle scene that parodies the great epic struggles. Employing the locale of a bawdy house, striking with all his farcical vigor and with an elaborate descriptive technique, Smollett plays out his lusty scene. Weapons like candlesticks "sing through the air," "winging" in "flight." Heroes, not to be outdone "in point of courtesy," hurl chandeliers, "smiting a large mirror"; or, taking advantage of lights extinguished, they "scamper off with infinite agility" (chapter 23).

But the mock-heroic is not restricted to a particular situation in the novel; it accompanies the language throughout.[32] Fathom is the "mirror of modern chivalry"; his bastard birth gives him the supernatural advantage of having "no mortal sire"; and his birthplace is as debatable as that of Homer. Smollett uses inflated diction, ornate style, to describe everything connected with him—his mother is an "English Penthesilea," that Queen of the Amazons killed by Achilles; her death, while robbing battlefield corpses, is "in point of courage . . . not inferior to Semiramis, Tomyris, Zenobia, Thalestris." When Fathom himself moves from his attempts at seduction into a forced military service, Smollett's chapter heading declares, "Our Hero departs from Vienna, and quits the Domain of Venus for the rough Field of Mars."

This particular statement is important because it neatly joins the mock-epic technique with the picaresque structure. If, at first, the inflated language of the former style seems at odds with the traditional realism of the latter, it is well to recall that the picaro himself is an antihero; and, consequently, he suggests in his own person something of the mock-epic intention. What Smollett is doing, then, is making a natural extension to the picaresque novel by relating it to the satiric tool of the mock-heroic.

In the same way, the didacticism in *Fathom* has its relation to the kind of picaresque being developed. It is true, as Knapp says, that the novel shows Smollett as a moralist;[33] but in the English picaresque—as evident in Defoe's novels and Smollett's *Peregrine Pickle*—no inconsistency exists between the satiric pillorying of abuses and the sermonizing on society's ills. Smollett, indeed, could find models in the traditions of the genre;[34] and he had good reason for extending what he found there. After all, one of the major criticisms of his earlier novels—unjustified, as Putney has shown for *Peregrine Pickle*—

had been their failure to condemn the vice that they described and their final rewarding of heroes who showed no contrition. In *Fathom* Smollett takes no chances that such criticism should be repeated; he openly speaks out against the calumny and deceit, the viciousness and cruelty of his character; and he concludes with Fathom's reformation.

Place in the Canon

Reading Smollett's novel carefully, then, we may possibly find a unity not generally granted to it, a consistency with Smollett's intentions as announced in his preface, and an interesting continuation of his experiments with the picaresque form. Whether it is a good novel is another matter. It is certainly a better novel than earlier criticism has pronounced it to be, if only for the way in which its structure is achieved. It also has small virtues that have been either neglected or denigrated. For example, Smollett wisely gains verisimilitude by narrating rather than dramatizing Fathom's powers of persuasion. Instead of presenting in scenic form Fathom's persuasive language that effects the conquest of Wilhelmina, Smollett summarizes: "so artfully did Fathom in the mean time manage the influence he had already gained over her heart, that before her passion could obtain a legal gratification, she surrendered to his wish, without any other assurance, than his solemn profession of sincerity and truth, on which she reposed herself with the most implicit confidence and faith" (49). Had Smollett used dialogue to convince others, he would have found greater difficulty in convincing his readers. He proceeds, too, in a realistic manner in such minor matters as introducing the names of characters only after they have been on the scene and acted and made it plausible for their names to be set forth. These concerns, to repeat, are small ones; but, along with the rest, they suggest that *Fathom* is something more than the dismal failure of a great novelist who has lost his creative power.

Chapter Five

Launcelot Greaves:
Quixotic Picaresque

What small interest has been expressed in Smollett's *The Adventures of Sir Launcelot Greaves* has generally had little to do with its merits as a novel, the work being primarily noteworthy as the first example of serialization by a major novelist. It is also cited as one of the many imitations of Cervantes' *Don Quixote* in the eighteenth century. Instead of taking it seriously as a work of art, most critics have been more concerned with its relation to Smollett's biography. How much of it, they have wanted to know, was written while Smollett was serving his sentence in King's Bench prison for having libeled Admiral Knowles? How accurately does his description of the character of Ferret conform to his old enemy Shebbeare? Smollett's political attitudes, regard for penal reform, and medical theories have gained the attention that critics have ordinarily declined to waste on the novelist's art. Only in such matters as the transition from Smollett's earlier style or his capitulation to the fashions in Gothicism and sentiment has critical comment customarily dealt with *Greaves* as a literary work.

The fact is that Smollett's first novel to be written after seven years devoted to journalism has generally been regarded as either his poorest work or as a close contender for that dubious honor with its immediate predecessor.[1] Written apparently to add to the popularity of the *British Magazine,* in which it appeared during 1760–61, *Greaves* served its purpose;[2] but, when published independently of the periodical in 1762, it "attracted a moderate amount of attention," and indeed there was no second London edition in Smollett's lifetime.[3] The *Monthly Review* dismissed it with a single sentence as "Better than the common Novels, but unworthy of the pen of Dr. Smollett," and his own *Critical Review* found little more to praise than its characters.[4] While Oliver Goldsmith complimented *Greaves,* it was by way of a puff to the magazine whose editorship he shared with the author;[5] and even the French reception it received was due only to its Toryism, which pleased the ultra-royalists.[6]

Even today, despite some slight stirring of interest in *Greaves,* the novel has received only minimal treatment by critics. A volume of essays devoted to Smollett's work all but ignores *Greaves,* and an assessment of the early English novelists dismisses it in a single paragraph that concludes, "it is a mere piece of copying, unworthy of Smollett's powers of invention."[7] Surveying Smollett's fiction in another collection of essays, Jerry C. Beasley devotes less than two pages to the work, finds its imitation of *Don Quixote* "a stale [conception], often tried . . ., and [argues that] Smollett had nothing new to add."[8] John Valdimir Price's more sympathetic account of *Greaves,* concerned largely with the author's expression of concern for "coaxing the reader into the novel,"[9] regards it as an "interesting failure," although one "more interesting than others in this category,"[10] and finds its importance chiefly in its role as a precursor of *Humphry Clinker.*

Yet some recent criticism justifies the comment of the novel's latest editor that, although "*Launcelot Greaves* is not a great novel by any means, . . . there are clear signs that it is more highly regarded today than at any time since its publication."[11] In his study of *The English Novel in the Magazines, 1740–1815* Robert D. Mayo makes a sensible evaluation of *Greaves* in the context of its publication. Comparing the work to novels that appeared from 1740 through the next eighty years in serial form, Mayo declares, "it represents a pinnacle of achievement, outstanding for its range of interest and allusiveness, its multiple relevance to contemporary life, and, however fluctuating, the maturity of its literary craftsmanship."[12] Whatever the faintness of such praise when set in the context of its judgment of periodical fiction that was in its infancy, Smollett's achievement *was* remarkable *because* his work had no genuine antecedents to build upon. Somehow, as Mayo notes, Smollett, the professional writer, accurately assessed "the requirements of serial publications"[13] and his novel admirably served the purpose for which it was originally created.

Considering the novel essentially apart from its serial publication, Damian Grant and Paul-Gabriel Boucé find merits that have previously been overlooked. Grant's study of its style and language illuminates Smollett's experimental techniques. He describes its "series of brilliant scenes" and its "vigorous exercise of language," and finds the "value of *Greaves*" in what Smollett himself called its "agreeable medley of mirth and madness, sense and absurdity."[14] For Grant, the novel's lack of "rebuttal of formal criteria" is "irrelevant." He points "to the natural affinity between [Smollett and Dickens] in their attitude to language,"[15] and relates the novel's "rhetorical effectiveness" to its "vigorous moral attitude."[16] Boucé argues effectively for the thematic unity and underlying symbolic pattern in *Greaves* that he perceives as centered in its concerns for madness and reason. Unlike Grant, who discounts Smollett's formal concerns, Boucé speaks of the novel's architecture, but he is in accord with Grant in his arguments for Smollett's "moral intentions."[17] Neither critic overrates Smollett's achievement in *Greaves* (indeed, Boucé terms it as "near failure")[18], but both give serious attention to a work whose literary merits have generally been underrated, if not totally ignored.

Yet there remain important and unnoticed levels to Smollett's satire, unobserved distinctions in his use of Cervantes, that make *Greaves* even more interesting than has already been suggested; and modern readers, along with Grant and Boucé, may even be inclined to conclude with Oliver Elton and George Saintsbury that the novel has some "genuine merits, which grow upon one as he rereads it."[19] They may even find a charm in Smollett's modern Quixote, who, driven to personal despair by the frustration of his marital plans, sets out in knight's costume to combat the evils that he discovers along the English countryside. In Smollett's gallery of caricatures—Crowe, the ex-sea captain who seeks to imitate Greaves; Crabshaw, the knight's Sancho Panza; and Ferret, the misanthropic pamphleteer and mountebank—there are still the novelist's appealing exaggerations and grotesques. There are, too, in the book Smollett's delight in play upon language, his sharp thrust at medical, legal, and political malpractices, and the old spirit of reform that denounces conditions in English prisons and madhouses.

Serialization

Without altogether eschewing the kind of earlier criticism that has been applied to *Greaves,* it is now possible to examine the novel on a more aesthetically critical basis than has heretofore been done. Serialization, for example, with the exception of Mayo's discussion, has been mentioned consistently without regard for its relation to the novel's structure, without consideration of the novelist's technique. Yet it would seem the most obvious point of departure for any critical discussion of the work.

Perhaps the matter has been largely ignored because the earliest descriptions of Smollett's composition of the novel offer so denigrating a picture of a hack at work that the novel has not been taken seriously. Smollett, according to Sir Walter Scott, "was residing at Paxton, in Berwickshire [Scotland], on a visit to the late George Home, Esq., and when post-time drew near, he used to retire for half an hour or an hour to prepare the necessary quantity of *copy,* . . . which he never gave himself the trouble to correct, or even to read over." Scott's accuracy in the account has been questioned,[20] but it—coupled with the fact that some of the chapters were written while Smollett was imprisoned and hence were thought of as merely journalism[21]—has left an enduring portrait of the creative process performed at its worst.

Yet whatever were Smollett's methods (Scott's story incidentally makes Smollett something of a superman to have composed so much copy in so little time), the criticism of his novel depends ultimately on the finished product, which to be sure may have suffered because of the manner of publication—but that remains to be seen. At any rate, it seems far more pertinent to ask how Smollett, without any genuine predecessors in the art, handles the matter of serialization.

For modern readers, accustomed to installment endings that keep them waiting impatiently for the subsequent chapter, Smollett's method may engender little suspense. He is still clearly working in the picaresque tradition, and the episodic technique that composes its structure out of minor narratives is hardly conducive to arousing anticipation from one chapter to the next. Moreover, Smollett's "imitation" of *Don Quixote* serves only to emphasize the individual episodes. Out of its twenty-five chapters, less than half may be said to create the excitement that comes from the continuity of the narrative; and these occur chiefly at the beginning of his novel where he can depend for interest on the introduction of Greaves and on revelations of the details of his situation.

Once into his story, Smollett shows less and less regard for creating what may be considered the customary suspense of serialization. Even where he ostensibly seeks to arouse such interest, he is perfunctory and uses rhetorical devices unlikely to yield such a result. "The reader," he declares, "if he be so minded, may partake [of the continuation of the narrative] in the next chapter" (17). Or again, "But as the reader may have more than once already cursed the unconscionable length of this chapter, we must postpone to the next opportunity the incidents that succeeded this denunciation of war" (30). But these devices appear strong compared to the anticlimax with which he rounds out his later episodes, and the way in which finally he becomes so absorbed in his social criticism that he evidently loses all sight of the main narrative itself.

Parody and Use of *Don Quixote*

Smollett, then, relies less on narrative suspense than on the particular episode to achieve his interest—a reliance hardly surprising for a picaresque writer, especially one following the scheme of *Don Quixote*. With Smollett's scheme, criticism has generally been dissatisfied. If critics have not ignored his use of Cervantes, as they have his serial technique, they have done it considerable harm by distorting to some extent its purpose and by calling it an "unfortunate imitation of Cervantes,"[22] a failure "to comprehend the spirit of its original,"[23] a "much attenuated" adaptation to English society,[24] and an "unimaginative and almost slavish imitation."[25]

In particular, Smollett's own words on the subject in the novel have been described as a "lame" excuse, anticipating the natural criticism that would follow.[26] The words come from Ferret: "What! you set up for a modern Don Quixote?—The scheme is rather too stale and extravagant.—What was an humorous romance and well-timed satire in Spain, near two hundred years ago, will make but a sorry jest, and appear equally insipid and absurd, when really acted from affectation, at this time of day, in a country like England" (12).

But for several reasons it is difficult to believe that Ferret speaks these words in order that Smollett may have a prepared defense for his novel. To begin with, no such defense was actually necessary. Not only was Smollett's own translation of Cervantes' novel reprinted several times before his death, indicating the popularity of the Quixote story, but Charlotte Lennox's *Female Quixote* (1752) and Richard Graves's *Spiritual Quixote* (1773) suggest that Smollett's audience was prepared to accept modern versions of the novel put to some particular contemporary use.

More to the point, it is Sir Launcelot's answer that seems truly important since it is he and not the villainous Ferret who generally speaks with Smollett's voice.[27] From Launcelot's response to Ferret, Smollett's purpose in using the device becomes clear:

"I am neither an affected imitator of Don Quixote, nor, as I trust in heaven, visited by that spirit of lunacy so admirably displayed in the fictitious character exhibited by the inimitable Cervantes. I have not yet encountered a windmill for a giant; nor mistaken this public house for a magnificent castle. . . . I quarrel with none but the foes of virtue and decorum, against whom I have declared perpetual war, and them I will every where attack as the natural enemies of mankind" (13).

Oddly, those very critics who lament Smollett's attempted imitation sometimes also criticize his plan as being inconsistent; yet Smollett is neither slavishly following Cervantes nor concerned with doing so. His is an endeavor to find, as Paulson has noted for another purpose, a proper vehicle for his satire.[28] Launcelot is reminding the reader of his role in that satire, as Smollett now takes another turn from the traditional picaresque to offer in still another way an attack upon medical, legal, and political practices. Launcelot is no mere imitation of Quixote; he is the picaro wearing yet another of his disguises.[29]

Where Smollett does specifically parody Cervantes' novel, he does so consciously to provide fun through recollections of the original. Smollett himself is quick to remind the reader of the originals by naming the knight's horse and his squire's nag, and by recalling the adventures of Sancho Panza and "Don Quicksot." Physical descriptions of Timothy Crabshaw, his cowardice, his talk, and his practical demands are all particularly intended to evoke memories of Sancho Panza. Battles—from those with irate townspeople who come armed with pitchforks and flails to that with Lord Sycamore, Launcelot's rival for Aurelia—are treated as mock-heroic comedy scenes. If Launcelot, as he has claimed, knows the difference between a windmill and a giant, an inn and a castle, Crabshaw does not always show the same discretion. "Sir Knight," he tells his master from his lodging in jail, "if you will slay the justice, hang the constable, release your squire, and burn the town, your name will be famous in story" (85).

In this particular instance, to be sure, Launcelot himself demonstrates no great hold on reality and stands ready to comply with his squire's wishes after learning that he too is a prisoner. However, the knight, for all his socalled madness, is not often shown in such a light. One of his primary functions throughout the novel is to allow Smollett to question what truly constitutes sanity within this corrupt world. When the novelist seeks to provide humor in the quixotic vein, he uses instead the figure of Captain Crowe, who looks upon Launcelot as a hero whom he hopes to imitate. In Cervantes' story the vigil of knighthood stands exposed as ludicrous, but in *Greaves* Sir Launcelot's test is described by Tom Clarke, nephew of Captain Crowe, who is impressed by the knight's bravery in entering a place "confidently reported . . . [as] haunted" (43). It is, instead, Crowe who is put to the test of a mock ceremony in a "haunted" church, who is incapable of recognizing the realities of the world, and who suffers the physical abuses visited upon Quixote in Cervantes' novel. The details of Smollett's story may resemble some of those in Cervantes', but he has a different purpose for his hero and saves him from some of the absurdities of Quixote so that he may otherwise use him profitably.

In one sense, of course, *Greaves* does closely parallel *Don Quixote*. Despite criticism that Smollett's work fails "to comprehend the spirit of its original,"[30] that proves to be the truest point of their relationship. Not that anything of the grand design exists in *Greaves,* for most assuredly it does not! Rather, Smollett attempts to give within a small compass what Cervantes renders on a large scale. Smollett is less concerned with parodying Cervantes than with raising chiefly for *his own time* the question of the line between illusion and reality. Some of the differences in the results come naturally enough from Cervantes' superior genius. Yet that is not all. Where Cervantes is a philosophical novelist, concerned with illusion and reality in some larger sense, despite his use of the tools of satire, Smollett is primarily a satirist who is bound by the problems of his own day, seeking measures to correct the particular ills of society, and limited in his vision of the human experience. There is nothing, therefore, of Don Quixote's timelessness in Greaves's character. To be sure, Smollett probably lacked the ability to create such universality; but nothing indicates that he is even seeking to achieve it. If Quixote serves as a lesson to men of all ages, Smollett plainly means Greaves to function only as a vehicle for his contemporary satire.

Such differences in function account for those in characterization in the two novels. Where the Don sets out to alter society radically, Sir Launcelot expresses his desire merely to deal with the "foes of virtue and decorum." Quixote is doomed to failure: if he prevents a master from beating his servant, the effect proves only momentary—merely an illusion rather than reality—because servitude is a condition of humankind. But Greaves can and does effect changes because Smollett, unlike Cervantes, is not describing universal conditions. Sir Launcelot can set right the wrongs of a Justice Gobble who has unfairly dealt with a town because he seeks personal gain. Confined to a madhouse because he is seeking his lady, also unfairly committed, Greaves can do something about their circumstances. In the end, the Don must die because his efforts ultimately are useless; and, whatever sympathy he has engendered, there is lunacy in his desire to correct the social order. For Launcelot, on the other hand, the conclusion proves happy. He has liberated those who are unfairly imprisoned, brought on an investigation of the asylums, and gained the hand of Aurelia, whose uncle, for his own selfish purposes, has wickedly kept the lovers apart.

Naturally, therefore, Greaves's character belongs to a different order from Quixote's. His madness has a simple, fairly realistic origin. When assured of Aurelia's love, he can put aside his knight's disguise. He knows the difference between benevolence and extravagance. Acting as Smollett's satirical voice—again that third voice of Horatian satire, the great public defender in the form of satirist—he must be capable of seeing the evils for what they are. His madness cannot afford to be all-encompassing, as indeed it is not. Like a picaro, although enlisted in the cause of good, Launcelot has assumed a role; and, mindful of its oddity, he explains it to the assemblage at the inn:

"The good company wonders, no doubt, to see a man cased in armour, such as hath been for above a whole century disused in this and every other country of Europe; and perhaps they will be still more surprised, when they hear that man profess himself a noviciate of that military order, which hath of old been distinguished in Great Britain, as well as through all Christendom, by the name of Knights Errant. Yes, gentlemen, in that painful and thorny path of toil and danger I have begun my career, a candidate for honest fame; determined, as far as in me lies, to honour and assert the efforts of virtue; to combat vice in all her forms, redress injuries, chastise oppression, protect the helpless and forlorn, relieve the indigent, exert my best endeavors in the cause of innocence and beauty, and dedicate my talents, such as they are, to the service of my country." (12)

Regardless of his appearance at any time, he is the one with strength in argument, the one who speaks political sense, who shrewdly recognizes that "madness and honesty are not incompatible" (60)—although this combination perhaps marks the greatest insanity in the face of reality.

Picaresque Satire

To be sure, problems of technique arise from Smollett's desire to use Sir Launcelot as a picaresque satiric voice. In order to put his character into action, to keep his story rolling, Smollett has to emphasize the madness of his behavior. But, to make the social comment significant and convincing, he has to provide Greaves with an awareness and grasp of reality that suggest inconsistency in the characterization. Smollett, aware of this problem, tries to account for it in a variety of ways—by insisting that the line between madness and sanity is not always clear and by making Sir Launcelot more obsessed than crazy. If these prove not altogether satisfactory explanations and if the duality remains, that was the price that Smollett had to pay for carrying out his satirical plan.

As for the objects of his satire, they have properly been identified by scholars as his characteristic grievances against society.[31] What critics have not always noted successfully is how much the Smollett of his later novels remains the same as the picaresque satirist in his earlier work. *Greaves* is frequently depicted as a turning point in his career—a yielding of the picaresque tradition, a mellowing of the harsh temperament, a foreshadowing of the more "romantic" *Humphry Clinker*.[32] A full discussion of the matter of such "transformation" may more appropriately be treated in regard to Smollett's final novel, but some major points must be made specifically about *Greaves*.

The subjects of Smollett's satire in the novel—the law, medicine, and politics—traditionally belong to the picaresque. At the time of composing his novel, however, Smollett was especially concerned with abuses of justice and prison conditions. Not only were parts of it written during his imprisonment, but he had been involved in the legalities of the Knowles libel case for more than a year prior to his beginning his novel.[33] His earlier experiences with the law had made him sensitive to its irregularities, and in *Greaves* he indicates how much its practitioners and their jargon irritated him. Even in describing the favorable character of Tom Clarke, nephew of Captain Crowe, Smollett strikes at lawyers and their occupation. Clarke's "goodness of heart" is such that "even the exercise of his profession had not been able to corrupt [him]" (2). And "Before strangers he never owned himself an attorney without blushing, though he had no reason to blush for his own practice" (2). His uncle contributes by denouncing the lawyer who has enabled his relatives to keep him from his rightful inheritance, and Tom has little to offer in defense of his colleagues.

But the eccentric Crowe's arguments about the inequities of the entail that have robbed him of his rightful inheritance concern themselves with comparatively minor abuses of the law. The real attack comes in the person of the malicious Justice Gobble, who "in the exertion of his authority . . . had committed a thousand acts of cruelty and injustice against the poorer sort of people, who were unable to call him to a proper account" (87). Smollett's descriptions of the prisoners' varying but legitimate grievances against the malefactor catalogue the atrocities committed in the name of the law. Smollett's is a far more poignant prison scene than the one that Goldsmith later presents in *The Vicar of Wakefield,* but Smollett remains characteristically wary of sentiment and balances it with a satirical attack on legal jargon, adding to the ridicule by coupling Gobble's windy language with grammatical deficiencies and malapropisms.

Smollett, moreover, strengthens his satirical technique by balancing the attack on Gobble's malpractices with a later idealized portrait of Justice Elmy, an acquaintance of Tom Clarke. Here Smollett argues that, to right the injustices of the law, it is not necessary to overturn the entire working system of government but only to put it into proper operation. Moreover, he uses the same device to offset the dismal picture of prison conditions by describing an institution properly supervised to provide a "comfortable asylum for the unfortunate" (164).

If Smollett's particular interest in this subject indeed results from his own circumstances at the time, his concern for medical practices was, of course, a continuing topic of attention to the man who had engaged in them prior to entering upon a literary career. Once more it is the material of the picaresque, indicating the continuity between his earliest and later work. Smollett's particular familiarity with quackery stands obvious in his exposure of the characters of Ferret, Kawdle, and the physician in the madhouse. Even as he was composing *Launcelot Greaves,* Smollett, as editor of the *Critical Review,* was pouncing upon the published information regarding absurd remedies and ludicrous nostrums that medical quacks were offering to the public. There is, in fact, despite the mixture of political with medical talk, something of his old enemy the notorious Dr. John Hill, as well as of the infamous Dr. Shebbeare, in his portrait of Ferret; and Hill is a favorite target of Smollett in the pages of the *Critical Review.*

Smollett again balances his satire with some sense of what honesty in the profession calls for, but even here the corruption remains plain. When Crabshaw, at the hands of an ignorant and avaricious apothecary and nurse, suffers from the ills of his treatment, the "honest" physician cures him by ridding him of the presence of the pair and their curatives. Nevertheless, the doctor, "at open war with the whole body of apothecaries," does not by any "means [find it in] his interest to disoblige" them; instead, he seems to resolve his anger in "witty sarcasms" and to find some solace in his mask as "a sort of cynic philosopher tinctured with misanthropy" (135).

While Smollett's attack on the operation of madhouses and the conduct of medical quacks seems clearly written in the spirit of reform, his general treatment of medicine in the novel may at times strike modern readers as no more than a sign of his coarseness. Arguments for Smollett's mellowing in his later novels tend to ignore the persistence of his chamber-pot humor, that insistent attention to physical detail that has come to be known in Swift as the "excremental vision." Yet here, as in Smollett's earlier work, its purpose proves more than sensationalistic excitation. In its most fundamental aim it seeks to give verisimilitude to the fanciful narrative, a fidelity to actuality. Seen against the background of popular medical literature, passages such as "the blood was seemingly viscous, and salt upon the tongue; the urine remarkably acrosaline; and the faeces atrabilious and foetid" (133) prove clearly satirical. They recall those reviews in the *Critical Review* of works in which practitioners meticulously set forth their findings on the number and characteristics of oral evacuations and bowel movements. For Smollett, the real object of satire here, as for Swift, is the kind of science that pays so much attention to details that it loses sight of their meaning.

In his political satire—another of the characteristic picaresque topics—Smollett does not appear much altered from the writer of *Peregrine Pickle* and *Roderick Random.* To be sure, this subject, like the law, takes on further interest because it was of particular interest to him just at this time. The novel was written at a moment when he was engaged in evaluating the merits of English policies at home and abroad in the Seven Years' War. The pages of his *Critical Review* abound in discussions of the virtues and defects of a militia, the obligations and disadvantages of the alliance with Frederick the Great of Prussia, the benefits and burdens of the king's Hanoverian connections. Smollett himself was still, despite his Tory sympathies, enchanted by the job that William Pitt, the Whig minister, had done in uniting the nation for a common purpose,[34] but the novelist was also only a few short months away from engaging in a political paper war in defense of Lord Bute, the minister of George III and the man who was the power behind the removal of the great Whig politician.

Spurred then, by very personal interests, Smollett concentrates his attention on politics at two points in the novel. In the first, he focuses upon Dr. John Shebbeare in the character of Ferret, whom he justly identifies as "a party-writer, not from principle, but employment" (6). Shebbeare was a notorious pamphleteer, whose scurrilous *Letters to the People of England,* attacked by Smollett in the *Critical Review,* inflamed the public passions against the government at a time when England was struggling against France and when Pitt was trying to keep the voices of faction from stirring up a revolution at home.[35] Despite his Toryism, Smollett supported Pitt, who had finally succeeded in bringing unity to the nation. The novelist's Pyrrhonism made him a natural opponent of those whose arguments threatened government stability. He certainly shared the sentiments of Greaves who deplores "the desperate emissaries of a party endeavour to poison the minds of his Majesty's subjects" (15). Even more than his character does, Smollett detested the French enemy.

And yet, oddly enough, some of Ferret's arguments express sentiments that Smollett himself professed. As Knapp has properly indicated,[36] Smollett himself opposed the war in Germany; and he surely did not disapprove of Ferret's criticism of an alliance that imposed the burden of taxation "to support two German electorates [Brunswick and Hanover]" (15). In only a matter of months Smollett not only finds kinder words for Shebbeare in the *Critical Review* but argues in the *Briton* for a cessation of the Continental alliance with Frederick and for a halt to the heavy expenditures of war. What irks him, however, in Shebbeare's work is what he feels to be the man's use of his writing as an "instrument of sedition" (16).

Smollett finds the same characteristics in "party spirit," and it leads him in *Greaves* to a hilarious attack on the absurdities of political parties. In a satirical chapter, brought on by Sir Launcelot's wandering about the countryside, Smollett presents an election contest between the extremist, "high-flying"

Tory party and the stockjobbing, money grabbers of the Duke of Newcastle's Whigs. Unquestionably the episode, while obviously a general satiric attack on politics, has genuine "counterparts in eighteenth-century political history."[37] Smollett's technique of moving from the particularities of reality to a broader satiric comment characterizes his methods throughout his fiction: caricature and the grotesque gain verisimilitude through the recognizability of material drawn from fact. The scene itself is a model of its kind, as Dickens recognized when he followed it some eighty years later in *Pickwick*.[38] Smollett regards his partisan groups as dangerous factions, subversive of the national interest; and he ridicules them with the broadest of his exaggerative powers. Between Sir Valentine Quickset, an empty-headed fox-hunter, speaking the party cant of dissent, excoriating foreigners in his country dialect, expressing the platitudes of the know-nothing country gentlemen, and Mr. Vanderpelft, standing on the corruption of what Smollett believed to be the dishonesty of the Duke of Newcastle, there is little to choose. Smollett permits each to state his case in the windy rhetoric of the politician, and each is received in the expected manner by his supporters without regard for the merits of his speech. In the midst of this meaningless nonsense the voice of the supposedly irrational Greaves offers the only sanity, warning that one man is the "dangerous tool . . . of a desperate faction" whose conduct would lead to anarchy, and that the other is "a sordid knave, without honour or principle," whose legacy to the nation is wholesale corruption (76–77).

Perhaps madness alone accounts for his political speech, reminding his countrymen of their responsibilities and obligations as a free people. Perhaps, indeed, the "real" world must regard such sentiments as at least naive if not altogether insane:

". . . you are this day assembled [he reminds the political gathering] to determine a point of the utmost consequence to yourselves and your posterity; a point that ought to be determined by far other weapons than brutal force and factious clamour. You, the free men of England, are the basis of that excellent constitution which hath long flourished the object of envy and admiration. To you belongs the inestimable privilege of choosing a delegate properly qualified to represent you in the high court of Parliament. This is your birth-right, inherited from your ancestors, obtained by their courage, and sealed with their blood. It is not only your birthright, which you should maintain in defiance of all danger, but also a sacred trust, to be executed with the most scrupulous care and fidelity" (75-76).

Within the context of the particular election, such idealism may indeed be madness; and Greaves receives his reward, of course—a stoning by partisans of both factions.

Concern for Language

Apart from these satiric subjects that traditionally belong to the picaresque, Smollett's satire in *Greaves* includes his familiar attack on abuses of the English language. This attack is another mark of the continuity between Smollett's early and late work; and, if there is any change in his treatment of the subject, it is merely in his heightened awareness of its possibilities for satire and in his more subtle manner, which leads ultimately to his finest achievement with it in *Humphry Clinker*.

Small wonder that the topic should interest Smollett. He had the outsider's sensitivity to that characteristic that perhaps most immediately distinguishes the alien in a society. As a Scot, Smollett was to be exposed in the next year to his old friend John Wilkes's barbs for whatever lapses occurred in his polemical use of the language in their political debate.[39] But he himself had been severe in the last few years with performances that came before him for review in the *Critical Review*—noting grammatical mistakes, scoring errors in diction, and reacting most vehemently to dialect forms whether from Ireland or from North of the Tweed.[40]

Yet personal reasons alone do not account for Smollett's interest. In part, it is a response to the general eighteenth-century concern for the "purity" of the language, one which many—from Swift's time on—felt should be the responsibility of an academy that like those in France and Italy could refine the language. This "prescriptive" attitude had some effect in giving such great authority to Dr. Johnson's *Dictionary* in 1755. It also encouraged the grammarians in activities that finally "codified" the language for the next hundred years or so.

In addition, of course, Smollett's concern for language came naturally to a serious novelist, particularly to a satirist. Bombast, pomp, and pedantry have universally been targets for socially conscious writers. Dialect has always been humorous to the sophisticated urbanite, and malapropisms had been material for comedy before Sheridan, with typical eighteenth-century scorn for class pretentiousness, had given it a name.

With all Smollett's former vigor and more extensive range, he attacks the subject in *Launcelot Greaves*. Some of his satiric intent has been described in relation to political rhetoric and the language of Justice Gobble. More interesting, however, is a comparison between Smollett's treatment of language in the characters of Gobble and young Tom Clarke. Clarke, like all Smollett's lawyers, cannot speak simply.[41] Attempting to recount Launcelot's early adventures, he promises to give the facts plainly; but his very preface betrays him as he asserts, "I shall tell, repeat, and relate a plain story—matters of fact, d'ye see, without rhetoric, oratory, ornament, or embellishment; without repetition, tautology, circumlocution, or going about the bush." The continuation proves even more verbose than the prologue, until Crowe, his uncle, threatens him unless he will take "a direct course, without yawing like a Dutch yanky" (18–19).

Yet the lawyer's sin is venial, a comment on the profession rather than the man; and Smollett bears him no malice. But, in scoring the ignorance of the justice's speech, Smollett indicates the stupidity and arrogance of his conduct for which others are made to suffer. What kind of intelligent performance of the law may be expected from a man who, even if he were well-disposed, much less a scoundrel, regards justice in the mutilated, bombastic language of Gobble?

"The laws of this land has provided—I says, as how provision is made by the laws of this here land, in reverence to delinquems and manefactors, whereby the king's peace is upholden by we magistrates, who represents his majesty's person, better than in e'er a contagious nation under the sun; but howsomever, that there king's peace, and this here magistrate's authority cannot be adequably and identically upheld, if so be as how criminals escapes unpunished. Now, friend, you must be confidentious in your own mind, as you are a notorious criminal, who have trespassed again the laws on divers occasions and importunities . . ." (93).

When coupled with the speech of his wife, Gobble's language devastatingly portrays those who have improperly gained an almost unassailable authority: "'Sirrah! sirrah! (cried she) 'do you dares to insult a worshipful magistrate on the bench?—Can you deny that you are a vagram, and a dilatory sort of person? Han't the man with the satchel made an affidavy of it? —If I was my husband. I'd lay you fast by the heels for your resumption, and ferk you with a primineery into the bargain'" (94).

But Smollett's satire on abuses of language proves not always so biting as in the portraits of Gobble and his wife. To be sure, he ridicules the country bumpkin dialect of Dolly, the innkeeper's daughter. Yet in her "'A-doan't maind what a-says, so a doan't, vor all his goalden jacket'" kind of talk (9), Smollett shows no malice toward the young lady, who later bears the responsibility of uniting Launcelot and his beloved Aurelia. If anything, the denouement, in which Dolly proves to be the knight's kinswoman, suggests that language is less a condition of blood than of circumstances; and, just as Smollett anticipates Shaw's *Pygmalion* in *Peregrine Pickle,* here, too, he notes that the difference between a lady and a servant girl is in the way she is treated.

There is the same good humor in Smollett's use of nautical language for the landlocked Captain Crowe—just as there is in the speech of Commodore Trunnion. In a sense Smollett attempts through the captain's jargon to give some degree of verisimilitude to the bizarre character. However ludicrous it may be to the situation, it always appears natural enough to the person. And, at the same time, it has a lively ring of its own, delightful in itself and capable of pithy expression, as in his rejection of Launcelot's arguments for the chivalric idealization of love and its infallibility: "'And I say unto thee,' (hallooed Crowe) 'if so be as how love pretends to turn his hawse-holes to the wind, he's no seaman, d'ye see, but a snotty-nose lubberly boy, that knows not a cat from a capstan—a don't'" (106).

Relation to Earlier Work

That "snotty-nose lubberly boy" recalls once more Smollett's earthiness, that characteristic that pervades his early novels and that has most frequently been described as his coarseness and vulgarity. He uses it here, as usual, to create realism in his unreal narrative. In fact, for all that has been said about the differences between the late and early Smollett, his manner in *Greaves,* as the picaresque qualities suggest and as the satire indicates, continues to be what it was in his earlier novels. Its liveliest scenes are farcical, frequently slapstick. Its tone is persistently satirical. Chamber pots still provide the material for his comedy. The very violence and tone of this passage in which the temporarily disordered mind of Launcelot's squire causes him to run amok might well have been drawn from Smollett's earlier novels:

The first object that presented itself to his disordered view was the figure of Ferret, who might very well have passed for the finisher of the law; against him, therefore, the first effort of his despair was directed. He started upon the floor, and seizing a certain utensil, that shall be nameless, launched it at the misanthrope with such violence, that had he not cautiously slipped his head aside, it is supposed that actual fire would have been produced from the collision of two such hard and solid substances. (42)

But once again the limited critical interest in the novel has focused its attention on those elements that are supposedly unlike Smollett's earlier novels, particularly on evidence of Gothicism and sentiment. To be sure, Gothic material and characteristics of the novel of sentiment run through *Launcelot Greaves;* but it is important to notice how they are treated by the satirist and how they fit into the overall plan and tone of the novel. Even where the Gothic influence seems strongest, as in the opening paragraphs about a howling wind in a rainstorm, the darkness of the savage night, and the "horror of divers loud screams," it becomes the material for comedy almost immediately in Captain Crowe's cries of "Avast, avast!" The violent knocking at the door, instead of culminating in a sense of terror, uncovers the preposterous figure of Crabshaw; and the whole incident is properly described as "the farce of Hamlet's ghost" (9).

In the two scenes of knightly vigil—Launcelot's described by Clarke, and Crowe's conceived as a trick—humor provides the dominant element. As Clarke tells the company of Greaves's experience, Smollett's stage directions make a mockery of the terror, without demeaning, to be sure, the knight himself. Dolly interrupts, with her comments giving rise to comedy because of her dialect; and Clarke's narrative concludes with a comic description of Greaves giving his squire a resounding thwack. The second vigil—by Crowe—is, of course, humorous from the outset. To see the difference between Smollett the satirist and the genuine Gothic novelists, it is only necessary to compare Crowe's experiences with the same material presented seriously by Clara Reeve in *The Old English Baron,* when Gothicism in the novel had truly come into fashion.

Smollett's apparitions invariably turn out the tools of the humorist; his supernatural, the material to evoke laughter. When Justice Gobble is confronted by the spirit of young Oakley, "pointing to a ghastly wound, which the doctor had painted on his forehead" (101), it is deception intended to ridicule the jurist into repentance for one of the victims of his iniquity. In the same way, not terror, but Gothic jest reigns when Dawdle, Lord Sycamore's squire, is frightened by the ludicrous figure of Crowe, whose bandaged head and battered appearance lend to him the grisly visage "of some murthered man" (150). And, finally, Crabshaw's perturbation at the sight of a ghost emerges from his own simplemindedness, from a night of excessive indulgence in rum punch and from "conversation turning upon hobgoblins, and God's revenge against murder" (177).

If Smollett, even in his satire, contributes something to the development of Gothic taste, it seems most inadvertent. He was too reasonable a man, too much concerned with common sense, to be seriously interested in the novel of supernatural terror. To be sure, as his plays, the war scenes in *Roderick Random,* and Lady Vane's confessions in *Peregrine Pickle* reveal, Smollett was not above seeking popular appreciation on such terms; but, if he intended to gain popularity through the appeal to a public taste already aroused by the "Graveyard Poets," it still had to be on his own satirical terms. In general, that seems, too, to have been his approach to the novel of sentiment.

It is, of course, difficult to be certain of what in *Greaves* is satirical of the sentimental novel. The genre too often is characterized by absurdities intended to be taken seriously. In Henry MacKenzie's *Man of Feeling* the hero who swoons at the sight of his lady and dies as much from an excess of emotion in her presence as from a fever is hardly a credible figure, but the author apparently regards him as such. *Greaves* is amply provided with similar material, but Smollett seems always to be mocking his own use of it.

As with his use of the Gothic, Smollett certainly was capable of capitalizing on the increasing popularity of sentiment in literature, and his inset story about the victims of Gobble's injustices who are driven to madness and near death, clearly anticipates Sterne's tragic sentimental tale of the Mad Maria in *Tristram Shandy.* But it hardly characterizes Smollett's use of sentiment in the novel. Characteristically, he depreciates sentiment by the pejorative connotations of his language or by farcical descriptions of his characters and their conduct. When, for example, Tom Clarke begins his account of Launcelot's early adventures and in his "melting mood" begins "to sob and weep plenteously," he is berated by his uncle, Captain Crowe, who, "not very subject to these tendernesses, damned him for a chicken-hearted lubber." Nor does the eccentric old man stand alone in his expression of annoyance; for Fillet, the surgeon, becomes equally "impatient" with the lawyer and urges him to get on with his story (17).

But not only in descriptions of Tom, "with tears in his eyes" and "bedewed" cheeks (51, 172), does Smollett mock the sentimental romances. His parody extends to most of the conventional devices of the genre and includes the behavior and language of the lovers. "On his knees before the young lady, and, pressing her hand to his lips, [breathing] the softest expressions which the most delicate love could suggest" (34), Greaves, in the circumstances, appears a ludicrous figure. His excessive emotion at their separation has a Byronic madness to it; and, in the language of their reunion, it seems impossible to miss the satire: "He looked and languished, she flushed and faultered. All was doubt and delirium, fondness and flutter" (123). Alliteration makes obvious what otherwise could not have been missed. And finally, at their surprise encounter on opposite sides of the wall in a madhouse, Smollett— playing upon the clichés of sentiment and punctuating a trifle too hysterically—indicates how much his tongue is in his cheek: "It was a strain of vocal music, more plaintive than the widowed turtle's moan, more sweet

and ravishing than Philomel's love warbled song." Then, there is the effect of
the voice on Sir Launcelot:

Through his ear it instantly pierced into his heart; for at once he recognized it to be
the voice of his adored Aurelia. Heavens! what was the agitation of his soul, when he
made this discovery! how did every nerve quiver! how did his heart throb with the
most violent emotion! He ran round the room in distraction, foaming like a lion in
the toil—then he placed his ear close to the partition, and listened as if his whole soul
was exerted in his sense of hearing. When the sound ceased to vibrate on his ear, he
threw himself on the bed; he groaned with anguish; he exclaimed in broken accents;
and in all probability his heart would have burst had not the violence of his sorrow
found vent in a flood of tears (191).

To recount in detail the various ways in which Smollett satirizes the form
of the sentimental romance seems scarcely necessary. A brief listing and a few
examples sufficiently demonstrate his technique. Beginning with Aurelia's
wicked uncle, who, to thwart her marriage to Launcelot, by forgery convinces
the lovers that each has been rejected by the other, Smollett develops the elements of the genre. Unable to get Aurelia to forget Greaves, the uncle tries to
arrange a match with Lord Sycamore, tricks her into the hands of a former
mistress of a bawdy house, and finally has her committed to an asylum. Near
meetings with Launcelot during her journey play directly upon the novels of
sentiment. Her final rescue and revelations of various sorts, including that of
Dolly's superior family connections, culminate in a grand recognition scene,
that stock ending for the genre. Added to these objects of literary satire—
some close to Fielding's technique in *Joseph Andrews*—there is Smollett's
play on the theme of the good-natured man, whose indiscriminate benevolence is a weakness disguised as a virtue.

But these are also the straight materials of romance. What makes it a parody is Smollett's treatment. It should be considered, for example, that little
more than halfway through the book, Smollett reveals the mysterious traveling lady as Aurelia Darnel. In the flatness of his language at the revelation,
his tone becomes apparent. Instead of continuing the elaborate contrivance of
suspense so common to the genre, he merely asserts, "We shall therefore,
without circumlocution, premise, that miss Meadows was no other than that
paragon of beauty and goodness, the all-accomplished Miss Aurelia Darnel."
Nor does he let the laudatory terms stand, for in the next statement he describes her weakness in submitting to her "uncle's tyranny" as having been the
result of a "meekness of resignation peculiar to herself" (114).

In the same way, when the lovers do meet after their long separation and before they settle down to their languishing and fluttering, they sit down to await the arrival of Greaves's portmanteau, so that he can demonstrate her uncle's forgery. Surely it is a comment on their romantic love that it takes documentary evidence to convince her of his affection and fidelity. Moreover, Smollett, at the height of this anticipation, resorts to a Popean anticlimax by announcing, "In the mean time tea was called" (123). Even before the subsequent description of their ardor, it has been exposed as a kind of mock-heroic.

What Smollett has done with the sentimental material in his novel compares somewhat to Goldsmith's technique in *The Vicar of Wakefield*. He both appeases the appetite for it and uses it as a target for satire. To perceive this use is to effect a change in attitude toward what are generally regarded as the weaknesses of the novel. Just as a better understanding of the picaresque technique and of Smollett's particular use of the Quixote theme accounts for much of the "looseness" in the plot construction, his satire on the romances explains his heavy use of foreshadowing, the artificiality of disguises, the mechanical features of his heroine's character and speech, and the often ludicrous use of coincidence. Upon closer examination, the novel's unity emerges from that same rhythmical use of its central character and its pervasive satirical viewpoint that serve in his earlier work. Smollett—with *The History and Adventures of an Atom*, the *Travels*, and *Humphry Clinker* still ahead of him—clearly has not slipped into mellowness in *Greaves*.

To forget that Smollett remains at all times a satirist is as destructive to an analysis of his techniques in this novel as it would be to ignore the effectiveness of "some [of the] fine sketches of humorous characters and some remarkable genre pieces" or the development of his prose style.[42] Praise has been accorded to his descriptions of inns and prisons, to his individual scenes of highway adventures and of an election, and particularly to the marvelous opening with its adroit maneuvering in medias res.[43] Some closer attention to the variety of its satiric purposes, some reduced emphasis on its Gothic and sentimental characteristics, as evidence of his yielding his satiric impulse, would place *Greaves* above its present low estate, not only in Smollett's canon, but in the ranks of eighteenth-century novels.

Chapter Six

Humphry Clinker:
The Picaresque Ménage

Generally well received at the time of its publication in 1771, Smollett's last novel, *The Expedition of Humphry Clinker*, has continued to grow in critical esteem until it is now ordinarily regarded as his masterpiece.[1] Its first edition of two thousand copies was followed by two more printings, with new typesettings, in the same year, and by a third in 1772. Contemporary criticism was generally favorable, with the only strong dissenting opinion coming from Smollett's adversaries on the *Monthly Review*.[2] If *Roderick Random* remained more popular until the early nineteenth century, *Humphry Clinker*, by the time of Hannay's biography in 1887, was being described "as not only, by general consent, the best of Smollett's works, but [as having] a manifold superiority to anything else he did in the course of his literary life."[3]

Recent critical opinions have carried Hannay's judgment even farther. Not merely is Smollett's final novel deemed better than his earlier writing; it is altogether different from it. Smollett's journalistic labors and increased interest in topical and historical subjects radically altered his fiction.[4] The differences are said to appear in structure and prose style; the distinctions, in values and point of view. This later Smollett—hints of whose changes come in the Gothic scenes of *Fathom* and in the sociological portions of *Launcelot Greaves*—supposedly eschewed the picaresque tradition followed in his three earliest novels. His prose technique became more simple and direct, his style more succinct and precise.[5] In his increasing mellowness—*The History of an Atom* and the *Travels* evidently prove no deterrent to such judgment— Smollett ostensibly yielded to the public taste for novels of sensibility. Tired and weary, broken in spirit—the *Ode to Independence* is ignored in such arguments—he capitulated to the demands created by the popularity of Jean-Jacques Rousseau's *La Nouvelle Héloise* and of Sterne's *Tristram Shandy* and A *Sentimental Journey*.[6] Even a critic arguing the general cohesiveness of Smollett's works emanating from the pervasiveness of his "conservative imagination" finds his final novel yielding "the rage and abrasiveness of the earlier novels."[7]

Without, for the moment, considering the question of the relative merits of Smollett's first and last novels, it would seem best to consider the differences of the two Smolletts and to examine in greater detail his technique in *Humphry Clinker*. To begin with the question of his use of the traditions of the picaresque seems most natural. How much, indeed, has he turned his back on the genre? Has he renounced it as his main device for satire? To be sure, as Byron Gassman has pointed out,[8] the particular achievement of *Humphry Clinker* is in its economical amalgamation of a variety of interests—its travel information, its interaction of characters, and its criticism of the milieu of the 1760s. But what permits Smollett to bring together these various interests is his adaptation of the picaresque to accommodate a new kind of quest in Matthew Bramble's journey in search of physical, moral, and spiritual health.

The Plot

The plot of Smollett's final novel indeed shows a remarkably strong resemblance to that of *Roderick Random,* and it suggests that Smollett was extending the possibilities of the picaresque rather than discarding it. Extending the possibilities of the genre, of course, involves transforming it, and that is precisely the process that he follows in his development from one novel to another.[9]

Humphry Clinker repeats from the earlier novel the elements of "the missing-father-found, estranged-lovers-united, paternal-estate-reclaimed, reward-for-everybody-ending."[10] But, what is even more important, the narrative holds together through the characteristic picaresque device of a journey motif used as a vehicle for social satire. No tight structural mold demands that the novel continue for its full length; no logical necessity requires the particular detailed order of travel; and few of its individual incidents prove so essential to the development of character, the movement of plot, or the elucidation of theme that in themselves they could not be jettisoned.

The plan, to be sure, seems simple enough and cast in a picaresque mold. It requires no detailed plot summary to follow the important lines of its action. What Smollett does is to take his small Welsh entourage of old, hypochondriacal Matthew Bramble and his family—his crotchety, husband-hungry sister Tabitha; his romantic-heroine niece Lydia; his stylishly cynical nephew Jery; and their maid Win Jenkins, an addict of malapropisms—and send them on a tour that includes London; Bath and other popular spas of England; and Scotland.

For each character there is a subplot. Matthew, in search of health, discov-

ers that Humphry Clinker, who joins the company along the way as a footman, is his son born of a youthful adventure and, therefore, a reminder of his
lusty younger days. Around the frantic efforts of Tabitha to secure a husband
revolve incidents of disappointment with the fortune-seeking Sir Ulic and
eventual satisfaction with the bizarre ex-soldier Obadiah Lismahago. Lydia,
meanwhile, experiences the conventional trials of the young heroine as she
meets a strolling player who eventually reveals himself as a young man of
good family and financial security. In still another variety of comic romance
Winifred Jenkins is provided for through the amorous interests of Humphry
and the competition he meets from a French valet. If there appears, at first,
no subplot for Jery, he shares in his role of spectator and commentator the
characteristics of the picaro who learns about the ways of life from others,
particularly in service to a master, who in Jery's case is his Uncle Matt.

Rhythm in Characterization

The insistence that *Humphry Clinker* employs a technique remote from the
picaresque emanates from a belief that the genre is incapable of subtle development. Once more uncritical assumptions focus upon the picaresque as a series of apparently unrelated incidents, loosely linked through interlocking
characters and some vaguely satirical aims. Those rhythmic devices through
which such things as character traits are both repeated and expanded upon
are ignored, and a charge of static structure is supported by a priori conclusions about the literary type itself. A masterpiece like *Don Quixote,* even
when it is most characteristically picaresque, ceases to be discussed in terms of
the genre when accounts are being made of its effectiveness, so that the manner in which Quixote himself retains his basic naïveté while growing in stature is attributed to something other than the possibilities of the picaresque
type. Lesser works within the genre, despite evidence of some dynamic process of growth, are either condemned for their picaresque limitations or treated
as belonging to another form. So it is with *Humphry Clinker,* which has variously been described as a "comic romance" (a nonexistent genre) and as an example of formal Roman satire.[11]

But to attempt to deny the essentially picaresque characteristics of
Smollett's last novel is to be misled by its overt epistolary form and to ignore
the manner in which its episodic narrative holds together. Its narrative outline
and its epistolary form may not indicate more inspiration than those of the
fashionable circulating-library novels of the eighteenth century, but they
allow Smollett to present yet another variation on the traditional
picaresque—one in which a group of picaros replaces the individual rogue-

hero. Through careful rhythmic development of his assemblage of unusually analytical picaros—particularly Jery and Matt—Smollett offers a deeper vision of society than he had ever before managed.

The best way to examine that rhythm in *Humphry Clinker* is through its characterization, which reveals the connection between Smollett's thematic concerns and the novel's basically picaresque structure. Primary consideration must be given to Matt Bramble, a picaro in the sense that Smollett uses him as an observer of society and that his observations are carried on as a result of the typical picaresque journey device. As with all picaros, Matt's characterization, if it is to emerge beyond static sterility, requires Smollett's adept use of rhythm, aided by the epistolary device. Because the theme of *Humphry Clinker* develops out of Matt's own growth—or at least the reader's understanding of the fullness and dimensions of the character—Smollett's technique has particular importance.

What Smollett reveals about Matthew Bramble in his very first letter encompasses, in actuality, everything that the reader will learn about him in the entire novel. However, the reader has at first no way to evaluate the justice of such a conclusion; nor can he assess the proportions of those revealed traits. Consequently, the initial attitude toward Matt remains unsettled and the significance of the elements in his character obscure. What Smollett intends the reader to feel about his protagonist and his role in the narrative and theme emerges only from the repetition and the modifications of individual points of characterization seen in a variety of contexts and in Matt's multiple relationships to other characters.

Illness, real or imagined, introduces Bramble's first letter to Dr. Lewis. Its connection with hypochondria is only suggested by his references to difficulties within his adopted family, and in his irascible tone and in his accusation that the physician knows less about the ailments than the patient does, Matt appears to be an unreasonable, selfish man. This impression seems confirmed in his next comment about having to assume responsibility for a sister's children: "As if I had not plagues enough of my own, those children of my sister are left me for a perpetual source of vexation—what business have people to get children to plague their neighbours?" (5) The evidence mounts as Bramble laments the fact that he will probably have to spend more time at Hot Well than he desires, a lament made even before he has set out for the place. Brusquely, he gives orders to his servants, but even here he begins to undercut the harsh image as he shows his concern for the poor. His desire to take vengeance on his purse-proud neighbor concludes with an injunction that he will dismiss action if the latter contributes instead to parish charity, and then Matt slips into an act of generosity to a needy widow, only to warn that he wants no one to know of it. Afraid, perhaps, of unveiling a sentimental soul, he ends with a request that suggests a distrust of others, except for the doctor whom he asks to lock his drawers and to put his papers in custody.

Development of the Picaresque

Intimations of Smollett's theme of a balance between benevolence and self-interest emerge in this first character portrayal, but throughout the novel application of rhythmic techniques to a picaresque structure develops both theme and characters. Through the journey motif and Jery's study of his uncle's ways, the suggested traits take full shape. To be sure, the epistolary device, with its variety of points of view, also contributes to Smollett's purpose. If Jery's servant relationship to Matt is of greater importance, it is nevertheless essential to note that such things as Tabitha's immediately subsequent letter, complete in its selfishness and irascibility, are used as a contrast to give perspective to Matt's character.

Yet the picaresque form dominates. Jery studies and analyzes his uncle, perhaps not with the picaro's concern for survival, but clearly with an effect on his own development. Despite his disclaimer that he suffers abuse to inherit Matt's estate, Jery's presence in the entourage hardly has another explanation. He calls attention to his uncle's unpleasantness, and, seemingly, for the sake of his own conscience, he attributes it to the old man's ailments. Remarking on the fact that Matt's "servants and neighbours . . . are fond of him, even to a degree of enthusiasm" (9), Jery admits that he cannot comprehend the reason for it; and that information—while increasing the reader's understanding of Matt—serves only to show Jery's rationalizing his toleration of his uncle's unpleasantness for the sake of some later gain. Development of Jery's character must take that self-interest as his starting point.

Again through a fine combination of the epistolary device and a kind of picaresque observation, Lydia, within the first series of letters, also invests the reader with knowledge about the duality in her uncle's character. Referring to the family's response to her aborted romance, she contrasts the conduct of Matt and Tabby. Matt, she says, began like her aunt to upbraid her for her conduct; but, whereas Tabby "continues to chide me severely when we are by ourselves," her uncle, "who was so dreadfully passionate in the beginning, has been moved by my tears and distress; and is now all tenderness and compassion" (9–10). Her judgment is immediately verified in Matt's next letter to Lewis, in which he describes Lydia as a "poor good-natured simpleton, as soft as butter." It is not, however, that she is a fool, but that she gives way to her emotions. For Matt there can be no more damning comment than to say that she "reads romances," and yet his own tenderness and his own emotions express themselves in the same letter as he admits: "You cannot imagine what I have suffered, partly from the indiscretion of this poor child, but much more from the fear of losing her entirely" (12, 14).

In his further instructions to Lewis, Matt goes on to reveal the full pattern of his character. His harsh exterior causes some of his inferiors—like Barns, who believes him capable of turning out penurious peasants—to mistake his intentions; and yet Matt makes quite apparent how mistaken such views are, as he writes, "I will not begin at this time of day to distress my tenants, because they are unfortunate and cannot make regular payments." He wants to be considered strong and tough-minded, for he would not be taken advantage of. Yet he detests tyranny and is easily moved to pity and benevolence. In many ways he resembles Goldsmith's Sir William in *The Vicar of Wakefield,* the good-hearted man who has found that the world abuses a charitable nature. Where Sir William hides behind an assumed name and a double role, Matt simply disguises his own character.

Once beyond the initial letters, the picaresque, using rhythmical repetition and progression, plays a major role in developing the facts of Matt's character and the principal theme of the novel. By the rapid series of adventures, the experiences provided by the journey, and Matt's reactions to them, the extent to which he is truly benevolent becomes clear; and the reasons for his disguise are apparent. At the same time, the narrative structure does not itself remain static; for, through the very devices used to explore character, a gradual development takes place, leading to a climax. It seems hardly necessary, however, to itemize the variety of incidents, told mainly by Jery, or their analysis, provided chiefly by Matt. A random sampling reveals how accruing evidence leads to a culminating impression that attests to the genuine benevolence of Smollett's hero and to his need to mask his generous nature.

Once Jery has witnessed Matt at work, he perceives easily the true nature of his uncle. "I think," Jery writes, "his peevishness arises partly from bodily pain, and partly from an excess of mental sensibility" (17). Having observed Matt's beneficence to a poor widow and his tender and delicate manner, his nephew, affected to the point of tears, can judge that the old man "affects misanthropy, in order to conceal the sensibility of a heart, which is tender, even to a degree of weakness" (28). Moreover, Matt's own cognizance of the dangers in such weakness is revealed by Jery's report on his uncle's comment about the unfortunate Mr. Serle, whose "fortune, which was originally small, has been greatly hurt by a romantic spirit of generosity, which he has often displayed, even at the expence of his discretion, in favour of worthless individuals" (69).

Bramble's charitable though gruffly disguised treatment of Clinker, his concern for the highwayman Edward Martin—whose letter to him remarks on his "heart warmed with beneficence and compassion" (160)—his satisfaction on finding humane prison conditions at York, his general patience with the vexatious Lismahago because of that soldier's misfortunes in an unfair military system—all demonstrate the balance between the natural goodness and the necessary prudence in Matt's character. The variety of incidents and settings provided by the picaresque makes such development of character and theme seem plausible, and the following conclusion unforced. In the contrasting situations of Baynard, whose unchecked benevolence in his treatment of his wife has led to ruin, and that of Dennison, whose properly balanced sentiment and wisdom have brought stability, Smollett brings to a climax the discussion of the relationship between reason or good sense and feeling or affections that has been the subject of his novel.

Without going into great detail it is possible to show how the picaresque displays the development of Jery's character. From the young man who, at the outset, obviously has his eye on his uncle's estate, he becomes at the end of the novel unselfish enough to react to the discovery of Humphry's true identity by shaking his "new-found cousin heartily by the hand" (318), although the revelation will likely deprive Jery of an inheritance. Allowing the heart its proper course with Humphry, Jery recognizes, in the Wilson-Dennison affair, the appropriate time to use his head. He who in passion had challenged Wilson, the strolling player, to a duel to protect his sister's honor matures through his experiences and accepts the discovery of Wilson's genuine character as George Dennison by fashioning a moral judgment upon himself: "I am . . . mortified to reflect what flagrant injustice we every day commit, and what absurd judgment we form, in viewing objects through the falsifying medium of prejudice and passion" (332). This problem has been Matt's: a balance between head and heart. While it is unusual for a picaro to learn from another's experience or to change fundamentally, in Smollett's combination of the epistolary and picaresque, Jery, as picaresque observer, has learned to strike a balance. Ultimately, it is not so different from Roderick's and Perry's learning how to live in the world.

To be sure, Smollett's use of the picaresque in *Humphry Clinker* does not follow along the close lines of the traditional genre, but then what eighteenth-century novel does? Smollett comes closest to it in *Roderick Random;* but, after that first venture, he plays upon the genre in various ways: the turn from first person and the removal to high life in *Peregrine Pickle;* the union with moral allegory in *Ferdinand Count Fathom;* the parodic affinities of *Launcelot Greaves*. Here, in his last novel, he extends the possibilities of the picaresque through his use of the epistolary technique and his company of picaros.

Aside from its importance to character, plot, and theme, the picaresque contributes in multiple ways to the novel. Even Frank W. Chandler, while insisting on its weakened presence in the work, indicates the variety of picaresque material left:

> If Miss Tabitha Bramble and her gaunt Lieutenant Lismahago are portraits in the burlesque style of Quevedo, and if the jests upon the latter and Mr. Justice Frogmore, or the confusion caused by fire at an inn, are souvenirs of Scarron, roguery has sunk to low ebb. Humphry possesses the varied talents of a picaro, makes as many blunders as the German jesters and moralizes like the Spanish Alonso; but when jailed on suspicion of a road-knight he simply exhorts his fellows to repentance. The highwayman who desires to reform is only the inverted ghost of a picaro; and Lismahago's early adventures in America as captive to the Indians, and finally as sachem of the Badger Tribe, but faintly revive those of Le Sage's Chevalier de Beauchêne.[12]

Chandler's arguments, noting as well the continuation of the "peripatetic notion" in the novel, are merely more evidence of the importance of the picaresque in *Humphry Clinker*. And, when Chandler concludes that "Smollett had outgrown the picaresque form, although he could not forget picaresque episodes," he gives less credit to Smollett's craftsmanship than it deserves. Not weakness, but Smollett's use of the traditional form for new purposes explains the presence of the many picaresque elements in the novel.

The Continued Satiric View

Implicit in Chandler's comments is that second suggested point of difference between the early and late Smollett: the mellowing of the satiric temper and the humanizing of the treatment of incidents. To be sure, scholars and critics have not altogether eradicated that ferocious satirist of the early novels, or ignored the persistence of his scatological satire;[13] but their insistence on the more sentimental characteristics gives an impression of kindness and gentility alien to Smollett's natural talents and hardly justified by the novel itself.

In his very opening sentence Smollett provides evidence that his vigorous style has lost none of its original humor, none of its delight in the hard realities of life. "The pills," Matt writes to Dr. Lewis, "are good for nothing—I might as well swallow snowballs to cool my reins—I have told you over and over how hard I am to move" (5). Following immediately upon this letter, the

puns wrought through Tabby's and Win Jenkins's spelling and malapropisms assure us that we are in the old Smollettian world. "Don't forget," Tabby
writes to her housekeeper, "to have the gate shit every evening before dark."
As for the maid, Mary Jones, Tabby assures her correspondent, "I know that
hussy . . . loves to be rumping with the men" (6). Then the artless,
simpleminded Winifred, describing the doctor's treatment of Chowder,
Tabby's dog, remarks, "he subscribed a repository, which did him great service" (7). Here is Smollett in the old vein.

Matt's letters carry the bulk of this chamber-pot humor. His comments on
the waters at Hot Well recall Laurence Sterne's description of Smollett as
"Smelfungus." Matt's olfactory sense responds particularly to the odors of
Bath; and, in an entire letter devoted to the subject, Matt denounces the place
with true Smollettian force. He vigorously deplores the "*compound of villainous smells,*" those "most violent stinks . . . mingled odours, arising from pu-
trid gums, imposthumated lungs, sour flatulencies, rank arm-pits, sweating
feet, running sores and issues, plasters, ointments, and embrocations" (66).

For those with a weak stomach Matt's remarks on London prove equally
strong. Whether he is describing the drinking water—"impregnated with all
the filth of London and Westminster—Human excrement [being] the least
offensive part"; or the bread, "a deleterious paste, mixed up with chalk,
alum, and bone-ashes"; or the food, cleaned "by a dirty barrow-bunter . . .
with her own spittle" (120, 122)—the result inevitably revolts in its details.
And, even as the company moves north towards Scotland, Matt continues his
abuse of the wells and spas that mark the halting places along the way.

But Smollett, by no means, limits this humor to Matt's comments. As
Win and Tabby continue in their malapropian way, the smell of the chamber
pot, the sexual innuendos, and the scatological suggestiveness that ground
Smollett's fiction in reality proceed apace. Writing "paleass" for "palace"
(108), describing the family as being in a "constipation" (155); dismissing
her unfaithful French lover as not worth a "farting" (220); and making a
"turd" of "third" and "ass of editida" of "asafetida" (338), Win does indeed
allow "her innocent pen [to] pursue its anal fixation."[14] In the same way,
Tabby refers constantly to the hired hands as "hinds," declares that she will
ignore Dr. Lewis's attempts to conciliate her "though he beshits me on his
bended knees" (156), and gets a great deal of unintended sexual meaning
into her description of Humphry: "our new footman, a pious young man,
who has laboured exceedingly, that [Win Jenkins] may bring forth fruits of
repentance. I make no doubt but he will take the same pains with that pert
hussy Mary Jones, and all of you; and that he may have power given to pene-

trate and instill his goodness, even into your most inward parts, is [my] fervent prayer" (274–75).

More of Smollett's characteristic humor comes through the comments of Jery in the details of a scene describing incidents of brutal behavior, scenes for which contemporaries and Victorians particularly rebuked Smollett.[15] Whether Jery is relating Matt's violent treatment of Negro servants, or a friend having drowned a dog out of malice, or the various embarrassments of Lismahago and Micklewhimmen—exposing bare posteriors for the attention of a company of scoffing onlookers or suffering the disastrous effects, in public view, of real or imagined cathartics—it is all humor that borders on the tasteless, a spirited coarseness and vulgarity, necessary to Smollett's purpose, but of a kind with that in the early novels. What could more suggest Smollett's characteristic style than Jery's description of their carriage accident outside Marlborough Downs? For Jery, looking into the coach, the first sight is of Jenkins's "nether end," and, when Matt appears, his means for making his ascent have been "poor Win's posteriors" (79). And, even as the novel begins with scatological comment, it continues almost to the very end with a practical joke that has its victim "enthroned on an easing-chair, under the pressure of a double evacuation" (303).

Some diminution of this Smollettian humor in the Scottish sections has been argued for by Louis Martz, who attributes it to the novelist's use of sources and to his desire to celebrate his birthplace in his valedictory novel.[16] Smollett, supposedly seeking to placate his irate countrymen, selects the more favorable material from his own account in the *Present State of All Nations,* in which the less personal approach creates a milder tone. Even so far as this appraisal is accurate, it serves only to argue for a continuance of the early Smollettian spirit in at least the English portions of the novel.

Yet this English-Scottish antithesis does not altogether hold up under examination.[17] To be sure, Matt's improved health, keeping him away from the spas and resorts that provided his primary targets earlier, affords fewer opportunities for that kind of satire; but he compensates for the loss with his severe criticism of Scottish inns and innkeepers. When, as in Edinburgh, the situations correspond to those in England, he proves no more gentle in his treatment; for he assails filth and pollution, adulterated food, and unsanitary disposal of waste that "offend[s] the eyes, as well as other organs of those whom use has not hardened against all delicacy of sensation" (218). Moreover, Smollett's desire to please his countrymen does not affect such satiric episodes as those concerning Lismahago and the Scottish advocate Micklewhimmen, scenes in which the full power of the creator of *Roderick Random* and *Peregrine Pickle* stands evident.

Smollett's satire, strongly scatological, was his trademark as a novelist; and he did not forsake it in his final work. *Humphry Clinker,* no less than his earlier novels, uses this harsh vision of life and society to shock the reader into a response. In Matt Bramble's hypochondriacal concern for purgatives, Humphry's exposed posterior, and Win Jenkins's playful malapropisms on suppositories Smollett employs vigorous obscenity to create his realism and to remove all of man's pretentiousness. "Smollett," as Sheridan Baker observes, "fixes upon the alimentary canal, revealing man's false front by his backside."[18]

But Smollett's satire is broader than any of his attacks on particular targets, and his technique is not limited to the scatological. As R. D. S. Jack summarizes the topic, "There is no doubt that Smollett intended to satirize eighteenth-century Britain, and in particular eighteenth-century England, as a land dominated at every level by false or superficial values."[19] That is the object of his persistent detailing of the discrepancies between appearance and reality throughout the novel. That is the point of his unveiling hypocrisy at every level of society. In its overall purpose, as John Sekora has demonstrated, *Humphry Clinker* is the culmination of Smollett's extensive assault on luxury, the eradication of which he regarded as essential to the maintenance of civilization.[20] Thus the evidence of Smollett's pervasive satire in his final novel is overwhelming, which makes inexplicable George Rousseau's comment that it is "an epistolary narrative with less satire in it than almost any other ingredient."[21]

Achievement in *Humphry Clinker*

Once these relationships between *Humphry Clinker* and Smollett's early novels have been made clear, the question of the relative merits of his final work becomes imperative. That his contemporaries should have found the novel attractive is not surprising. Much in its form had contemporary appeal, particularly the travel letters that Smollett had found success with in his *Travels through France and Italy.* Not only did travel books enjoy enormous vogue, but the epistolary novel itself had reached a height of popularity unequaled until late in the century.[22] A commercial writer, aware of what his age demanded, Smollett constantly makes use of the fashionable—but for his own purpose.

Not unnaturally, then, he employs sentiment in his last novel as in *Fathom* and *Greaves,* appealing to his audience's taste at the same time that he holds it up to ridicule. Among a variety of parodies in *Clinker,*[23] Smollett offers a play upon the sentimental novel. Lydia, for example, parodies such romantic heroines as Richardson's Pamela and Clarissa. Like those women, Lydia is prone to faint at the slightest provocation. Her letters gush with the tenderest emotions; and, when she grieves because of the frustrations of her romance, Matt fears she may fade away and die. Yet she *is* a warm and sympathetic figure; she is properly grateful for Matt's concern and perceptive enough to distinguish between his external gruffness and his natural compassion. Despite the satirical portrait, she emerges as the most attractive of Smollett's heroines, one likely to please Smollett's most romantic readers.

Parody and gratification of public taste run through the other characters in the novel. No champion of the "noble savage," Smollett, in Humphry and Lismahago, offers readers an opportunity to indulge their taste for Jean-Jacques Rousseau's natural man. Whatever Humphry's absurdities, he possesses the attractive qualities of loyalty, honesty, and sincerity; and in the melodramatic plot that Smollett uses to parody contemporary romances and sentimental drama Humphry finds his virtues properly rewarded. Smollett plays the same game with Lismahago. If he is a comic figure, if his experiences with the American Indians satirize the vogue for that "noble savage," Lismahago, nevertheless, like Don Quixote, engages the reader's sympathies through his stubborn resistance against social conventions. While Smollett's technique typically undercuts "the mood [of sentiment] by the introduction of a ludicrous detail,"[24] the novelist presents sufficient sentiment to meet a public demand for the material made popular by Richardson and Sterne.

Beyond making these appeals to his contemporaries, Smollett displays a craftsmanship in his epistolary style that greatly accounts for his novel's continuing popularity. Much has been made of his using a "diversity in reactions of a group of travellers"—a device probably derived from Christopher Anstey's *New Bath Guide* (1776), letters written in rhyme by a family staying at Bath.[25] Although to some degree the importance of this particular technique has been overemphasized,[26] where Smollett uses the contrasting views, he does it to excellent effect, uniting the varied views of his individual letter writers with stylistic distinctions appropriate to their characters.[27]

Bath provides the best example. For Matt, Bath is a disappointment and an irritant to his "crusty humours." Its "avenues . . . are mean, dirty, dangerous"; the open chairs used for transportation are "boxes of wet leather," producing "infinite mischief to the delicate and infirm." Even its architecture is monstrous, the construction of "some Gothic devil." Crowds jostle and push impudently on their way—"a mass of ignorance, presumption, malice, and brutality" (33ff). Old and irritable, Matt finds no charm or excitement, only "scrophulous ulcers," "sweat and dirt," "rotten bones and carcasses" (45–46).

But to romantic young Lydia, Bath appears "a new world." Here "all is gayety, good-humour, and diversion." She sees the best fashions, hears the pleasantest sounds. Manners are appealing, and what Matt describes as rudeness becomes a symbol of democratic living, where "the highest quality, and the lowest trades folk, jostling each other, without ceremony, [are examples of] hail-fellow well-met." To be sure, she requires some adjustment to its excitement, and she never accepts the Bath waters or is able to hide her embarrassment at the bathers; yet, all in all, she can say of Bath that it "is an earthly paradise" (38ff).

If not quite an "earthly paradise" for Jery, Bath seems at least "a place so crowded with entertainment and variety" that London does not exceed it. Its very chaos appears "a source of infinite amusement," for he can observe a variety of characters. He reports most of the same conduct and scenes as had aroused Matt's ire; but, as he puts it, "Those follies, that move my uncle's spleen, excite my laughter" (49). The difference between them is not so much one of temperament as of years; for, as Matt says, "The longer I live, I find the folly and the fraud of mankind grow more and more intolerable." Having seen it all, he can only wish that he had not left his home at Brambleton-hall (47). But Jery, who luxuriates in that first real excitement of youth, can taste all experience with relish.

In a lesser key, Win Jenkins offers her opinions of Bath, according to her own interests and desires. Writing to Mary Jones, who knows nothing of the great world, Win passes on information as from on high. "O Molly!" she writes, "you that live in the country have no deception of our doings at Bath." Amid the family gossip, she boasts of "all the fine shews" she has seen (42), the fashions she has observed, and the flirtations she has experienced. Properly shocked by the morals she reports on, she suggests her delight in the very moralizing with which she bids it adieu: "O Molly! the sarvants at Bath are devils in garnet—They lite the candle at both ends—Here's nothing but ginketting, and wasting, and thieving and tricking, and trigging; and then they are never content" (70). Poor Molly—to have missed it.

Only Tabby does not indicate her views. Partly, she is restricted from doing so because her correspondence concerns business affairs; partly, her reticence results from her natural reluctance to deal with the particular events. Whether writing to Mrs. Gwyllim, her housekeeper, or Dr. Lewis, Matt's friend, she can hardly be expected to describe her husband-chasing activities, which the other letters recount.

Smollett's exceptional skill with the epistolary technique, however, extends well beyond this mere novelty of the contrasting views of his travelers. In his characters' awareness of their relationships to their correspondents Smollett provides the necessary picaresque comment on society and its val-

ues. Not only does Tabby remain silent about her activities because she is neither willing to admit them to herself nor perhaps even to recognize them for
what they are; she simply cannot tell these things to Mrs. Gwyllim, her
housekeeper and social inferior. Tabby's tone, gruff and dictatorial, echoes
her natural character and social consciousness. Win, on the other hand, writing to Mary Jones, addresses her social equal. Whatever the sense of superiority derived from her travels, she generally speaks plainly to one who shares her
interests and who can be relied on to view things from a common vantage
point.

If the effect of the differences between Win and Tabby is to assure a variety
in the events covered by their letters, Lydia's correspondence, offering still another social point of view, promises to add another dimension. In Miss Willis,
a romantic young lady, Lydia has a naturally sympathetic audience for the
outpourings of the love-smitten heroine. Once more, however, Smollett
demonstrates, in characteristic picaresque observation, how society's values
govern the individual. To balance Lydia's letter from Clifton to Miss Willis
about her aborted romance with "Wilson," Smollett offers another directed
to her governess, Mrs. Jermyn. Although the letters cover the same subject,
that to Mrs. Jermyn concerns itself with matters of honor, innocence, and
prudence; but the one to her friend discloses the pains of a broken heart.

Even the style is affected by the nature of the recipients. With Mrs.
Jermyn, Lydia—although remaining naturally warm—affects a more formal manner; careful of sentence structure and diction, she omits even the hint
of an exclamation point. Her tone is the decorous, studied diction of a school-
girl addressing her teacher. But when writing to "O, my dear Letty!" (10–
11), Lydia explodes in passion. Exclamation points, dashes for indecision or
despair, and conjunctions as sentence openers mark the signs of friendship,
peer to peer.

While the letters of Matt and Jery display the same sense of awareness of
their correspondents and of social values as do the others, Smollett uses them
for other purposes as well. These are his picaresque observers; and, while his
epistolary technique has its difficulties, it also allows him to use Matt and Jery
in their roles to give greater breadth to the genre. At first glance Smollett's
problem would seem insoluble: how to have two commentators cover essentially the same ground without repeating the same information and without re-
sorting to artificial, unbelievable explanations. Smollett, in fact, does not
always achieve his purpose. When Jery summarizes, in two or three sentences,
Tabitha's altercation with Lady Grisken because of Tabby's farcical belief that
she herself is the object of Lydia's suitor, Smollett employs his method to escape
repetition of Matt's preceding letter to Dr. Lewis. Yet Jery, with his narrative

rather than analytical interests, would hardly keep such a delightful tale from his curious correspondent. In the same way, Matt writes to Dr. Lewis: "I have been engaged in a ridiculous adventure, which I shall recount at meeting" (285). The lame excuse for the delay enables Smollett to omit material contained in Jery's previous letter to his friend Phillips.

Yet such instances are relatively few, and Smollett's achievement in *Humphry Clinker* comes in the way in which he has combined his epistolary and picaresque forms, allowing the narrative to arise naturally out of his two major characters and their relationship to their correspondents. To be sure, as with Tabby, Matt and Jery occasionally omit material out of modesty or self-interest; but generally they cover those things that interest them and their correspondents. Writing to Dr. Lewis, Matt has a reader receptive to information about ailments, health resorts, and manners and customs. Advanced in years, they settle into the contemplative survey of scenes and manners as well as of assessments of the general characteristics of man. Jery, on the other hand, addresses himself to Sir Watkin Phillips, of Jesus College, Oxford, a person likely to be interested in the escapades described in Jery's narrative technique. For Jery and Phillips, young and active, experience means adventures—the way and how rather than the why of things. How appropriate it is, then, for the bulk of Matt's correspondence, especially in Scotland, to be expository rather than narrative,[28] while Jery's contributes—consistently with his predominantly picaresque function—most to the story line.

While Smollett's skillful manipulation of his picaresque tale in an epistolary framework allows him to give greater depth to characterization and greater perceptiveness to his theme than he manages in *Roderick Random,* something else helps to account for the superiority of *Humphry Clinker.* Smollett, in his last novel, reflects the wise experience gained from a lifetime of activity and observation. His spirit remains the same as in youth, but his understanding and his perceptiveness are marked by his maturity and wisdom.[29]

Unlike the characters in his earliest novel, those in *Humphry Clinker* have warmth as well as bite.[30] Matt Bramble at his worst never irritates the reader as Roderick does in his treatment of Strap or Peregrine in his cavalier use of others. Even Jery, whose age corresponds to that of Smollett's earlier heroes, never shows himself to be as mean-spirited as they. Smollett's dual protagonists of his final novel exhibit together a generosity and a warmth that do not lessen their picaresque quality, but in some ways these make them as attractive as the traditional rogues of earlier literature.

Smollett also achieves better balance with Lydia. And in this respect, the epistolary method, even more obviously than with his two protagonists, contributes to his effect. Despite the burlesque of Richardson's Pamela and Clarissa, Lydia has a life and richness that make her more than the conventional romantic heroine. Although Smollett's heroines, generally, have a functional purpose beyond what critics have been willing to accord them, their human characteristics, with the exception of Emilia's in *Peregrine,* seem lacking. Lydia, as a result of the epistolary technique which forces the revelations of a character's mind, has a fullness and depth that yield a higher degree of verisimilitude than can be claimed for Narcissa, Aurelia, or even Emilia. Lydia—crying her hurt out to Letty, posing bravely to Mrs. Jermyn, scheming after "Wilson," and evaluating the characters of her aunt and uncle—does not want for realism.

Even the comic character of Lismahago demonstrates the increased understanding of Smollett the man and writer. If he, as Kahrl has argued, emphasizes the eccentric features of the real-life Robert Stobo, from whom his humorous ex-lieutenant is supposedly drawn,[31] he nevertheless creates a sympathy for his character that is not often evoked in his earlier humor. In Lismahago there is a Don Quixote attractiveness so that, despite the Scot's wrongheaded, vain, and ridiculous behavior, Matt and the reader respond kindly to him. Moreover, while Smollett uses his character to achieve his customary farcical comedy, he also employs him to initiate much of the debate about the question of Scottish or English superiority.

The extent to which Smollett's development as a writer and his lifetime of experience enabled him to surpass his earliest achievements in the novel is nowhere more evident than in this comic treatment. *Humphry Clinker* belongs to the tradition of the picaresque, a tradition that Smollett explores and develops in different ways in each of his novels. The picaresque objects of satire in *Roderick Random* Smollett pursues with continued fervor to the end; the difference is in the technique and experience that he brings to the task.

That interest, for example, in language, apparent in each of his works, develops to a high point in *Humphry Clinker.* The complexity of the pun on Humphry's surname itself suggests how much Smollett is an eighteenth-century anticipation of James Joyce. To begin with, "clinker" signified a "blacksmith," so that Humphry's name derived naturally from the profession of his foster father. Recently it has been suggested that at the time "clinker" signified "he who or that which clinches," which would define the character's role in unifying the group of travelers.[32] However, the word was also scatological slang and appropriate to Smollett's general satire in the novel. In its further reference to "the fetters of prison," the name suggests Humphry's poverty—a point strengthened, in turn, by the slang significance of "Duke Humphrey" as a commonplace for "impoverished nobility." More-

over, the sense of "clinker" as a "crafty fellow," a play upon Humphry's character through inversion, gives some sense of Smollett's linguistic ingenuity
that must impress the most skeptical.[33]

But who can be skeptical after reading the letters of Tabby and Win? The
richness of their play on words, already described in some detail, has been related by Giorgio Melchiori to what is now known as Joycean love of language. Melchiori has noted how the process begins in simple and obvious
malapropisms and becomes more and more complex until the "new compos-
ite words with a higher concentration of meaning . . . tell a story on different
levels, implying in it two separate trains of thought.[34] Smollett's linguistic ingenuity, particularly in Win's letters, provides one of the novel's major pleas-
ures as well as achievements.[35]

For the old familiar targets of the picaresque—medical, literary, and political abuses—Smollett in his final novel has not only the same vigorous attacks
but an added sense of considerable experience and familiarity with his subjects.
Whereas *Roderick* represents the picaro freshly exposed to the hypocrisies and
deceits of society, *Humphry* offers the picaro grown wise through experience.
Behind the criticism of Bath and the other spas lies Smollett's *Essay on the External Use of Water.* In the discussion of politics Smollett draws upon lessons
learned during his editing of the *Briton* and *Critical Review,* experiences already expressed in the general revulsion of the *Atom.*[36] When he writes of the
practices of adulterating food, he recalls passages in the *Critical,* and the descriptions of Grub Street life clearly reflect his own involvement in literary circles. All these are also subjects in his earlier novels, but now Smollett brings to
them the authenticity of a lifetime's experiences.

It is difficult, therefore, to read *Humphry Clinker* and not to think of
Smollett the man. To be sure, the novel is no more autobiographical than
Roderick Random; but neither is it less so. McKillop is right to warn that
Smollett draws upon books as well as life for his characters,[37] and the many
models Smollett uses, himself included, are, after all, transformed by art.[38]
Appraising the points of identity between Matt and Smollett, however,
Knapp concludes that in general terms old Bramble is a picture of the novelist in his final years.[39] At least he is as much a self-portrait of the aging
Smollett as Roderick is of the young man setting out for London in search of
adventure. It seems fitting that it should be so—that the last novel, like the
first, should fictitiously somewhat represent autobiography and bring the literary life, like the physical one, to its close. To have rounded it out so would
have been achievement enough, but to have done it so well is the ultimate
satisfaction.

Afterword

Smollett's importance as a mid-eighteenth-century novelist stands secure. As a young man he had to challenge the established reputations of Richardson and Fielding, which he successfully did by grasping a large portion of the public interest with *Roderick Random*. At the end of his career Smollett had to confront the popularity of Sterne, whose appeal to readers suggested a turn in literary taste, a demand to feed an appetite for sentiment that would balance the customary harsh diet of satire. Smollett responded with *Humphry Clinker*, a novel that could not detract from Sterne's substantial hold upon the public's enthusiasm; but, nevertheless, it managed to make a highly respectable place for itself within the new climate of opinion.[1] To discuss the eighteenth-century novel without considering Smollett's contribution to the genre would, therefore, be as impossible as discussing the poetry of the age without giving full attention to the work of Pope.

But what *was* Smollett's contribution to the novel of his own time? To be sure, his methods of characterization offered none of the fine psychological probing of Richardson's, and his plots had none of the dramatic sense that Fielding brought from his plays to the novel. Smollett lacked the wild imaginativeness of Sterne that even two hundred years later makes *Tristram Shandy* still seem a daring fictional experiment. And yet Smollett gave much to the new genre, helped to shape it for his own period, and directed it in ways that continue to have significance today.

For his own time Smollett, together with Fielding, demonstrated that the novel was an appropriate means for carrying on the Augustan tradition of satire. Pope had made poetry an effective instrument for satirizing society; Swift had accomplished the same purpose with a variety of prose parodies. By introducing the Continental picaresque form into the eighteenth-century English novel, Smollett provided another method for attacking the social vices and abuses that had aroused the wrath of his Augustan predecessors. Like Pope and Swift, he turned to a traditional genre instead of initiating a new one; but, also like them, he adapted and altered what he took so that it became something quite different from what it originally had been.

Smollett's technique of adapting the picaresque to new purposes has been the source of major twentieth-century scholarly controversy. George Rousseau and Paul-Gabriel Boucé, in particular, have savagely attacked the idea that Smollett was a picaresque writer,[2] but in the process have ignored the manner of generic change. As Rosalie L. Colie has demonstrated in her study of genre theory in the Renaissance,[3] it is erroneous to conceive of genre as a static rather than a process form of literature. She has described in detail the progress of genre resulting from cultural change, the effects of mixing genres, the grafting of one genre, or subgenre, on another. She has emphasized, as her title indicates, *The Resources of Kind*. Writing at a time when the novel as a form had barely taken shape, Smollett, in his use of the picaresque, offers a paradigm of the development of a genre.

Various genres of fiction (embryonic to the later novel) existed in the early eighteenth century as forms of subcultural or popular literature, and a novelist like Smollett, eager to achieve popularity, was likely to exploit them in his writing. His use of the picaresque, combined with varieties of rogue literature, criminal biographies and the like; his employment of the romances as well as anti-romances; his adaptation, as Paulson suggests, of formal verse satire;[4] his reliance on travel literature and family pilgrimages—all these represent his dependence on the authority of the appeal of various genres familiar to his public, and his changes reflect his own talent and genius, his own desire to create literary forms that are particularly his own. In consequence, one finds in his novels a reflection of genre theory—a dependence on what has already emerged formally—and an example of how genre itself develops and adapts according to cultural, national, and chronological conditions. For the eighteenth-century novel, a new form that had neither established an aesthetic rigidity nor even developed a critical terminology, the example is particularly meaningful.

Roderick Random comes closest to the traditional Continental picaresque, but its preface suggests Smollett's dissatisfaction with *Gil Blas* as an adequate work both for Smollett's British audience and for a vehicle to express his own vision of society. The long romantic coda, so often criticized, reflects his need to satisfy the didactic demands of his own conscience and his audience's taste. The changes from the picaresque in *Peregrine Pickle* indicate his unwillingness to repeat what he had done in his first novel. He chooses the third person in order to broaden his point of view; he includes the *Memoirs of a Lady of Quality* to take advantage of the public desire for scandalous literature (exemplified in the genre at least as early as *The New Atalantis*); he uses formal verse satire because that is consistent with his own artistic purposes; and he employs the Grand Tour material to appeal to popular interest in the subject. In *Ferdinand Count Fathom* he is aware of the general taste for criminal biography (*pace* Fielding's *Jonathan Wild*); he extends the possibilities of the picaresque by including dramatic material and the didactic fable; and he recognizes, in the use of Gothic machinery and the long second-half romance, the developing taste for sentiment among his readers. With *Sir Launcelot Greaves* Smollett attempts to capitalize on the interest in *Don Quixote,* an interest propelled in part by his own translation of Cervantes' work, and he carries on both his own and his public's concern for social, political, and religious comment, depending for part of his appeal on Hogarth's popular prints, particularly the series on *Hudibras.* At the same time, his methods sustain his continuing regard for the possibilities of the picaresque genre and its elements as reflected in *Don Quixote.* The *Atom* uses the popular device of the experiences of a peripatetic animal or an inanimate object as hero, a literary form consistent with that of the picaresque (and exploited successfully in Charles Johnstone's *Chrysal; or the Adventures of a Guinea* and Coventry's *Adventures of Pompey the Little*), but he also relies on the topical interest of politics and chinoiserie to capture the attention of his audience. *Humphry Clinker,* while using the devices of the picaresque, expands the form to gain attention through its variety of relationships with the established appeal of sentiment, the continuing regard for travel literature, the traditional vehicle of the family pilgrimage, and a host of topical concerns in religion and politics.[5] A fine example in the novel of Smollett's reliance on and modification of traditional genres is reflected in his treatment and development of the character of Matt Bramble, which depends upon but extends the characteristics of the figure of the benevolent misanthrope.[6]

Throughout his work Smollett remains essentially a picaresque novelist, but one whose own literary interests and desire for fame lead him to develop the genre in a remarkable number of ways. In "Smollett and the Old Conventions" Michael Rosenblum argues that Smollett's novels are "reworkings" of the romance conventions to "construct a satiric fiction [which] suggests that like any other serious writer Smollett had to find a way to use and go beyond the language of the fiction that he inherited."[7] While Rosenblum, like Rousseau and Boucé, specifically denies that Smollett is a picaresque novelist, he ignores the fact that the picaresque is simply a form of romance, and it is that form that Smollett transforms from novel to novel.

In a variety of other ways Smollett gave added breadth to the eighteenth-century novel. His nautical characters in *Roderick Random* and *Peregrine Pickle* introduced a new type into English fiction. In his Gothic scenes in *Ferdinand Count Fathom* Smollett first brought the materials of romantic Jacobean and Elizabethan drama into the novel; and he did so a dozen years before the publication of Horace Walpole's *Castle of Otranto.* Although not the first example of novel serialization, *Launcelot Greaves* was indeed the first by a major novelist. Finally, with *Humphry Clinker* Smollett demonstrated how the epistolary form could gain effectiveness from presenting the same materials from multiple points of view.

Smollett's importance as a novelist, however, is not limited to the role he played in the eighteenth century. His work has had an enduring interest and significance, not only for the realistic portrait that it gives of so much of his own society, but also for the effect that it has had on the tradition of the novel. In the early years of the nineteenth century, before Victorian prudery rebuked Smollett for what had come to be regarded as his unsavory coarseness, his novels enjoyed their greatest reputation and influenced both major and minor writers. For Walter Scott and Charles Dickens, as well as Bulwer-Lytton, Frederick Marryat, and Charles Lever, Smollett was in the front rank of novelists, on a par with Henry Fielding, and usable in varied ways. Dickens specifically acknowledged his indebtedness to Smollett; and *The Pickwick Papers,* as Dickens's contemporaries recognized, bore Smollett's stamp and depended on the older novelist's technique of picaresque realism.[8] Just as Dickens learned style and comic characterization from Smollett,[9] other nineteenth-century novelists used Smollett's sea material as a study for their art.[10]

While the indebtedness of twentieth-century writers to Smollett cannot be traced so directly as his influence on the nineteenth-century novel, it exists in no uncertain terms. Perhaps James Joyce's play upon language owes no more to Smollett's *Humphry Clinker* than Shaw's *Pygmalion* does to Smollett's "nymph of the road" episode in *Peregrine Pickle.*[11] Although these are perhaps merely examples of literary parallelism, the resurgence of the picaresque form in the modern novel could not have taken place had Smollett not transferred the Continental rogue adventures to English soil and had he not demonstrated the adaptability of the picaresque narrative to more modern social satire. Smollett was heir to a tradition; and, by reshaping, reforming, and refurbishing what he had borrowed, he became ancestor to a new tradition that includes such writers as Saul Bellow, John Barth, and Joyce Cary.[12]

In the long run, however, a writer's greatness depends less on his influence—even when that influence, like Smollett's, is international[13]—than upon his own fictional accomplishments. Smollett bears up well in this respect. Along with his creation of a gallery of comic characters rivaled only by those of Dickens, Smollett has left two novels—*Roderick Random* and *Humphry Clinker*—that have an enduring worth of their own. Readable and significant in their own time, they remain among the finest novels written in English. Not many novelists have equaled that achievement.

Notes and References

ABBREVIATIONS USED IN THE NOTES

BNYPL	*Bulletin of the New York Public Library*
CE	*College English*
ECS	*Eighteenth-Century Studies*
ELH	*English Literary History*
ELN	*English Language Notes*
JEGP	*Journal of English and Germanic Philology*
MLN	*Modern Language Notes*
MP	*Modern Philology*
N&Q	*Notes and Queries*
PBSA	*Papers of the Bibliographical Society of America*
PLL	*Papers on Language and Literature*
PMLA	*Publications of the Modern Language Association*
PQ	*Philological Quarterly*
RES	*Review of English Studies*
SECC	*Studies in Eighteenth-Century Culture*
SEL	*Studies in English Literature*
SP	*Studies in Philology*

Preface

    1. George S. Rousseau, *Tobias Smollett. Essays of Two Decades* (Edinburgh: T. and T. Clark; New York: Seabury, 1982), 89.

Chapter One

    1. George M. Kahrl, *Tobias Smollett, Traveler-Novelist* (Chicago: University of Chicago Press, 1945), 78.

    2. *Letters of Tobias George Smollett: A Supplement to the Noyes Collection,* ed. Francesco Cordasco (Madrid, Avelino Ortega, Cuesta de Sancti Spiritusy, 1950), 22. This collection contains forged letters, but no textual references in this study concern any of these. See, also, *The Letters of Tobias Smollett,* ed. Lewis M. Knapp (Oxford: Clarendon Press, 1970), 33; hereafter cited as Knapp, *Letters.*

    3. Kahrl, *Tobias Smollett,* 76.

4. Lewis M. Knapp, *Tobias Smollett, Doctor of Men and Manners* (Princeton: Princeton University Press, 1949), 84.

5. For the relationship between Smollett's conservative nature and his satiric writing, see Michael Rosenblum, "Smollett as Conservative Satirist," *ELH* 42 (Winter 1975):556–79.

6. Kahrl, *Tobias Smollett*, 184ff. Despite his position as outsider, Smollett never advocates the radicalism described in Donald Bruce's account (*Radical Dr. Smollett* [Boston: Houghton Mifflin, 1965]). Like Pope and Swift, whose eighteenth-century "optimism" Bruce fails to understand, Smollett feared the anarchistic nature of man and believed that for all their corruptness, the institutions of society are necessary to regulate man's conduct. Comparing Smollett and Swift in their view that "the wickedness of the world" is "axiomatic," Bruce (195ff.) does not recognize the conservative basis of their attitudes.

7. Fred W. Boege, *Smollett's Reputation as a Novelist* (Princeton: Princeton University Press, 1947), 14, n.1.

8. References to the text of Smollett's poems and plays in this chapter, unless otherwise noted, are to volume 6 of the twelve-volume edition of Smollett's *Works* (London: Otridge & Rackham, 1824). Line references, where required, appear at appropriate points in the text. For comments on style, see Howard S. Buck, *Smollett as Poet* (New Haven: Yale University Press; London: Oxford University Press, 1927), 10.

9. Knapp, *Tobias Smollett*, 108.

10. David Hannay, *Life of Tobias George Smollett* (London: Walter Scott, 1887), 23.

11. Knapp, *Tobias Smollett*, 107.

12. Arnold Whitridge, *Tobias Smollett, a Study of His Miscellaneous Works* (New York: n.p., 1925), 4.

13. Howard S. Buck, *A Study in Smollett, Chiefly "Peregrine Pickle"* (New Haven: Yale University Press, 1925), 54.

14. Whitridge, *Tobias Smollett*, 20.

15. Buck, *Smollett as Poet*, 49. Resemblances between the sea lieutenant and Lieutenant Bowling are noted by C. E. Jones, *Smollett Studies* (Berkeley and Los Angeles: University of California Press, 1942), 64.

16. Harold F. Watson, *The Sailor in English Fiction and Drama* (New York: Columbia University Press, 1931), 156.

17. Knapp, *Tobias Smollett*, 196.

18. Ibid., 309.

19. Buck, *Smollett as Poet*, 84.

20. Ibid., 30. For a recent discussion of the relationship of Smollett's poetry to his novels, see Frederick M. Keener, "Transitions in *Humphry Clinker*," *SECC* 16 (1986):149–63.

21. Buck, *Smollett as Poet*, 23.

22. Hannay, *Life of Smollett*, 50.

23. Cf. Ronald Paulson, "Satire in the Early Novels of Smollett," *JEGP* 59 (July 1960):390.

24. For a discussion, see Buck, *Smollett as Poet,* 39–40, and Knapp, *Tobias Smollett,* 66. For discussion of Smollett's attitudes on homosexuality, see Robert Adams Day, "Sex, Scatology, Smollett," *Sexuality in Eighteenth-Century Britain,* ed. Paul-Gabriel Boucé (Totowa, N.J.: Barnes & Noble, 1982), 225–43.

25. Buck, *Smollett as Poet,* 37.

26. Knapp, *Tobias Smollett,* 63.

27. Buck, *Smollett as Poet,* 75.

28. Ibid., 78.

29. Boege, *Smollett's Reputation,* 55.

30. Paulson, "Smollett's Early Satire": 390–91; Buck, *Smollett as Poet,* 46ff. and passim.

31. Kahrl, *Tobias Smollett,* and Louis L. Martz, *The Later Career of Tobias Smollett* (New Haven: Yale University Press, 1942).

32. Martz, *Later Career,* 34ff. The quotations are from 34, 36, 38, 42.

33. Ibid., 23–24, 26.

34. See Martz, *Later Career,* and his "Tobias Smollett and the *Universal History,*" *MLN* 56 (January 1941):1–14.

35. Knapp, *Letters,* 65. For the following quotation, see Hannay, *Life of Smollett,* 137.

36. Hannay, *Life of Smollett,* 82–83. Earlier, however, Hannay (45–46) attributes Smollett's Toryism to his work on the history.

37. Donald Greene, "Smollett the Historian: A Reappraisal," *Tobias Smollett: Bicentennial Essays Presented to Lewis M. Knapp,* ed. G.S. Rousseau with P.G. Boucé (New York: Oxford University Press, 1971), 30. Hereafter cited as *Bicentennial Essays.*

38. Ibid., 34.

39. Knapp, *Letters,* 65.

40. *Letters of Tobias Smollett,* ed. Edward S. Noyes (Cambridge, Mass.: Harvard University Press, 1926), 166.

41. Robin Fabel, "The Patriotic Briton: Tobias Smollett and English Politics, 1756–1771," *ECS* 8 (Fall 1974):100–14.

42. John Sekora, *Luxury: The Concept in Western Thought, Eden to Smollett* (Baltimore and London: Johns Hopkins University Press, 1977), 140.

43. R.D. Spector, "Smollett and Admiral Byng," *N&Q* 200 (February 1955): 66–67. Buck, *Study in Smollett,* 75.

44. Knapp, *Letters,* 73; Noyes, *Letters,* 173, n.5.

45. Hannay, *Life of Smollett,* 137.

46. Cordasco, *Supplement to Letters,* 17.

47. Carmine Rocco Linsalata, *Smollett's Hoax: Don Quixote in English* (Stanford: Stanford University Press, 1956), 13.

48. Jones, *Smollett Studies,* 82.

49. Ibid., 107ff. and R. D. Spector, "Attacks on the *Critical Review*," *Periodical Post Boy* (June 1955):7–8; "Further Attacks on the *Critical Review*," *N&Q* 200 (December 1955):535; "Additional Attacks on the *Critical Review*," *N&Q* 201 (October 1956):425; "Attacks on the *Critical Review* in the *Court Magazine*," *N&Q* 203 (July 1958):308; "Attacks on the *Critical Review* in the *Literary Magazine*," *N&Q* 205 (August 1960):300–301.

50. R. D. Spector, "The *Monthly* and Its Rival," *BNYPL* 64 (March 1960):159–61.

51. Derek Roper, "Smollett's 'Four Gentlemen': The First Contributors to the *Critical Review*," *RES* n.s. 10 (February 1959):38–44. Knapp, *Tobias Smollett*, 177.

52. Alice Parker, "Tobias Smollett and the Law," *SP* 39 (July 1942):545–58; Lewis Knapp, "Rex *versus* Smollett: More Data on the Smollett-Knowles Libel Case," *MP* 41 (May 1944):221–27.

53. For background see George Nobbe, *The North Briton: A Study in Political Propaganda* (New York: Columbia University Press, 1939); R. D. Spector, "Eighteenth-Century Political Controversy and Linguistics," *N&Q* 200 (September 1955):387–89; Eugène Joliat, *Smollett et la France* (Paris. Librairie Ancienne Honoré Champion, 1935). For the most complete account of Smollett and the *Critical Review*, see Robert D. Spector, *English Literary Periodicals and the Climate of Opinion during the Seven Years' War* (The Hague: Mouton, 1966).

54. Byron Gassman, "The *Briton* and *Humphry Clinker*," *SEL* 3 (Summer 1963):398. For a contrary view, see Fabel, "The Patriotic Briton." Fabel examines Smollett's views throughout his career, but focuses on the later years. For this period he concludes—I believe erroneously—that Smollett was essentially nonpolitical, inconsistent in his support of political groups or individual politicians, and strongly opposed to political parties.

55. Gassman, "The *Briton* and *Humphry Clinker*," 397.

56. Hannay, *Life of Smollett*, 149; Whitridge, *Tobias Smollett*, 80; E. A. Baker, *The History of the English Novel* (London: Witherby, 1930), 4: 226; Martz, *Later Career*, 68, 88.

57. Knapp, *Letters*, 117–18, 125–26.

58. Ibid., 117–18.

59. See Baker, *History of the Novel*, 4: 226, and Hannay, *Life of Smollett*, 149, for the Sterne view.

60. Robert D. Spector, "Smollett's Traveler," *Bicentennial Essays*, 233.

61. John F. Sena, "Smollett's *Persona* and the Melancholic Traveler," *ECS* 1 (Summer 1968):353–69.

62. Scott Rice, "Smollett's Seventh Travel Letter and the Design of Formal Verse Satire," *SEL* 16 (Summer 1976):503.

63. Scott Rice, "The Satiric *Persona* of Smollett's Travels," *Studies in Scottish Literature* 10 (July 1972):40.

64. *Travels through France and Italy*, ed. Frank Felsenstein (London: Oxford

University Press, 1979), 245; hereafter page references cited in the text are to this edition.

65. See, particularly, Kahrl, *Tobias Smollett,* 104ff., and Martz, *Later Career,* 68ff.

66. See Kahrl, *Tobias Smollett,* 117–18, and Martz, *Later Career,* 67–68.

67. Kahrl, *Tobias Smollett,* 96, n.2.

68. Ibid., 96, n.1.

69. Robert E. Moore, *Hogarth's Literary Relationships* (Minneapolis: University of Minnesota Press; London: Oxford University Press, 1948), 174, describes Smollett's judgments on art as "absurd pronouncements."

70. Kahrl, *Tobias Smollett,* 110.

71. Ibid., 113.

72. Boege, *Smollett's Reputation,* 143.

73. V. S. Pritchett, *The Living Novel* (New York: Chatto and Windus, 1947), 35.

74. Boege, *Smollett's Reputation,* 28.

75. Knapp, *Tobias Smollett,* 280.

76. Alan D. McKillop, *The Early Masters of English Fiction* (Lawrence, Kansas: University of Kansas Press, 1956), 170.

77. Whitridge, *Tobias Smollett,* 118.

78. Ibid.

79. Robert Adams Day, "The Authorship of the *Atom,*" *PQ* 59 (Spring 1980):187.

80. Wayne J. Douglass, "Done after the Dutch Taste: Political Prints and Smollett's *Atom,*" *Essays in Literature* 9 (Fall 1982):175, 178.

81. Damian Grant, *Tobias Smollett. A Study in Style* (Manchester, England: Manchester University Press; Totowa, N.J.: Roman & Littlefield, 1977), 145.

82. Ibid., 58, 83.

83. James R. Foster, "Smollett and the *Atom,*" *PMLA* 68 (December 1963):1032-46.

84. See Wayne J. Douglass, "Smollett's Authorship of the *Atom,*" *ELN* 17 (March 1980):183–84, and notes 79 and 81 above.

Chapter Two

1. Boege, *Smollett's Reputation,* 2.

2. Knapp, *Tobias Smollett,* 94, 102.

3. Knapp, *Tobias Smollett,* 96; Moore, *Hogarth's Literary Relationships,* 164.

4. Boege, *Smollett's Reputation,* 12.

5. McKillop, *Early Masters,* 147–48; Knapp, *Letters,* 7–9.

6. Boege, *Smollett's Reputation,* 44.

7. Knapp, *Letters,* 56, and *Tobias Smollett,* 102.

8. Moore, *Hogarth's Literary Relationships,* 176ff.; Knapp, *Tobias Smollett,* 101–2.

9. Buck, *Smollett as Poet*, 13–14; Knapp, *Tobias Smollett*, 4.

10. Knapp, *Tobias Smollett*, 49, 53; Buck, *Study in Smollett*, chap. 3.

11. Knapp, *Tobias Smollett*, 155. See, also, 12.

12. Ibid., 15.

13. Kahrl, *Tobias Smollett*, 114 and 22.

14. Damian Grant, "*Roderick Random*: Language as Projectile," in *Smollett: Author of the First Distinction*, ed. Alan Bold (London: Vision Press; Totowa, N.J.: Barnes & Noble, 1982), 129.

15. See, for example, Baker, *History of the Novel*, 4: 207, and Hannay, *Life of Smollett*, 75–76.

16. Quoted in Knapp, *Tobias Smollett*, 10.

17. Noyes, *Letters*, xv.

18. *The Adventures of Roderick Random*, ed. Paul-Gabriel Boucé (London: Oxford University Press, 1979), 149; hereafter page references cited in parentheses in the text.

19. Jones, *Smollett Studies*, 40.

20. Ibid., 73.

21. McKillop, *Early Masters*, 149; Watson, *Sailor in Fiction*, 166.

22. Kahrl, *Tobias Smollett*, 21.

23. Knapp, *Tobias Smollett*, 34–35.

24. Louis Martz, "Smollett and the Expedition to Carthagena," *PMLA* 56 (June 1941):428–46. The quotations are from Martz, *Later Career*, 13, and the article, 437, 442.

25. Martz, "Smollett and the Expedition to Carthagena," 441.

26. Robert Alter, *Rogue's Progress* (Cambridge, Mass.: Harvard University Press, 1963), ix, 57, 59. Quotations are from viii, 3.

27. Ibid., 72, 74.

28. Paul-Gabriel Boucé, "'Snakes in Ireland': The 'Picaresque' in Smollett's *Roderick Random* (1748)," *Caliban* 22 (1983):34ff.

29. Alice Green Fredman, "The Picaresque in Decline: Smollett's First Novel," *English Writers of the Eighteenth Century*, ed. John H. Middendorf (New York and London: Columbia University Press, 1971), 181–207.

30. Robert Giddings, *The Tradition of Smollett* (London: Methuen, 1967), 97.

31. Philip Stevick, "Smollett's Picaresque Games," *Bicentennial Essays, 112.*

32. Jones, *Smollett Studies*, 68; F. W. Chandler, *The Literature of Roguery* (Boston and New York: Houghton Mifflin, 1907), 2:311.

33. Kahrl, *Tobias Smollett*, 25-26; Paulson, "Smollett's Early Satire," 387; M. A. Goldberg, *Smollett and the Scottish School* (Albuquerque: University of New Mexico Press, 1959), 30.

34. Goldberg, *Smollett and the Scottish School*, 30; Paulson, "Smollett's Early Satire," 387.

35. Paulson, "Smollett's Early Satire," 386.

36. Watson, *Sailor in Fiction*, 168.

37. Alter, *Rogue's Progress*, 75–76. Alter points out weaknesses in Smollett's treatment.

38. Goldberg, *Smollett and the Scottish School*, 36ff.

39. Dorothy Van Ghent, *The English Novel: Form and Function* (New York: Rinehart, 1953), 6–7.

40. Chandler, *Literature of Roguery*, 2:310, makes this point.

41. Paul-Gabriel Boucé, *The Novels of Tobias Smollett*, trans. P. G. Boucé and Antonia White (London and New York: Longman, 1976), 111, 122–23.

42. E. K. Brown, *Rhythm in the Novel* (Toronto: University of Toronto, 1950); E. M. Forster, *Aspects of the Novel* (New York, 1927).

43. Kahrl, *Tobias Smollett*, 23.

44. Moore, *Hogarth's Literary Relationships*, 183.

45. Hannay, *Life of Smollett*, 102.

46. W. B. Piper, "The Large Diffused Picture of Life in Smollett's Early Novels," *SP* 60 (January 1963):45–56.

47. See McKillop, *Early Masters*, 160, and Baker, *History of the Novel*, 4:213.

48. Edward C. Mack, "Pamela's Stepdaughters: The Heroines of Smollett and Fielding," *CE* 8 (March 1947):295.

49. Alter, *Rogue's Progress*, 84.

50. Ibid., 69, 30.

51. Ibid., 28–29.

52. Goldberg, *Smollett and the Scottish School*, 12–13.

53. Ibid., 22.

54. Ibid., 36ff.

55. Alter, *Rogue's Progress*, 68.

56. Piper, "Smollett's Early Novels":50–51.

57. Ibid., 52.

58. Alter, *Rogue's Progress*, 65–66, 69.

59. Ibid., 78.

60. Boucé, *The Novels of Tobias Smollett*, 124.

61. Alter, *Rogue's Progress*, 5.

62. Paulson, "Smollett's Early Satire," passim, argues that Smollett's satire follows Roman rather than picaresque models.

63. Alter, *Rogue's Progress*, 64, refutes Paulson's arguments regarding the Roman originals of Smollett's satire.

64. Paulson, "Smollett's Early Satire," 383–84.

65. Ibid., 384.

66. Knapp, *Tobias Smollett*, 93. Smollett's comment was made after the novel was complete, but before publication.

67. Paulson, "Smollett's Early Satire," 382–83.

68. Grant, "*Roderick Random*: Language as Projectile," 131.

69. Alter, *Rogue's Progress*, 64. See, too, McKillop, *Early Masters*, 155.

70. Cited by Boege, *Smollett's Reputation*, 3.

71. Alter, *Rogue's Progress*, 59ff.

72. Jones, *Smollett Studies*, 54–55, 58–59.

73. Albrecht B. Strauss, "On Smollett's Language: A Paragraph in *Ferdinand Count Fathom*," in *Style in Prose Fiction: English Institute Essays, 1958* (New York: Columbia University, 1959), 49–50.

Chapter Three

1. For reception, see Buck, *Study in Smollett*, 2, 8; Boege, *Smollett's Reputation*, 6ff.; Knapp, *Tobias Smollett*, 119–21; Moore, *Hogarth's Literary Relationships*, 177. Knapp and Moore attribute its success mainly to nonliterary considerations.

2. Buck, *Study in Smollett*, 2–3.

3. Knapp, *Tobias Smollett*, 118–19.

4. Rousseau, *Essays of Two Decades*, 5–6, 105.

5. Buck, *Study in Smollett*, 8; Boege, *Smollett's Reputation*, 6–8.

6. Baker, *History of the Novel*, 4:209.

7. McKillop, *Early Masters*, 159.

8. Goldberg, *Smollett and the Scottish School*, 62.

9. McKillop, *Early Masters*, 157.

10. Knapp, *Tobias Smollett*, 318.

11. Kahrl, *Tobias Smollett*, 41.

12. Ronald Paulson, "The Pilgrimage and the Family: Structures in the Novels of Fielding and Smollett," *Bicentennial Essays*, 58.

13. J. L. Clifford, "Introduction" to *The Adventures of Peregrine Pickle*, ed. J. L. Clifford, (London: Oxford University Press, 1964), xxvii; subsequent quotations from this novel are from this edition and are cited parenthetically in the text.

14. Hannay, *Life of Smollett*, 108.

15. See Clifford, "Introduction," xxvii–xxviii.

16. For the suggestion that Perry's mother's behavior is a result of his illegitimate birth, see R. G. Collins, "The Hidden Bastard: A Question of Illegitimacy in Smollett's *Peregrine Pickle*," *PMLA* 94 (January 1979):91–105.

17. See Ronald Paulson, "Smollett and Hogarth: The Identity of Pallet," *SEL* 4 (Summer 1964):351–59; H. S. Buck, "Smollett and Akenside," *JEGP* 31 (January 1932):10–26, and Buck, *Study in Smollett*, 104.

18. Clifford, "Introduction," xxvii.

19. Ibid., xxiv–xxv.

20. Boucé, *The Novels of Tobias Smollett*, 127.

21. See *Monthly Review* 4 (March 1751):355–64; Knapp, *Tobias Smollett*, 120.

22. Alter, *Rogue's Progress*, 58–59.

23. Chandler, *Literature of Roguery*, 2:312; Buck, *Study in Smollett*, 19.

24. McKillop, *Early Masters*, 160.

25. Goldberg, *Smollett and the Scottish School,* 67ff.; Rufus Putney, "The Plan of *Peregrine Pickle,*" *PMLA* 60 (December 1945):1051–65.

26. Boucé, *The Novels of Tobias Smollett,* 122–24.

27. Putney, "The Plan of *Peregrine Pickle*": 1058.

28. For a helpful commentary on some of the picaresque characteristics of both *Roderick Random* and *Peregrine Pickle,* see Stevick, "Smollett's Picaresque Games," 111–30.

29. Ian Campbell Ross, "'With Dignity and Importance': Peregrine Pickle as Country Gentlemen," in *Smollett, Author of the First Distinction,* ed. Alan Bold, 149–51.

30. The text used is that of the first edition. See n. 13.

31. Buck, *Study in Smollett,* 8–9; Hannay, *Life of Smollett,* 60; Knapp, *Tobias Smollett,* 311; Moore, *Hogarth's Literary Relationships,* 185; McKillop, *Early Masters,* 162.

32. Knapp, *Tobias Smollett,* 312.

33. Putney, "The Plan of *Peregrine Pickle,*" 1053, 1059.

34. Ibid., 1058.

35. Buck, *Study in Smollett,* 6–7.

36. Putney, "The Plan of *Peregrine Pickle,*" 1053.

37. Paulson, "Smollett's Early Satire," 397.

38. Buck, *Study in Smollett,* offers a collation of the editions.

39. Kahrl, *Tobias Smollett,* 40.

40. *New Letters of David Hume,* ed. D. Mossner and R. Klibansky (London: Oxford University Press, 1955), 174.

41. Buck, *Study in Smollett,* 66.

42. Noyes, *Letters,* 157; Knapp, *Tobias Smollett,* 126; Buck, *Study in Smollett,* chap. 3.

43. Knapp, *Tobias Smollett,* 125ff. Quotations, 129.

44. Her name suggests cuckolding of her husband.

45. David L. Evans, "Peregrine Pickle: The Complete Satirist," *Studies in the Novel* 3 (Fall 1971):258–74.

46. Noyes, *Letters,* 128–29; Goldberg, *Smollett and the Scottish School,* 67–68; Hannay, *Life of Smollett,* 86.

47. Grant, *A Study in Style,* 48.

48. W. Austin Flanders, "The Significance of Smollett's *Memoirs of a Lady of Quality,*" *Genre* 8 (June 1975):147.

49. Rufus Putney, "Smollett and Lady Vane's *Memoirs,*" *PQ* 25 (April 1946): 120ff.; Clifford, "Introduction," xxvi; Buck, *Study in Smollett,* 36ff.

50. Goldberg, *Smollett and the Scottish School,* 67–68.

51. Buck, *Study in Smollett,* 26; James R. Foster, *History of the Pre-Romantic Novel in England* (New York: Modern Language Assn., 1949), 122.

52. Clifford, "Introduction," xxvi.

53. David K. Jeffrey, "Smollett's Irony in *Peregrine Pickle*," *Journal of Narrative Technique* 6 (Spring 1976):142.

54. Ibid., 139.

55. Flanders, "The Significance of Smollett's *Memoirs of a Lady of Quality*," 147, 157.

56. Noyes, *Letters,* 128–29. See, too, Lewis M. Knapp and Lillian de la Torre, "Smollett, MacKercher, and the Annesley Claimant," *ELN* 1 (September 1963):28–33.

57. Putney, "The Plan of *Peregrine Pickle*," 1053, 1059. See Boucé's discussion in *The Novels of Tobias Smollett.*

58. Buck, *Study in Smollett,* provides a complete account of the changes made in the revised edition.

Chapter Four

1. Knapp, *Tobias Smollett,* 158.

2. Ibid., 158–59; Boege, *Smollett's Reputation,* 15, 18.

3. Strauss, "On Smollett's Language," 25.

4. Ibid.

5. Hannay, *Life of Smollett,* 90–91; Knapp, *Tobias Smollett,* 158, 318–19; Goldberg, *Smollett and the Scottish School,* 96–97.

6. Baker, *History of the Novel,* 4:215.

7. Damian Grant, "Introduction" to *The Adventures of Ferdinand Count Fathom,* ed. Damian Grant (London: Oxford University Press, 1971), xxi. See, too, Grant, *A Study in Style.* Subsequent quotations from this novel are from this edition and are cited parenthetically in the text.

8. Grant, "Introduction," xvi-xvii.

9. Paul-Gabriel Boucé, "The Thematic Structure of *Ferdinand Count Fathom*," in *Smollett. Author of the First Distinction,* ed. Alan Bold, 170.

10. T. O. Treadwell, "The Two Worlds of *Ferdinand Count Fathom*," in *Bicentennial Essays,* 137.

11. Ibid., 153.

12. Giddings, *The Tradition of Smollett,* 125.

13. Thomas R. Preston, "Disenchanting the Man of Feeling: Smollett's *Ferdinand Count Fathom*," in *Quick Springs of Sense: Studies in the Eighteenth Century,* ed. Larry S. Champion (Athens: University of Georgia Press, 1974), 227.

14. Jerry C. Beasley, "Smollett's Novels: *Ferdinand Count Fathom* for the Defense," *PLL* 20 (Spring 1984):166.

15. Ibid., 184.

16. Martz, *Later Career,* 13.

17. Kahrl, *Tobias Smollett,* 53.

18. Rousseau, *Essays of Two Decades,* 87–88.

19. Thomas R. Preston, "The 'Stage Passions' and Smollett's Characterization," *SP* 71 (January 1974):105–25.

20. Baker, *History of the Novel,* 4:216.

21. Kahrl, *Tobias Smollett,* 51; Putney, "The Plan of *Peregrine Pickle,*" 1052. On the seriousness with which the preface is now regarded, see Beasley, n.14, Boucé, n.9, and Preston, n.13 above. Only Grant, in his "Introduction" and his study of Smollett's style (n.7 above) argues to the contrary.

22. McKillop, *Early Masters,* 164–65.

23. Knapp, *Tobias Smollett,* 151–53, quotation, 154.

24. Ibid., 155.

25. References run throughout the novel. See Goldberg, *Smollett and the Scottish School,* 90.

26. Strauss, "On Smollett's Language," 32.

27. Baker, *History of the Novel,* 4:215; Moore, *Hogarth's Literary Relationships,* 179.

28. Paulson, "Smollett's Early Satire," 384–85.

29. Knapp, *Tobias Smollett,* 156.

30. Foster, *History of the Pre-Romantic Novel in England,* 130. See Strauss, "On Smollett's Language," 25; Baker, *History of the Novel,* 4:217; McKillop, *Early Masters,* 165; Paulson, "Smollett's Early Satire," 399.

31. Strauss, "On Smollett's Language," passim; Hannay, *Life of Smollett,* 78; Paulson, "Smollett's Early Satire," 399.

32. References too numerous to note specifically. Bruce, *Radical Dr. Smollett,* 200, notes the use of the mock-heroic, but does not indicate the extent.

33. Knapp, *Tobias Smollett,* 158.

34. Hannay, *Life of Smollett,* 64.

Chapter Five

1. See, for example, Baker, *History of the Novel,* 4:215; Alter, *Rogue's Progress,* 59; Hannay, *Life of Smollett,* 143; Martz, *Later Career,* 14.

2. Knapp, *Tobias Smollett,* 223.

3. Martz, *Later Career,* 14; Boege, *Smollett's Reputation,* 23–24, quotation, 23.

4. Knapp, *Tobias Smollett,* 244.

5. Ibid., 223.

6. James R. Foster, "Smollett's Pamphleteering Foe Shebbeare," *PMLA* 57 (December 1942):1100.

7. John Butt, "Smollett's Achievement as a Novelist," in *Bicentennial Essays,* 19.

8. Jerry C. Beasley, "Smollett's Art: The Novel as 'Picture,'" in *The First English Novelists. Essays in Understanding,* ed. J. M. Armistead (Knoxville: University of Tennessee Press, 1985), 166.

9. John Valdimir Price, "Smollett and the Reader in *Sir Launcelot Greaves,*" in *Smollett, Author of the First Distinction,* ed. Alan Bold, 207.

10. Ibid., 206.

11. David Evans, "Introduction," *The Life and Adventures of Sir Launcelot Greaves,* ed. David Evans (London: Oxford University Press, 1973), xix.

12. Robert D. Mayo, *The English Novel in the Magazines, 1740–1815* (Evanston, Ill.: Northwestern University Press; London: Oxford University Press, 1962), 280.

13. Ibid.

14. Grant, *A Study in Style,* 53.

15. Ibid., 94.

16. Ibid., 174.

17. Ibid., 179.

18. Boucé, *The Novels of Tobias Smollett,* 99.

19. Knapp, *Tobias Smollett,* 320.

20. Ibid., 228–30. Scott's quotation is from *Lives of the Novelists* (New York: A. Denham, 1872), 137.

21. Knapp, *Tobias Smollett,* 234–36; Foster, "Shebbeare," 1054.

22. Martz, *Later Career,* 14.

23. Chandler, *Literature of Roguery,* 2:319.

24. McKillop, *Early Masters,* 169.

25. Kahrl, *Tobias Smollett,* 59.

26. Ibid., 59; Foster, "Shebbeare," 1054.

27. Foster, "Shebbeare," 1099.

28. Paulson, "Smollett's Early Satire."

29. See Boucé, *The Novels of Tobias Smollett,* 92–99, for a discussion of Smollett's use of *Don Quixote.* He describes in some detail likenesses and differences between the works, emphasizing the differences between the heroes.

30. Chandler, *Literature of Roguery,* 2:319.

31. Knapp, *Tobias Smollett,* 244; Martz, *Later Career,* 14; Baker, *History of the Novel,* 4:222.

32. Martz, *Later Career,* vii, 12, 15–16; Foster, *History of the Pre-Romantic Novel in England,* 125, 127.

33. See n. 52 for chap. 1.

34. See Lewis Knapp, "Smollett and the Elder Pitt," *MLN* 59 (April 1944): 250–57.

35. For Smollett's relations with Shebbeare, see Foster, "Shebbeare."

36. Knapp, *Tobias Smollett,* 244. Bruce, *Radical Dr. Smollett,* 107–8, notes Smollett's double spokesmen.

37. George S. Rousseau and Roger Hambridge, "Smollett and Politics: Originals for the Election Scene in *Sir Launcelot Greaves,*" *ELN* 14 (September 1976):33.

38. Baker, *History of the Novel,* 4:222; McKillop, *Early Masters,* 169.

39. See n. 53 for chap. 1.

40. R. D. Spector, "Language Control in the Eighteenth Century," *Word Study* 27 (October 1951):1–2.

41. See Roger A. Hambridge, "Smollett's Legalese: Giles Jacob's *New Law Dictionary* and *Sir Launcelot Greaves*," *Revue des Langues Vivantes* 44 (1978): 37–44 for Smollett's source.

42. Quotation is from McKillop, *Early Masters*, 169; see Kahrl, *Tobias Smollett*, passim.

43. Knapp, *Tobias Smollett*, 321; Kahrl, *Tobias Smollett*, 57.

Chapter Six

1. Baker, *History of the Novel*, 4:215; Knapp, *Tobias Smollett*, 321; Martz, *Later Career*, 15; Strauss, "On Smollett's Language," 54; McKillop, *Early Masters*, 180.

2. Boege, *Smollett's Reputation*, 29ff.

3. Hannay, *Life of Smollett*, 152.

4. Martz, *Later Career*, vii.

5. Ibid., 12, 15, 16.

6. Foster, *History of the Pre-Romantic Novel in England*, 120–21, 128.

7. Rosenblum, "Smollett as Conservative Satirist," 560, 575.

8. Byron Gassman, "The Economy of *Humphry Clinker*," in *Bicentennial Essays*, 155–68.

9. John Valdimir Price's objections to the limits of the phrase "extending the possibilities of the picaresque" and his suggestion that Smollett *transformed* the genre are presented in *Tobias Smollett: "The Expedition of Humphry Clinker"* (London: Edward Arnold, 1973), 17. Price argues that the novel is "emphatically not a picaresque," but does not deny its many picaresque elements.

10. Paulson, "Smollett's Early Satire," 382.

11. Goldberg, *Smollett and the Scottish School*, 153ff., sees the work as another example of Smollett's providing a synthesis of the values of Scottish Common Sense philosophers. Paulson, "Smollett's Early Satire," 382ff., argues that Smollett's work shows the influence of formal Roman satire; however, Paulson does see a continuity between the early and late novels. Sheridan Baker, "*Humphry Clinker* as Comic Romance," *Papers of the Michigan Academy of Science, Arts, and Letters* 46 (1961): 645–64, describes the work as belonging to an unacknowledged genre of "comic romances." Bruce, throughout *The Radical Dr. Smollett*, treats Smollett as a consistently radical opponent of social abuses. However, he does not specifically relate his argument to Smollett's literary technique. He virtually dismisses (165–67) the picaresque from consideration.

12. Chandler, *Literature of Roguery*, 2:320.

13. See, particularly, Baker, "*Humphry Clinker* as Comic Romance," passim.

14. Ibid., 654.

15. Boege, *Smollett's Reputation*, 110, 132, 140, 144.

16. Martz, *Later Career*, 104–5, 125–26, 131, 138ff., 170. Martz notes that Smollett's impartial treatment in the *Present State of All Nations* irked his Scottish friends.

17. Ibid., 170–71; Goldberg, *Smollett and the Scottish School,* 145ff.

18. Baker, *"Humphry Clinker* as Comic Romance," 651. It is interesting that contemporaries raised objections to the novel's indecencies (Boege, *Smollett's Reputation,* 30).

19. R. D. S. Jack, "Appearance and Reality in *Humphry Clinker,"* in *Tobias Smollett. Author of the First Distinction,* ed. Alan Bold, 222.

20. Sekora, *Luxury.*

21. Rousseau, *Essays of Two Decades,* 84.

22. Kahrl, *Tobias Smollett,* 101; Martz, *Later Career,* 132–33; Goldberg, *Smollett and the Scottish School,* 144; Boucé, *The Novels of Tobias Smollett,* 192–93.

23. See Foster, "Shebbeare," 1076; Baker, *History of the Novel,* 4:236; McKillop, *Early Masters,* 176; Kahrl, *Tobias Smollett,* 130.

24. Strauss, "On Smollett's Language," 33.

25. The quotation is from Kahrl, *Tobias Smollett,* 128. See Baker, *History of the Novel,* 4:215, 229.

26. McKillop, *Early Masters,* 173–74; Lewis M. Knapp, "Smollett's Self-Portrait in *The Expedition of Humphry Clinker,"* in *The Age of Johnson: Essays Presented to Chauncey Brewster Tinker,* ed. Frederick W. Hilles (New Haven: Yale University Press, 1949), 151. The percentage of letters is Bramble, 40, and Jery, 50. However, the length of their letters compared with the others increases the proportion.

27. Strauss, "On Smollett's Language," 53–54; Grant, *A Study in Style,* 59ff.

28. See Martz, *Later Career,* for the amount of material Smollett used from his *Present State of All Nations* in Matt's exposition.

29. See Knapp, "Self-Portrait," 149.

30. McKillop, *Early Masters,* 172, sees this as central to the novel. See, too, 174–75.

31. Kahrl, *Tobias Smollett,* 142–43.

32. Boucé, *The Novels of Tobias Smollett,* 250.

33. Baker, *"Humphry Clinker* as Comic Romance," 646.

34. Giorgio Melchiori, *The Tightrope Walkers* (London: Macmillan, 1956), 46–48, 51.

35. For further discussion of Smollett's play on language in the novel, see Arthur W. Boggs, "A Win Jenkins' Lexicon," *BNYPL* 68 (May 1964):323–30, and "Dialectal Ingenuity in *Humphry Clinker,"* *PLL* 1 (Autumn 1965):327–31. For a contrary view, see Arthur Sherbo, "Win Jenkins' Language," *PLL* 5 (Spring 1969): 199–204.

36. For the relationship between the *Briton* and *Humphry Clinker,* see Byron Gassman, "The *Briton* and Humphry Clinker," *SEL* 3 (Summer 1963):397–414.

37. McKillop, *Early Masters,* 147. McKillop is not, however, in disagreement with Knapp on the generally autobiographical features in Bramble's portrait.

38. For a few examples, see: Baker, *History of the Novel,* 4:234; Foster, "Shebbeare," 1068–69; Buck, *Smollett as Poet,* 13–14.

39. See, for example, Knapp, "Self-Portrait," 153ff.

Chapter Seven

1. See Boege, *Smollett's Reputation,* passim, and Knapp, *Tobias Smollett,* 309–24, for comments on Smollett's reputation and his contribution to the novel.

2. Rousseau, *Essays of Two Decades,* 55–79.

3. Rosalie L. Colie, *The Resources of Kind. Genre-Theory in the Renaissance,* ed. Barbara L. Lewalski (Berkeley, Los Angeles, London: University of California Press, 1973).

4. Paulson, "Smollett's Early Satire," 381–402.

5. Gassman, "The Economy of *Humphry Clinker,*" 155–68.

6. Thomas R. Preston, "Smollett and the Benevolent Misanthrope Type," *PMLA* 79 (March 1964):51–57.

7. Michael Rosenblum, "Smollett and the Old Conventions," *PQ* 55 (Summer 1976):401.

8. Edgar Johnson, *Charles Dickens* (New York: Simon and Schuster, 1952), 155, 174, 716.

9. Baker, *History of the Novel,* 4:238; Allen, *The English Novel,* 72.

10. Boege, *Smollett's Reputation,* 100; Allen, *The English Novel,* 72.

11. Allen, *The English Novel,* 72; see E. S. Noyes, "A Note on *Peregrine Pickle* and *Pygmalion,*" *MLN* 41 (May 1926):327–30.

12. Allen, *The English Novel,* 72.

13. See E. Joliat, *Smollett et la France.*

Selected Bibliography

PRIMARY SOURCES

Miscellaneous Works of Tobias Smollett. Edinburgh: David Ramsey, 1790. 6 vols. Includes biographical sketch, novels, poems, plays, and *Travels*.
Miscellaneous Works of Tobias Smollett. Edinburgh: Mundell, 1796. 6 vols. Includes Robert Anderson's memoir on Smollett's life and writing. Later editions: 1800, 1806, 1811, 1817, 1820.
Miscellaneous Works of Tobias Smollett. London: Otridge & Rackham, 1824. 12 vols. Contains memoir and includes *Atom*.
Works. Edited by David Herbert. Edinburgh: William P. Nimmo, 1870. Introduction stresses Smollett's realism.
Works. Edited by W. E. Henley and T. Seccombe. Westminster: Constable, 1899–1901. Complete works, unsympathetic introductions.
Works. Edited by George Saintsbury. London: Gibbings, 1899–1903. 12 vols. Apologetic introductions.
Works. New York: G. D. Sproul, 1902. 12 vols. Interesting introductions by G. H. Maynadier.
Travels through France and Italy. Edited by Thomas Seccombe. London: Oxford University Press, 1907. Text no longer acceptable, but offers a spirited introduction.
Works. Oxford: Blackwell, 1925–1926. 11 vols. Shakespeare Head edition of the novels, standard prior to Oxford English Novels editions.
Letters of Tobias Smollett. Edited by E. S. Noyes. Cambridge, Mass.: Harvard University Press, 1926. Still valuable for its notes.
An Essay on the External Use of Water. Edited by C. E. Jones. Baltimore: Johns Hopkins Press, 1935. Smollett's medical interests.
The Adventures of Peregrine Pickle. Edited by J. L. Clifford. London: Oxford University Press, 1964. Unexpurgated text of the first edition, with good introduction, notes, and bibliography. Rev. for Oxford World Classics by P. G. Boucé, 1983.
The Expedition of Humphry Clinker. Edited by L. M. Knapp. London: Oxford University Press, 1966. Based on first edition, includes good introduction, notes, and bibliography. Rev. for Oxford World Classics by P. G. Boucé, 1984.
Letters of Tobias Smollett. Edited by Lewis M. Knapp. Oxford: Clarendon Press, 1970. Standard edition of 108 letters.
The Adventures of Ferdinand Count Fathom. Edited by Damian Grant. London: Ox-

ford University Press, 1971. Follows first edition and includes informative critical introduction, bibliography, and notes.

The Life and Adventures of Sir Launcelot Greaves. Edited by David Evans. London:
Oxford University Press, 1973. Text from *British Magazine* with the original
illustrations. Includes introduction, notes, and bibliography.

The Adventures of Roderick Random. Edited by Paul-Gabriel Boucé. London: Oxford
University Press, 1979. Based on first edition, with the "Apologue" from the
fifth edition. Excellent introduction, bibliography, and notes.

Travels through France and Italy. Edited by Frank Felsenstein. London: Oxford University Press, 1979. Standard text. Appendices on sources and a description of
earlier editions.

A scholarly edition of Smollett's novels, including the *Atom,* is forthcoming from the
University of Georgia Press.

SECONDARY SOURCES

1. Bibliographical

Bevis, Richard W. "Smollett and *The Israelites.*" *PQ* 45 (April 1966):387–94. Attribution to Smollett on basis of circumstantial evidence.

Boege, Fred W. *Smollett's Reputation as a Novelist.* Princeton: Princeton University Press, 1947. Full account of contemporary through twentieth-
century criticism.

Brack, O. M. Jr., and James B. Davis. "Smollett's Revisions of *Roderick Random.*"
PBSA 64 (Third Quarter 1970):295–311. Considers changes in second
through fourth editions.

Day, Robert Adams. "The Authorship of the *Atom.*" *PQ* 59 (Spring 1980):187–93.
Argues Smollett's authorship based on external evidence.

Deutsch, O. E. "Poetry Preserved in Music: Bibliographical Notes on Smollett and
Oswald, Handel, and Haydn." *MLN* 63 (February 1948):73–88. Publishes
Smollett's first printed poem and lyrics of *Alceste.*

Douglass, Wayne J. "Smollett's Authorship of the *Atom.*" *LN* 17 (March 1980):
183–84. Offers internal evidence of Smollett's authorship.

Foster, James R. "Smollett and the *Atom.*" *PMLA* 68 (December 1953):1032–46.
From internal evidence argues Smollett's authorship.

Norwood, L. F. "The Authenticity of Smollett's *Ode to Independence.*" *RES* 17 (January 1941):55–64. Conclusive proof of Smollett's authorship.

Smith, Albert H. *"The Adventures of Peregrine Pickle,* 1758 and 1765." *Library* Series 5, 28 (March 1973):62–64. William Strahan's role in publication of second and third editions.

_____. "A Duplicate Setting in the Second Edition of Smollett's *Roderick Ran-*

dom." Library, Series 5, 28 (December 1973):309–18. Relates bibliographical evidence to increased demand for the novel.

————. "The Printing and Publication of Smollett's *Peregrine Pickle." Library*, Series 5, 26 (March 1971):39–52. William Strahan's role in publishing and distributing the first edition.

————. *"Sir Launcelot Greaves:* A Bibliographical Survey of Eighteenth-Century Editions." *Library*, Series 5, 32 (September 1977): 214–37. Publication details from *British Magazine* through British, Irish, and unauthorized editions.

Spector, Robert D. *Tobias Smollett: A Reference Guide*. Boston: G. K. Hall, 1980. Annotated chronological bibliography covering secondary works from 1746 through 1978.

Wagoner, Mary. *Tobias Smollett: A Checklist of Editions of His Works and an Annotated Secondary Bibliography*. New York and London: Garland, 1984. Thorough coverage of secondary sources with helpful annotation.

2. Biographical and Critical

Alter, Robert. *Rogue's Progress*. Cambridge, Mass.: Harvard University Press, 1963. Study of the picaresque contains excellent chapter on *Roderick Random*.

Andres, Sophia. "Tobias Smollett's Satiric Spokesman in *Humphry Clinker." Studies in Scottish Literature* 13 (1978):100–10. Use of Matt Bramble in classical satiric tradition attacks individual evils and argues for social stability.

Auty, Susan G. *The Comic Spirit of Eighteenth-Century Novels*. Port Washington, N.Y.: Kennikat Press; London: National University Publications, 1975. Sees Smollett as a comic rather than satiric novelist.

Baker, Ernest A. *The History of the English Novel*. vol. 4. London: W. E. and G. Witherby, 1930. General survey, but old-fashioned criticism.

Baker, Sheridan. *"Humphry Clinker* as Comic Romance." *Papers of the Michigan Academy of Science, Arts, and Letters* 66 (1961):645–54. Good discussion of Smollett's scatological satire and its purpose.

Batten, Charles L. *"Humphry Clinker* and Eighteenth-Century Travel Literature." *Genre* 7 (December 1974):392–408. Argues that the work should be read as a fictional adaptation of the travel book.

Beasley, Jerry C. "Smollett's Art: The Novel as 'Picture,'" In *The First English Novelists. Essays in Understanding*, edited by J. M. Armistead, 143–83. Knoxville: University of Tennessee Press, 1985. Solid brief survey of Smollett's novels describes him as an experimental novelist.

————. "Smollett's Novels: *Ferdinand Count Fathom* for the Defense." *PLL* 20 (Spring 1984):165–84. *Fathom*, a considerable achievement, despite flaws ranks behind the masterful *Roderick Random* and *Humphry Clinker*.

Bertelsen, Lance. "The Smollettian View of Life." *Novel* 11 (Winter 1978):115–27. Smollett's use of a drive for human communication to provide unity achieves success in *Humphry Clinker*.

Bjornson, Richard. *The Picaresque Hero in European Fiction*. Madison: University of

Wisconsin Press, 1977. Smollett's alterations in plan, tone, and characterization differentiate *Roderick Random* from the traditional picaresque.

Bloch, Tuvia. "Smollett's Quest for Form." *MP* 65 (November 1967):103–13. Smollett unsuccessfully attempts to adapt Fielding's methods prior to achieving own form in *Humphry Clinker.*

Boggs, W. Arthur. "A Win Jenkins' Lexicon." *BNYPL* 68 (May 1964):323–30. Explicates difficult or unusual puns in letters in *Humphry Clinker.*

Bold, Alan, ed. *Smollett: Author of the First Distinction* London: Vision Press; Totowa, N.J.: Barnes & Noble, 1982. Four essays on general topics and one on each of the five novels attempt to rescue Smollett's reputation.

Boucé, Paul-Gabriel. "The Duke of Newcastle's Levee in Smollett's *Humphry Clinker.*" *Yearbook of English Studies* 5 (1975):136–41. Shows Smollett's rendering of reality into fiction.

————. *The Novels of Tobias Smollett.* Translated by P. G. Boucé and Antonia White. London and New York: Longman, 1976. Excellent examination of the structure of Smollett's novels includes thorough discussion of his realism, comedy, and style.

————. "'Snakes in Ireland': The 'Picaresque' in Smollett's *Roderick Random* (1748)." *Caliban* 22 (1983):29–39. Whatever its thematic and conceptual indebtedness to an altered form of picaresque, the novel has no significant relationship to the genre.

Brooks, Douglas. *Number and Pattern in the Eighteenth-Century Novel: Defoe, Fielding, Smollett and Sterne.* London and Boston: Routledge & Kegan Paul, 1975. Smollett's use of numerology in patterning his novels.

Bruce, Donald. *Radical Dr. Smollett.* London: Victor Gollancz, 1964: Boston: Houghton Mifflin, 1965. Unconvincing argument about Smollett's "radicalism," but interesting facts about the times.

————. "Smollett and the Sordid Knaves." *Contemporary Review* 220 (February 1972):133–38. Although favoring Tories, Smollett is less interested in politics than in social reform.

Buck, Howard S. "Smollett and Dr. Akenside." *JEGP* 31 (January 1932):10–26. Considers their relationship and reason for attack on Akenside in *Peregrine Pickle.*

————. *Smollett as Poet.* New Haven: Yale University Press; London: Oxford University Press, 1927. Only full commentary on Smollett's poems.

————. *A Study in Smollett, Chiefly "Peregrine Pickle."* New Haven: Yale University Press, 1925. Collates first and second editions and gives account of Smollett's quarrels recorded in the novel and in *The Regicide.*

Bunn, James H. "Signs of Randomness in *Roderick Random.*" *ECS* 14 (Summer 1981):452–69. Extent of Smollett's contribution to a developing eighteenth-century epistemology related to probability theory.

Chandler, Frank W. *The Literature of Roguery.* 2 vols. Boston and New York:

Houghton Mifflin, 1907. Includes discussion of influences on Smollett's novels.

Collins, R. G. "The Hidden Bastard: A Question of Illegitimacy in Smollett's *Peregrine Pickle*." *PMLA* 94 (January 1979):91–105. Reasonable argument that Peregrine was illegitimate.

Day, Robert Adams. "Sex, Scatology, Smollett." In *Sexuality in Eighteenth-Century Britain,* edited by Paul-Gabriel Boucé, 225–43. Manchester: Manchester University Press; Totowa, N.J.: Barnes & Noble, 1982. Interesting attempt to demonstrate the relationship of Smollett's scatology to "the sexual element of his fantasy world."

—————. "*Ut Pictura Poesis?* Smollett, Satire, and the Graphic Arts." *SECC* 10 (1981):297–311. Pictorial character in the novels ranges from caricature to landscape and the picturesque.

De la Torre, Lillian. "New Light on Smollett and the Annesley Cause," *RES,* n.s., 22 (August 1971):274–81. Demonstrates accuracy of treatment of the Annesley cause in *Peregrine Pickle.*

Donovan, Robert Alan. *The Shaping Vision: Imagination in the English Novel from Defoe to Dickens.* Ithaca, N.Y.: Cornell University Press, 1966. Describes Smollett's transformation of factual material into imaginative fictional form through characterization in *Humphry Clinker.*

Douglass, Wayne J. "Done after the Dutch Taste: Political Prints and Smollett's *Atom.*" *Essays in Literature* 9 (Fall 1982):170–79. Rich account of "the background of political iconography" in the *Atom.*

Driskell, Leon V. "Looking for Dustwich." *Texas Studies in Literature and Language* 9 (Spring 1967):85–90. Relates prefatory material in *Humphry Clinker* to theme of disparity between appearance and reality.

Ellison, L. M. "Elizabethan Drama and the Works of Smollett." *PMLA* 44 (September 1929):842–62. Chiefly Shakespeare's and Jonson's influence on Smollett's characterization.

Evans, David L. "Peregrine Pickle: The Complete Satirist." *Studies in the Novel* 3 (Fall 1971):258–74. Not only is the novel a satire, but it is also a study of satire and combines the conventions of the novel with those of satire.

Fabel, Robin. "The Patriotic Briton: Tobias Smollett and English Politics, 1756–1771." *ECS* 8 (Fall 1974):100–14. Finds Smollett nonpartisan in politics, a reformist opposed to radical change.

Flanders, W. Austin. "The Significance of Smollett's *Memoirs of a Lady of Quality.*" *Genre* 8 (June 1975):146–66. Unable to create unity from characters' varied experiences, Smollett resorts to conventional endings for his novels.

Folkenflik, Robert. "Self and Society: Comic Union in *Humphry Clinker.*" *PQ* 53 (April 1974):195–204. Unity results from use of a multiple point of view as characters attempt to resolve self-interest and social union.

Foster, James R. *History of the Pre-Romantic Novel in England.* New York: Modern

Language Association, 1949. Good general survey of major and minor eighteenth-century novels.

————. Smollett's Pamphleteering Foe Shebbeare." *PMLA* 57 (December 1942): 1053–1100. On Smollett's work on the *Critical Review* and his relationship with the notorious John Shebbeare.

Franke, Wolfgang. "Smollett's *Humphry Clinker* as a 'Party-Novel.'" *Studies in Scottish Literature* 9 (October-January 1971–1972):97–106. Sees the novel as propaganda to convey a favorable image of Scotland.

Fredman, Alice Green. "The Picaresque in Decline: Smollett's First Novel." In *English Writers of the Eighteenth Century,* edited by John H. Middendorf, 189–207. New York and London: Columbia University Press, 1971. Describes elements in *Roderick Random* that indicate a falling off from traditional picaresque.

Gassman, Byron. "The *Briton* and *Humphry Clinker.*" *SEL* 3 (Summer 1963):397–414. Discusses consistency of Smollett's political ideas in his work.

————. "*Humphry Clinker* and the Two Kingdoms of George III." *Criticism* 16 (Spring 1974):95–108. Novel contrasts a real and ideal world and reflects in the latter the views of the population at the accession of George III.

————. "Smollett's *Briton* and the Art of Political Cartooning." *SECC* 14 (1985): 243–58. Literary techniques in the *Briton* reflect those of contemporary political cartoonists.

Giddings, Robert. *The Tradition of Smollett.* London: Methuen, 1967. Relationship of Smollett's novels, particularly *Roderick Random* and *Peregrine Pickle,* to the picaresque.

Goldberg, Milton A. *Smollett and the Scottish School: Studies in Eighteenth-Century Thought.* Albuquerque: University of New Mexico Press, 1959. Argues that the novels attempt to reconcile antithetical ideas of Scottish Common Sense school of philosophy.

Grant, Damian. *Tobias Smollett: A Study in Style.* Manchester: Manchester University Press; Totowa, N.J.: Rowman & Littlefield, 1977. First full-length study of Smollett's style rejects previous generalizations and analyzes specific qualities, particularly techniques for achieving moral statements.

Griffith, Philip Mahone. "Fire Scenes in Richardson's *Clarissa* and Smollett's *Humphry Clinker:* A Study of a Literary Relationship in the Structure of the Novel." *Tulane Studies in English* 11 (1961): 39–51. Smollett's fire scenes parody Richardson's scene and contribute to rhythmic structure of *Clinker.*

Hambridge, Roger A. "Smollett's Legalese: Giles Jacob's *New Law Dictionary* and *Sir Launcelot Greaves.*" *Revue des Langues Vivantes. Tijdschrift voor Levende Talen* 44, no. 1 (1978):37–44. Jacob's work a source for legal jargon in Smollett's novel.

Hannay, David. *Life of Tobias George Smollett.* London: Walter Scott, 1887. Readable, sympathetic biography and criticism.

Hopkins, Robert. "The Function of Grotesque in *Humphry Clinker.*" *Huntington Li-*

brary Quarterly 32 (February 1969):163–77. Unity derives from Smollett's
effective use of the grotesque as a means of satire.

Iser, Wolfgang. *The Implied Reader: Patterns of Communication in Prose Fiction from
Bunyan to Beckett.* Baltimore and London: Johns Hopkins University Press,
1974. Combination of the epistolary novel, travel book, and picaresque in
Humphry Clinker achieves a perspective of reality related to associational psychology and Scottish empirical philosophy.

Jeffrey, David K. "'Ductility and Dissimulation': The Unity of *Ferdinand Count
Fathom.*" *Tennessee Studies in Literature* 23 (1978):47–60. Use of image clus-
ters provides the novel's structural and thematic unity.

————. "Smollett's Irony in *Peregrine Pickle.*" *Journal of Narrative Technique* 6
(Spring 1976):137–46. *Memoirs of a Lady of Quality* contrasts with the main
narrative and theme and enhances the character of Peregrine.

Joliat, Eugène. "Smollett, Editor of Voltaire." *MLN* 54 (June 1939):429–36.
Smollett's role in editing translation of Voltaire's works.

————. *Smollett et la France.* Paris: Librairie Ancienne Honoré Champion, 1935.
Full account of experiences, reputation, and sources in France; includes bibliography of European translations of Smollett's work.

Jones, Claude E. *Smollett Studies.* Berkeley and Los Angeles: University of California
Press, 1942. Important study of Smollett's naval experiences and editorial
work on the *Critical Review.*

Kahrl, George M. "The Influence of Shakespeare on Smollett." In *Parrott Presentation Volume,* 399–420. Princeton: Princeton University Press, 1935. Notes
Smollett's conscious use of Shakespeare.

————. *Tobias Smollett, Traveler-Novelist.* Chicago: University of Chicago Press,
1945. Studies fiction and *Travels* against background of travel literature, journalism, and personal experience.

Keener, Frederick M. "Transitions in *Humphry Clinker.*" *SECC* 16 (1986):149–63.
Emphasizes the metaphorical construction of the novel.

Kline, Judd. "Three Doctors and Smollett's Lady of Quality." *PQ* 27 (July 1948):
219–28. Neither Smollett nor Shebbeare, but Dr. Peter Shaw was Dr. S. in
the *Memoirs.*

Knapp, Lewis M. "Early Scottish Attitudes toward Tobias Smollett." *PQ* 45 (January 1966):262–69. Valuable biographical material about Smollett's Scottish associations.

————. "The Keys to Smollett's *Atom.*" *ELN* 2 (December 1964): 100–102.
Prints key to the novel found in 1769 edition.

————. "The Naval Scenes in *Roderick Random.*" *PMLA* 49 (June 1934):593–98.
Evaluates accuracy of Smollett's treatment.

————. "Rex *versus* Smollett: More Data on the Smollett-Knowles Libel Case." *MP*
41 (May 1944):221–27. On Smollett's trial and conviction for libel in *Critical Review.*

_____. "Smollett and the Elder Pitt." *MLN* 59 (April 1944):250–57. Account of Smollett's changing attitudes over the course of twenty-five years.

_____. "Smollett's Self-Portrait in *The Expedition of Humphry Clinker.*" In *The Age of Johnson,* edited by Frederick W. Hilles, 149–158. New Haven: Yale University Press, 1949. Cites autobiographical features in characterization of Matthew Bramble.

_____. *Tobias Smollett. Doctor of Men and Manners.* Princeton: Princeton University Press, 1949. Excellent standard biography.

_____, and Lillian de la Torre. "Smollett, MacKercher, and the Annesley Claimant." *ELN* 1 (September 1963): 28–33. Concludes that Smollett's material for the case in *Peregrine Pickle* came from MacKercher, Annesley's supporter.

Korte, Donald M. "Smollett's *Advice* and *Reproof:* Apprenticeship in Satire." *Studies in Scottish Literature* 8 (April 1971):239–53. Relates formal verse satire of the poems to the novels.

_____. "Tobias Smollett's *Advice* and *Reproof.*" *Thoth* 8 (Spring 1967):45–65. Smollett's indebtedness to Pope.

Linsalata, Carmine Rocco. *Smollett's Hoax: Don Quixote in English.* Stanford: Stanford University Press, 1956. Demonstrates Smollett's extensive use of Charles Jarvis's translation of *Don Quixote* for his own work.

Mack, Edward C. "Pamela's Stepdaughters: The Heroines of Smollett and Fielding." *CE* 8 (March 1947):293–301. Describes Smollett's heroines as the eighteenth-century conception of the ideal woman.

McKillop, Alan D. *The Early Masters of English Fiction.* Lawrence, Kans.: University of Kansas Press, 1956. Contains a long chapter on Smollett's novels.

_____. "Notes on Smollett." *PQ* 7 (October 1928):368–74. Outlines Smollett's controversy with the poet Charles Churchill.

Martz, Louis L. *The Later Career of Tobias Smollett.* New Haven: Yale University Press, 1942. Studies the significance of Smollett's journalistic career for his later fiction.

_____. "Smollett and the Expedition to Carthagena." *PMLA* 56 (June 1941): 428–46. Compares Smollett's accounts of the battle in various works and relates these to the historical truth.

_____. "Tobias Smollett and the *Universal History.*" *MLN* 56 (January 1941):1–14. Smollett's role as editor and author of large commercial publication.

Mayo, Robert D. *The English Novel in the Magazines, 1740–1815.* Evanston, Ill.: Northwestern University Press; London: Oxford University Press, 1962. Significant discussion of *Sir Launcelot Greaves* as first work by a major author to be serialized in a periodical.

Moore, Robert E. *Hogarth's Literary Relationships.* Minneapolis: University of Minnesota Press; London: Oxford University Press, 1948. Includes a chapter on Smollett's indebtedness to Hogarth and the relationship of their artistic techniques.

Nemoianu, Virgil. "The Semantics of Bramble's Hypochondria: A Connection between Illness and Style in the Eighteenth Century." *Clio* 9 (January 1979):39–51. Suggest reasons for Smollett's choice of hypochondria and gout as Matt Bramble's ailments.

Orowitz, Milton. "Smollett and the Art of Caricature." *Spectrum* 2 (Fall 1958):155–67. Discusses Smollett's methods of characterization.

Park, William. "Fathers and Sons—*Humphry Clinker*." *Literature and Psychology* 16, nos. 3–4 (1966):166–74. Relates imagery in the novel to the archetypical characteristics in its mythic structure.

Parker, Alexander A. *Literature and the Delinquent: The Picaresque Novel in Spain and Europe. 1599–1753*. Edinburgh: Edinburgh University Press, 1967. Sees Smollett as last important European novelist to use the picaresque significantly—in *Roderick Random* and *Fathom*.

Parker, Alice. "Tobias Smollett and the Law." *SP* 39 (July 1942):545–58. Account of Smollett's legal entanglements and their relationship to his personality and novels.

Paulson, Ronald. "Satire in the Early Novels of Smollett." *JEGP* 59 (July 1960): 381–402. Influence of formal Latin verse satire on the early novels.

————. *Satire and the Novel in Eighteenth-Century England*. New Haven and London: Yale University Press, 1967. Traces development in Smollett's novels from early use of picaresque for satire to later characters who function as various types of satirists.

————. "Smollett and Hogarth: The Identity of Pallet." *SEL* 4 (Summer 1964): 351–59. Describes Hogarth as the original of the painter in *Peregrine Pickle*.

Piper, William B. "The Large Diffused Picture of Life in Smollett's Early Novels." *SP* 60 (January 1963):45–56. Studies characters in first three novels and their use in order to explore Smollett's vision of society.

Pratt, T. K. "Linguistics, Criticism, and Smollett's *Roderick Random*." *University of Toronto Quarterly* 42 (Fall 1972):26–39. Linguistic approach to an analysis of the style of the novel.

Preston, Thomas R. *Not in Timon's Manner. Feeling, Misanthropy, and Satire in Eighteenth-Century England*. University, Ala.: University of Alabama Press, 1975. Interesting examination of the relationship of Smollett's novels to the tradition of the man of feeling. Incorporates Preston's earlier articles on *Fathom* and *Humphry Clinker*.

————. "Smollett among the Indians." *PQ* 61 (Summer 1982):231–41. Smollett's use of "Indian matter" for his details of Lismahago's adventures in *Humphry Clinker*.

————. "The 'Stage Passions' and Smollett's Characterization." *SP* 71 (January 1974):105–25. Smollett's methods of characterization influenced by drama and eighteenth-century acting theory.

Price, John Valdimir. *Tobias Smollett: "The Expedition of Humphry Clinker."* London: Edward Arnold, 1973. Excellent pamphlet on form and content considers epistolary technique, characterization, point of view, and theme.

Punter, David. "Smollett and the Logic of Domination." *Literature & History,* no. 2 (October 1975):60–81. Smollett, an outsider, describes contradictions between expressed ideals and actual practices of British capitalism.

Putney, Rufus D. S. "The Plan of *Peregrine Pickle.*" *PMLA* 60 (December 1945): 1051–65. Argues for the harmonious structure of the novel through the unity of Peregrine's moral history.

————. "Smollett and Lady Vane's *Memoirs.*" *PQ* 25 (April 1946):120–26. Argues for Smollett's authorship of the *Memoirs* in the first edition of *Peregrine Pickle.*

Reid, B. L. "Smollett's Healing Journey." *Virginia Quarterly Review* 41 (Autumn 1965):549–70. Discusses the spiritual and moral journey of the characters in *Humphry Clinker.*

Rice, Scott. "The Satiric Persona of Smollett's *Travels.*" *Studies in Scottish Literature* 10 (July 1972):33–47. Persona of the satiric *Travels* provides its unity.

————. "Smollett's Seventh Travel Letter and the Design of Formal Verse Satire." *SEL* 16 (Summer 1976):491–503. *Travels* combines the genres of Grand Tour travel literature and classical formal verse satire.

Roper, Derek. "Smollett's 'Four Gentlemen': The First Contributors to the *Critical Review.*" *RES* 10 (February 1959):38–44. From marked copy of first two volumes, identifies the contributors.

Rosenblum, Michael. "Smollett as Conservative Satirist." *ELH* 42 (Winter 1975): 556–79. Smollett's satire is designed to preserve order and stability in society.

————. "Smollett and the Old Conventions." *PQ* 55 (Summer 1976):389–402. Smollett consciously reworks traditional modes of the romances to achieve satiric fiction.

Ross, Angus. "The 'Show of Violence' in Smollett's Novels." *Yearbook of English Studies* 2 (1972): 118–29. Evaluates importance of violence in Smollett's fictional world.

Ross, Ian Campbell. "Language, Structure and Vision in Smollett's *Roderick Random.*" *Etudes Anglaises* 31 (January-March 1978):52–63. Unity achieved through Smollett's persistent vision of a disordered world.

Rothstein, Eric. "Scotophilia and *Humphry Clinker:* The Politics of Beggary, Bugs, and Buttocks." *University of Toronto Quarterly* 52 (Fall 1982):63–78. Perceptive analysis of how Smollett's treatment of Humphry Clinker responds to English anti-Scottish sentiments.

————. *Systems of Order and Inquiry in Later Eighteenth-Century Fiction.* Berkeley, Los Angeles, London: University of California Press, 1975. Examines the relationship of form in *Humphry Clinker* to Smollett's skeptical epistemology.

Rousseau, George S. *Tobias Smollett: Essays of Two Decades.* Edinburgh: T. and T. Clark; New York: Seabury, 1982. Includes fifteen previously published essays, notes, and reviews on Smollett and Smollett criticism. Particularly important on connections between Smollett's work and medicine.

————, with Paul-Gabriel Boucé, eds. *Tobias Smollett: Bicentennial Essays Pre-

sented to Lewis M. Knapp. New York: Oxford University Press, 1971. Ten essays on Smollett's novels, history, travels, and use of the picaresque and caricature.

Sekora, John. *Luxury: The Concept in Western Thought, Eden to Smollett.* Baltimore and London: Johns Hopkins University Press, 1977. Portrays Smollett as exponent of the classical attitude that considered luxury as the basic human vice.

Sena, John F. "Smollett's Matthew Bramble and the Tradition of the Physician-Satirist." *PLL* 11 (Fall 1975):386–96. Smollett's use of the literary tradition of the physician-satirist relates physical ailments to moral sickness.

———. "Smollett's Persona and the Melancholic Traveler: An Hypothesis." *ECS* 1 (Summer 1968):353–69. Relates Smollett's persona in the *Travels* to an eighteenth-century type and describes the medical sources for the character.

Sherbo, Arthur. "Win Jenkins' Language." *PLL* 5 (Spring 1969):199–204. Questions the extent of the ingenuity in Win's language in *Humphry Clinker.*

Siebert, Donald T., Jr. "The Role of the Senses in *Humphry Clinker.*" *Studies in the Novel* 6 (Spring 1974):17–26. Smollett's imagery follows from Locke's epistemological assumptions that argue that the senses provide the basis for knowledge.

Spector, Robert Donald. *English Literary Periodicals and the Climate of Opinion during the Seven Years War.* The Hague: Mouton, 1966. Extensive discussion of Smollett's labors on the *Briton, British Magazine,* and *Critical Review.*

———. "The *Monthly* and Its Rival." *BNYPL* 66 (March 1960):159–61. Describes the effect of Smollett's *Critical Review* on the older periodical.

Starr, Nathan. "Smollett's Sailors." *American Neptune* 32 (April 1972):81–99. Describes the reality of Smollett's nautical material and offers sources for his characters and scenes.

Stevick, Philip. "Stylistic Energy in the Early Smollett." *PQ* 64 (October 1967): 712–19. First three novels gain effect from hyperbolic style rather than characterization and narrative.

Strauss, Albrecht B. "On Smollett's Language: A Paragraph in *Ferdinand Count Fathom.*" In *Style in Prose Fiction: English Institute Essays, 1958,* 25–54. New York: Columbia University Press, 1959. Examines Smollett's style to determine the characteristic strengths and weaknesses of the novelist.

Underwood, Gary N. "Linguistic Realism in *Roderick Random.*" *JEGP* 69 (January 1970):32–40. Smollett's use of dialect to create realism.

Warner, John M. "The Interpolated Narratives in the Fiction of Fielding and Smollett: An Epistemological View." *Studies in the Novel* 5 (Fall 1973):271–83. Relationship of interpolations and main narrative shows Smollett's achievement of unity in *Humphry Clinker.*

———. "Smollett's Development as a Novelist." *Novel* 5 (Winter 1972): 148–61. Influence of Locke's epistemology on Smollett's quest for form.

Wasserman, Earl R. "Smollett's Satire on the Hutchinsonians." *MLN* 70 (May

1955):336–37. Smollett satirizes John Hutchinson as Sir Mungo Barebones in *Fathom* as part of a satirical portrait of the Hutchinsonian sect.

Watson, Harold F. *The Sailor in English Fiction and Drama, 1550–1800.* New York: Columbia University Press, 1931. Includes material on Smollett's nautical characters in his plays and novels.

Weinsheimer, Joel. "Defects and Difficulties in Smollett's *Peregrine Pickle*." *Ariel, A Review of International English Literature* 9 (July 1978):49–62. Novel fails as satire, Bildungsroman, or a combination of both.

———. "Impedance as Value: *Roderick Random* and *Pride and Prejudice*." *PTL: A Journal for Descriptive Poetics and Theory of Literature* 3 (1978):139–66. Smollett's novel fails to engage the reader.

Whitridge, Arnold. *Tobias Smollett, A Study of His Miscellaneous Works.* New York: n.p., 1925. A readable study of Smollett's work, excluding the novels, but offering an excellent account of the *Atom*.

Index

Absent Man, The, 6
Adventures of Ferdinand Fathom, 67–84, 110, 122–23, 124; Augustan satire in, 82–84; characterization in, 72–76; plot of, 71–72; satire, 76–82; Smollett's intentions with, 69–71
Adventures of Peregrine Pickle, The, 9, 44–66, 81, 83, 100–101, 110, 122, 123; Augustan satire in, 60–63; autobiographical material in, 58–60; comparison of with *Roderick Random*, 45–49; picaresque in, 49–52; point of view in, 64–65; revision of, 66; satire in, 52–58; use of insets in, 63–64
Adventures of Roderick Random, The, 2, 3, 5, 9, 22, 23, 24–43, 45–49, 53, 57–58, 60, 64, 65, 81, 99, 100–101, 104, 105, 110, 118, 119, 121, 122, 123, 124; autographical material in, 27–30; characterization in, 34–40; plot of, 25–27; satire in, 40–43; use of picaresque in, 30–34
Advice, 8–9
Akenside, Mark, 13, 44, 47
Alceste, 6
Alter, Robert, 31–32, 33, 36, 37, 42; *Rogue's Progress*, 31–32
Annesley, 44, 48, 64
Anstey, Christopher: *New Bath Guide*, 115
antihero, 31, 73
art and literature, satire of, 60–61, 120
Augustan satire, 9, 60–63, 82–84; *see also* satire
autobiographical material, 27–30, 58–60

Baker, Ernest, 67, 69
Baker, Sheridan, 114
Barth, John, 124
Beasely, Jerry C., 68, 86
Bellow, Saul, 124

Boswell, James, 1
Boucé, P. G., 33, 39, 64, 68, 86, 87, 122, 123
Bower, Archibald, 15, 56
British Magazine, the, 85
Briton, the, 13, 16, 17, 18, 95, 120
Brown, E. K., 34
Buck, Howard, 5, 7, 9
Bulwer-Lytton, Edward, 124
Bute, Lord, 12, 13, 15, 16–17, 22, 95

Canning, Elizabeth, 67
caricature. *See* grotesque, the
Carlyle, Alexander, 2
Cary, Joyce, 124
Cervantes Saavedra, Miguel de, 3, 6, 87, 91; *Don Quixote*, 13, 85, 86, 88–92, 123
Chandler, Frank W., 111
characterization, 34–40, 62, 72–76, 106–8, 121
Chesterfield, Lord, 59
Churchill, Charles, 15, 16, 17
Cleland, John, 5, 49, 52
Colie, Rosalie: *The Resources of Kind*, 122
Compendium of Authentic and Entertaining Voyages, A, 11, 29
Complete History of England, The, 11, 12, 17, 29
Cope, Sir John, 8–9
criminal biography, 122–23
Critical Review, the, 10, 13, 14, 16, 17, 56, 85, 94, 95, 97, 120

Day, Robert, 23
Dickens, Charles, 34, 96, 124; *Bleak House*, 54; *The Pickwick Papers*, 96, 124
didacticism, 76, 83–84, 123
Douglass, Wayne, 21, 22–23
Dryden, John, 69
Duke of Newcastle, 15, 96
dulce et utile, 16, 19

Ellison, Ralph: *Invisible Man*, 32
Elton, Oliver, 87
epistolary technique, 108, 111, 115–18, 124
Essay on the External Use of Water, An, 120
Evans, David, 62
Examiner, the, 17
Expedition of Humphrey Clinker, The, 3, 11, 17–18, 23, 24, 28, 62, 65, 70, 86, 92, 97, 103, 104–20, 121, 124; achievement in, 114–20; characterization in, 106–8; picaresque in, 108–11; plot of, 105–6; satire in, 111–14

Fabel, Robin, 12
Fielding, Henry, 3, 13, 22, 44, 52, 60, 66, 121; *Jonathan Wild*, 65, 68, 79; *Joseph Andrews*, 24, 65, 102; *Tom Jones*, 24, 46, 60, 65
Fleury, Cardinal, 79
Forster, E. M., 34
Foster, James R., 22
Francklin, Thomas, 13
Frederick of Prussia, 15, 95

Garrick, David, 1, 5, 13, 44, 59, 66
Gassman, Byron, 17, 18, 105
Giddings, Robert, 68
Gilbert and Sullivan: *H. M. S. Pinafore*, 7
Goldberg, M. A., 33, 37
Goldsmith, Oliver, 1, 3, 8, 85, 93; *The Vicar of Wakefield*, 93, 103, 109
Gordon, John, 27
Gordon, Peter, 70
Gothicism, 76, 77, 81–82, 85, 99–100, 123
Grand Tour, the, 18, 48, 56, 58, 61, 122
Grant, Damian, 21, 23, 28, 67–68, 86, 87
Graves, Richard, 60; *Spiritual Quixote*, 89
Greene, Donald, 12
Griffith, Ralph, 14, 67
Groom, Edward, 70
grotesque, the, 34–35

Hamilton, Archibald, 14
Hannay, David, 5, 12, 13, 104

heroines, 35–36, 114–15, 119
Hill, Dr. John, 14, 40–41, 44, 94
History and Adventures of an Atom, The, 11, 13, 21–23, 103, 104, 120, 123
Hogarth, William, 24, 41, 47, 71; *The Harlot's Progress*, 41, 42; *Hudibras*, 123
Hume, David, 3, 12, 13
Hunter, Dr. William, 15

Jack, R. D. S., 114
Jeffrey, David, 64
Jerrold, Douglas: *Black Eyed Susan*, 7
Johnson, Samuel: *Dictionary*, 97
Johnstone, Charles: *Chrysal; or, the Adventures of a Guinea*, 22
Joyce, James, 62, 119, 120, 124

Kahrl, George, 2, 11, 19, 20, 28, 29, 68–69, 119
Knapp, Lewis, 2, 5, 7, 14, 24, 27, 45, 69–70, 77, 83, 95, 120
Knowles, Admiral Charles, 10, 15, 85, 93

language, satire of, 61–62, 81, 97–99, 111–14, 119–20
law, satire of, 78–79, 92–93
Lennox, Charlotte: *Female Quixote*, 89
Le Sage, Alain René, 3, 6, 22, 29, 33, 40; *The Adventures of Gil Blas*, 13, 24, 30, 31, 49, 122
Lever, Charles, 124
Lewis, John, 27
Life and Adventures of Sir Launcelot Greaves, The, 13, 78, 85–104, 110, 123, 124; language in, 97–99; parody in, 88–92; picaresque satire in, 92–97; relation of to earlier work, 99–103; serialization of, 87–88
Lucian, 22
Lyttelton, Lord George, 13, 44, 52, 66; *Monody*, 60

MacKenzie, Henry: *Man of Feeling*, 101
MacKercher, Daniel, 44, 48, 64, 66
McKillop, Alan, 45, 49, 69, 120
Mann, Thomas: *Felix Krull*, 32
Marryat, Frederick, 124

Martz, Lewis, 11, 19, 29, 68–69, 113
Mayo, Robert D.: *The English Novel in the Magazines, 1740–1815*, 86, 87
medical practice, satire of, 54–55, 77–78, 93–94, 120
Melchiori, Giorgio, 120
Memoirs of a Lady of Quality, The (inset to *Peregrine Pickle*), 44–45, 48, 63, 66, 122
mock-heroic, the, 82–84, 103
Monthly Review, the, 5, 14, 49, 69, 85, 104

nationalism and nationality, 2, 20, 57–58, 113
"noble savage," the, 115
North Briton, the, 16
Noyes, Edward, 12

Ode to Independence, 10, 104

parody, 88–92, 114–15
Paulson, Ronald, 18, 32, 41, 75, 89, 122
Petronius: *Satyricon*, 48
Philosophical Transactions of the Royal Society, 9, 55, 61
picaresque, the, 2, 30–34, 36–37, 40–41, 49–52, 67–69, 71–72, 73, 88, 92–97, 104–5, 106–7, 108–11, 121–24
Piper, William, 37, 49
Pitt, William, 15, 16, 22, 95
point of view, narrative, 49, 164–65, 122
politics, satire of, 41–42, 55–56, 94–97, 120
Pope, Alexander, 8, 10, 12, 61, 76, 83, 121; *Dunciad*, 60
Present State of All Nations, 113
Preston, Thomas R., 68, 69
Price, John Valdimir, 86
pride, 36, 50–52, 70
Pritchett, V. S., 20
progression, narrative, 34, 75, 109; *see also*, repetition; rhythm
Putney, Rufus, 49–50, 52, 64

Quin, James, 13, 44, 59

Reeve, Clara: *The Old English Baron*, 100
Regicide, The, 4–6, 27, 59

religion, satire of, 56–57, 79–81, 120
repetition, narrative, 34, 42, 51, 75, 107, 109; *see also* progression; rhythm
Reprisal, The or *The Tars of Old England*, 6–7
Reproof, 8, 9–10
revenge, 36
rhythm, narrative, 34, 38, 39, 50, 52, 75–76, 103, 106–8; *see also* progression; repetition
Rice, Scott, 18–19
Richardson, Samuel, 68, 115; *Clarissa*, 24
Roper, Derek, 14
Rosenblum, Michael: "Smollett and the Old Conventions," 123
Ross, Ian, 50
Rousseau, G. S., 69, 114, 122, 123
Rousseau, Jean-Jacques, 115; *La Nouvelle Heloise*, 104

Saintsbury, George, 67, 87
satire, 2–3, 8–10, 21–23, 40–43, 52–63, 76–84, 92–97, 111–14, 121
scatology, 42, 111–14
Scott, Sir Walter, 87, 124
Scottish Common Sense Philosophy, 49
Sekora, John, 12, 114
Sena, John F., 18
sentimentalism, 39, 63, 68, 76, 77, 81, 82, 85, 100–103, 111, 114–15, 121, 123
serialization, 87–88, 124
Seven Years' War, 15–16, 21
sexual perversion, 8–9
Shakespeare, William, 5, 6, 73; *Julius Caesar*, 5; *Othello*, 5, 73
Shaw, George Bernard: *Pygmalion*, 54, 99, 124
Shebbeare, Dr. John, 13, 14, 15, 66, 85, 94, 95; *History of the Sumatrans*, 72
Shelburne, Lord, 58
Shenstone, William, 60
Smollett, Tobias George: as editor, translator, and publisher, 13–18; as journalist and historian, 11–13; as outsider, 1–3; as physician, 2, 3, 19–20, 54–55, 93–94; plays of, 4–7; poetry of, 7–10; politics of, 11–13; 15–18, 21–22, 55–56, 94–97; as

prisoner, 10, 15, 85, 93; as satirist,
21–23; as seaman, 2, 28–30; as travel
writer, 18–20; as writer, 3, 121–24

WORKS: NONFICTION
*Compendium of Authentic and
Entertaining Voyages, A*, 11, 29
Complete History of England, The, 11,
12, 17, 29
Essay on the External Use of Water, An, 120
Present State of All Nations, 113
Travels through France and Italy,
18–20, 103, 104, 114

WORKS: NOVELS
Adventures of Ferdinand Fathom,
67–84, 110, 122–23, 124;
Augustan satire in, 82–84;
characterization in, 72–76; plot of,
71–72; satire, 76–82; Smollett's
intentions with, 69–71
Adventures of Peregrine Pickle, The, 9,
44–66, 81, 83, 100–101, 110, 122,
123; Augustan satire in, 60–63;
autobiographical material in, 58–60;
comparison of with *Roderick
Random*, 45–49; picaresque in,
49–52; point of view in, 64–65;
revision of, 66; satire in, 52–58; use
of insets in, 63–64
Adventures of Roderick Random, The, 2,
3, 5, 9, 22, 23, 24–43, 45–49, 53,
57–58, 60, 64, 65, 81, 99,
100–101, 104, 105, 110, 118, 119,
121, 122, 123, 124; autographical
material in, 27–30; characterization
in, 34–40; plot of, 25–27; satire in,
40–43; use of picaresque in, 30–34
Expedition of Humphrey Clinker, The, 3,
11, 17–18, 23, 24, 28, 62, 65, 70,
86, 92, 97, 103, 104–20, 121, 124;
achievement in, 114–20;
characterization in, 106–8;
picaresque in, 108–11; plot of,
105–6; satire in, 111–14
History and Adventures of an Atom, The,
11, 13, 21–23, 103, 104, 120, 123
*Life and Adventures of Sir Launcelot

Greaves, The, 13, 78, 85–104, 110,
123, 124; language in, 97–99;
parody in, 88–92; picaresque satire
in, 92–97; relation of to earlier work,
99–103; serialization of, 87–88

WORKS: PLAYS
Absent Man, The, 6
Alceste, 6
Regicide, The, 4–6, 27, 59
*Reprisal, The or The Tars of Old
England*, 6–7

WORKS: POETRY
Advice, 8–9
Ode to Independence, 10, 104
Reproof, 8, 9–10
Tears of Scotland, 7–8

Sterne, Laurence, 18, 75, 112, 115, 121;
Sentimental Journey, 104; *Tristram
Shandy*, 24, 46, 104, 121
Strauss, Albrecht, 75
Strobo, Robert, 119
structural unity, 34; *see also*
characterization; progression; repetition;
rhythm
Swift, Jonathan, 1, 9, 12, 17, 22, 61, 76,
83, 94, 121; *Tale of a Tub*, 48

Tears of Scotland, 7–8
Thackeray, W. M., 29
Toryism. *See* Whigs and Tories
Travels through France and Italy, 18–20,
103, 104, 114
Treadwell, T. O., 68

Vane, Frances Viscount, 44, 66
Van Ghent, Dorothy, 33
Voltaire, 13; *Micromegas*, 22

Walpole, Horace, 3; *Castle of Otranto*, 123
Walpole, Sir Robert, 77
Wells, H. G., 13
Whigs and Tories, 11–12, 15–18, 22, 85,
95–97
Whitridge, Arnold, 5, 21
Wilkes, John, 3, 16, 17, 97